D1561483

THE GERMAN
OFFICER CORPS
1890–1914

Oxford University Press, Ely House, London W.1

GLASGOW   NEW YORK   TORONTO   MELBOURNE   WELLINGTON
CAPE TOWN   SALISBURY   IBADAN   NAIROBI   LUSAKA   ADDIS ABABA
BOMBAY   CALCUTTA   MADRAS   KARACHI   LAHORE   DACCA
KUALA LUMPUR   HONG KONG   TOKYO

THE GERMAN OFFICER CORPS
1890–1914

BY

MARTIN KITCHEN

CLARENDON PRESS · OXFORD
1968

© *Oxford University Press* 1968

MADE AND PRINTED IN GREAT BRITAIN BY
WILLIAM CLOWES AND SONS, LIMITED
LONDON AND BECCLES

TO BRIGITTE

ACKNOWLEDGEMENTS

I AM most grateful to the staffs of the following institutions for providing me with archival material, a task made all the more arduous by the destruction of the German military archives in 1945; as a result of their efforts a wealth of material was made available to me: the Bundesarchiv, Koblenz; the Bayerisches Hauptstaatsarchiv, Munich; the Staatsarchiv, Ludwigsburg; the Heeresarchiv, Stuttgart; and the Deutsches Zentralarchiv, Potsdam and Merseburg.

The Wiener Library, London, made some important pamphlet material available to me, and helped me in many other ways.

The Central Research Fund of London University gave me a travel grant to visit the archives in Potsdam and Merseburg.

The Government of Rhineland-Palatinate awarded me a generous scholarship which enabled me to spend one year of research in Germany. I am most deeply grateful.

My thanks are also due for the helpful criticisms and suggestions of Mr James Joll, Professor W. N. Medlicott and of my colleague Dr Warren E. Williams.

I have also profited greatly from lengthy discussions of many aspects of this book with Dr Dietrich Aigner.

Laurence and Susan Olivier undertook the mammoth task of suggesting improvements to my prose, which suffered badly from an over-exposure to the writings of Wilhelmine officers.

My greatest debts, however, are two: to Professor F. L. Carsten for his unfailing advice and encouragement and for his incisive and scholarly criticism; and lastly to my wife who has helped me in so many ways that I find it impossible adequately to express my thanks.

CONTENTS

ABBREVIATIONS

AApA   Abteilung für allgemeine Armee und für persönliche Angelegenheiten

AKO   Allerhöchste Kabinett Order

Bayr.HSA   Bayerisches Hauptstaatsarchiv

BA   Bundesarchiv

DZA   Deutsches Zentralarchiv

GPEK   *Grosse Politik der europäischen Kabinette*

HZ   *Historische Zeitschrift*

JM   Justiz-Minister

KA   Kriegsarchiv

KM   Kriegsminister

Mil.Kab.   Militär-Kabinett

RT   Reichstag

WKM   Württembergischer Kriegsminister

ZfGW   *Zeitschrift für Geschichtswissenschaft*

INTRODUCTION

THE essential character of the Prussian, and later the German Officer Corps, was determined by the efforts of the Kings of Prussia to make the Junkers serve a centralized monarchical state. In spite of the efforts of the Great Elector, it was Frederick William I who first successfully forced the sons of the East Elbian nobility into the cadet schools and thence into the Prussian Officer Corps. Although the nobility had at first vigorously protested against such heavy-handed action by the monarchy, soon any doubt as to the determination of the king to have his way was dispelled, and at the same time they were given very real social and material advantages. Although they may have lost much formal independence they remained the first estate in the land, feudal barons in an age that had turned its back on feudalism, owing direct allegiance to the king with whose interests they had come to identify themselves. Frederick William I had achieved his aim of crushing the autonomy of the Junkers, and of establishing his sovereignty like a 'rocher von bronze'.

Frederick the Great continued the policy of Frederick William I, but with even more radical determination. Although the Prussian Officer Corps was decimated in the Seven Years War, Frederick was determined to maintain its social exclusiveness. He purged the Officer Corps of any bourgeois elements, and preferred to import foreign aristocrats as officers, rather than draw upon the burghers to whom he allotted the role of building up Prussia's mercantile and industrial strength.

This system of recruitment to the Officer Corps was geared to the needs of the 18th-century state, with a fundamental ideology which went back to even earlier times. After the French Revolution and the startling successes of the Napoleonic mass army it became apparent to anyone but a purblind conservative that the old order was quite inadequate for the requirements of modern warfare. Furthermore the organization of the army was hopelessly ineffectual, with the higher commanders virtually independent of any sort of central control. By 1806, the fateful year of Jena and Auerstädt, the average age of the Officer Corps was so advanced that four generals were over 80, and 25 per cent. of the regimental and battalion commanders were over 60.

The disastrous defeat of the old army in 1806 meant that a drastic reform of its structure and organization could no longer be postponed, and even the arch-conservatives realized that Prussia could not be saved from her humiliating situation without fundamental changes in the military system. In Stein, Scharnhorst, Gneisenau, Boyen and Grolman, Prussia had statesmen and soldiers who were admirably equipped to instigate such reforms, inspired by a vision that went far beyond the purely military problem of freeing Prussia from French domination.

The reformers realized that the central problem was political rather than military. They attributed Napoleon's successes as much to the fact that the French army had managed to bridge the gulf between the state machine and the nation at large, as to the brilliance of Napoleon as a commander. Thus, just as the original form of the Officer Corps had been moulded by the Prussian kings' desire for political unity, so the reformers realized that without a degree of liberalization the army could not hope to be militarily effective. The aristocratic domination of the Officer Corps would have to end.

Personal serfdom was abolished in 1807, and in the following year local government was reformed, while at the same time the army was also reorganized. An ordinance of 6 August 1808 stipulated that officers should be appointed on merit rather than aristocratic lineage. Also in 1808 the War Ministry was formed with overall control of military affairs, headed by Scharnhorst and by a conservative, Graf Lottum, who was entirely overshadowed by Scharnhorst's forceful personality. Scharnhorst's most able disciple, Boyen, with Grolman as his Chief of Staff, began his work on the Landwehr in 1813. Boyen designed the Landwehr as a reserve army with a bourgeois Officer Corps that was to be largely independent of the regular army, thus helping to end the Prussian dichotomy between army and nation. Boyen's reforms became law in 1814, with a three-year service in the regular army, and two years in the active reserve. This was followed by seven years in the first levy of the Landwehr, which was designed to serve with the regular army in time of war, and a further seven years in the second levy, which was allotted a purely defensive role. The Landwehr was greeted enthusiastically by the liberals, but was and remained anathema to the regular officers.

Liberal hopes that these reforms, which had proved their worth on the battlefields of Europe, would herald a new era of liberalization in Prussia were dashed when Napoleon was safely interned at St Helena and reaction set in throughout Europe. As early as 1816 only the sons of officers who had been killed in the war, or young men to whom the king wished to show favour, were allowed to become officers. This meant that for some years the Officer Corps drew its members from the traditional aristocratic families, for few commoners who had served as officers during the war had sons old enough to become officers. In 1819 the Landwehr lost much of its semi-autonomous position, and both Boyen and Grolman resigned in protest against a measure that was clearly designed to turn back the clock and to undo the influence of Scharnhorst's liberal reforms. Similarly Scharnhorst's War Ministry was reconstituted by the creation of a Military Cabinet in 1816, and in 1821 the General Staff was separated from the War Ministry; but both bodies remained under the nominal control of the War Ministry, although the way was now open for the tensions and divisions between the three highest military institutions, which became characteristic of the following century. This was to weaken the unity of command within the army, which had always been the driving force behind Scharnhorst's reforms.

In the reactionary Germany of the Carlsbad decrees there was no room for the likes of Scharnhorst, the son of a humble Hanoverian peasant, and the army returned to the aristocratic and exclusive days it had enjoyed before 1806. The Officer Corps regarded itself once again as a privileged order, and looked down with contempt on the humble civilians. The gulf between the Officer Corps and the nation, which the reformers had tried so hard to bridge, was as wide as ever. The army was now to function as a bulwark against liberalism and revolution; thus it became increasingly aristocratic so as to be politically safe from dangerous liberal elements, and at the same time anxious to avoid any military engagement outside the borders of Prussia. Thus Prussian policy was paralysed both at home and abroad. Prussia was humiliated at Olmütz and wavered during the Crimean crisis, and the liberals looked upon the army as a militarily ineffective weapon which could only be used as an instrument of domestic oppression.

The growing antagonism between the army and the liberals had come to a head in 1848. The Frankfurt parliament made sweeping demands for army reform, for an Officer Corps open to the talents, for the abolition of the exclusive cadet schools and military academies, and for parliamentary control over the army. In the face of such demands the Officer Corps rallied even closer round the king, and even the Landwehr which had seemed so dangerously liberal to regular officers proved impeccably loyal, though militarily of questionable value. Although some officers took an oath to the constitution, many of them under duress, the Officer Corps was not prepared to make any concessions to such alarming ideas as the introduction of soldiers' councils, the appointment of officers by the votes of the men, or the abolition of saluting. With nothing but the quixotic 'Bürgergarde' to give force to their arguments the liberals were unable to achieve any of their proposed reforms in the structure and organization of the army.

The constitution of 1848 was resented by the Officer Corps as an unwarranted restriction on the royal prerogative, from which sprang their own unique position in the state, and officers regarded the parliamentarians, other than those of rigid conservative principles, as their sworn enemies. In King William I the army got a warlord who was as sincere in his love for the army as he was in his hatred of anything that smacked of liberalism. He believed that a soldier was a being who was in every way superior to, and different from, the mere civilian. He was intent on restoring the old Frederician army, and to purge the Officer Corps of any remnants of the attitudes of the war of liberation. In his own phrase he wanted soldiers and not drilled peasants. The army was to be the keystone of the monarchical state, a 'rocher von bronze'.

The problem of the army was the central issue over which the disputes of the 'New Era' were fought. Prince William, appointed regent in 1858, ousted the old conservative ministry, and replaced it by right-wing liberals. The election of 1859 gave the liberals a majority in the Prussian Landtag. The liberals hoped that William would lead the country into a new era of liberalism, but their hopes were soon dashed. The conservatives remained powerful at court and in the army, and the liberals in the ministry proved themselves more eager to show their loyalty to the crown than to liberal principles.

Any doubts as to a real change of heart in the government were dispelled when the issue of army reform was raised. William had spent all his life in the army, and military affairs were almost his sole interest. He was determined to reorganize the army, which Frederick William IV had neglected, in a bold programme of reform, which included a drastic increase in the size of the annual intakes. Military reform, he argued, was long overdue. It was the first important attempt to reform the army since 1814. Although the population since that date had increased from 10 to 18 million, the size of the army had remained the same. It was thus proposed to increase the annual intake by 23,000 men. But it was not so much the increase in the size of the army that aroused the hostility of the liberals, although some carped at the increased expenditure involved. The main objection was to the proposal further to reduce the significance of the Landwehr, for the Landwehr remained the pride of the liberals, the central measure of Boyen's liberal reforms. The regular officers on the other hand despised the Landwehr as being militarily useless, and a hot-bed of liberal ideas. They were determined to end its semi-autonomous status and to bring it under the direct control of the regular army. Equally objectionable to the liberals was the proposal to increase the length of regular service from two to three years.[1] Here, they were convinced, was further proof of the reactionaries' determination to use the army as a means of thrusting a conservative ideology down the throats of raw recruits.

Although fundamental issues as to the political future of Prussia determined the struggles between conservatives and liberals in the 'New Era', it was the question of the army which gave rise to the most violent passions. The towns objected to the

---

[1] The length of service had been three years since 1814. It was then shortened to two years, and after 1856 was again three years. The measure was therefore designed to perpetuate the existing terms of service established in 1814.

increased costs of quartering which they would have to pay. Industrialists objected to the wasteful drain on manpower which the three-year service would cause. Although the liberals themselves were uncertain as to what they wished to do with the army, they were united in their determination to resist this attempt to strengthen the army as the bastion of a reactionary state, to purge it of any liberal institutions, and to make the Officer Corps even more autonomous than before. The struggle was further exacerbated by the fact that the government was unwilling to make any concessions to the liberals in other fields, which alone might have made the army reform palatable to them. Further, many liberals, such as the historian von Sybel, knew that the fundamental conflict, liberalism versus conservatism, could never be decided in favour of the liberals unless the army backed the constitution, and this they knew was highly improbable.

Not even the army stood united behind William's programme. The War Minister, von Bonin, was forced to resign, having pointed out that the reforms would cause the mass of the population to lose confidence in the army, and drive the army and the civilians into separate and hostile camps. On the other wing Manteuffel, the Chief of the Military Cabinet, urged the king seriously to consider the possibility of revolution from below, or a *coup d'état* from above. But the liberals, remembering 1848, had no wish for a fight which they were bound to lose, and the king, although his heart was with the army, threatened to abdicate rather than instigate a blood-bath. A war of attrition began, but most of the cards were in the government's hands.

Thanks to Bismarck's brilliant and unscrupulous manoeuvrings, the army emerged unscathed from the conflict, and after the successful campaigns against Denmark in 1864, Austria in 1866, and France in 1870–1, it rode on the crest of a wave of patriotic enthusiasm. In 1866 the opposition capitulated by granting the act of indemnity which gave parliamentary sanction to the army's desire to remain a state within the state. After the foundation of the Reich in 1871 there were few who criticized an army that had achieved a feat that inspired nationwide admiration and enthusiasm. But the army raised objections to the constitution of the North German Federation of 1867, and to the universal manhood suffrage it introduced.

The wars marked a growing tension between the army and the civilian government. Moltke, who had been made Chief of the General Staff in 1857, first rose to real prominence during the Danish war, when he acted as Chief of Staff to Prince Frederick Charles. By 1866 he was the dominating figure in the army. Moltke had no political ambitions, and turned down all overtures by political groups to bring him into the political arena. In 1861 the Crown Liberals made advances to Moltke in the hope that he might solve the constitutional crisis. After 1862 many National Liberals, who resented Bismarck's autocratic ways, hoped that Moltke could be persuaded to enter politics. During the Kulturkampf those conservatives who objected to Bismarck's attacks upon the Church hoped that he could be replaced by Moltke. But the Chief of the General Staff insisted that, although in war he was as hard as steel, as a politician he would be too weak and indecisive. Although Moltke had no wish to challenge Bismarck's political position in peace-time, he resented any form of political control over the conduct of war, thus helping to increase the animosity between the politicians and the army.

The wars against Denmark and Austria passed without any major clash between Bismarck and Moltke. Moltke realized that both wars were fought within the context of a complex diplomatic situation and thus was prepared to accept Bismarck's supremacy. The success in the Austrian war increased Moltke's confidence, and he looked forward to leading the army against France. Thus he quarrelled with Bismarck in 1867 over the results of the London conference which guaranteed the neutrality of Luxemburg, Moltke insisting that this weakened Prussia's military position, and was a part of Bismarck's misguided attempt to conciliate France, instead of fighting the inevitable battle for supremacy in Europe.

Thus for Moltke the Franco-Prussian war was a straightforward duel between two nations, with none of the diplomatic complications of 1864 or 1866. He was determined to have complete control over military operations until France had been utterly defeated. Only then would he relinquish control to Bismarck. Bismarck was determined to resist these demands. He feared that the powers might intervene if the war was prolonged, and was anxious to leave France, even in defeat, with a viable government. Thus he wished to bring fighting to an end as soon as possible, and was prepared to impose relatively mild peace terms on the French so as not to hamper the work of the new French government.

The struggle between the two men broke out openly soon after Sedan. While Bismarck wanted mild terms for the defeated armies, and toyed with the idea of restoring Napoleon III, Moltke called for a war of extermination against the French, and thought in terms of a military dictatorship for France, rejecting any idea of restoring the Emperor. Other quarrels between the two developed over the future of Alsace-Lorraine, Bismarck being prepared to give up Metz if peace could be brought about more quickly, Moltke demanding Alsace and Lorraine in entirety as a necessary defence against a future threat from France. Bismarck demanded the bombardment of Paris, again in the hope that it would end the war sooner by underlining the futility of the efforts of the Army of National Defence. Moltke feared the possible German losses in a storming of the French capital, and thought that Paris could easily prove to be a second Sebastopol. Moltke continued to demand a war of extermination, a fatal policy which Bismarck was only just able to avert. It was Bismarck who eventually concluded the terms for a cease-fire with Favre, the provisional Foreign Minister of France, Moltke's negotiations with Trochu, the army commander in Paris, having come to nothing.

By concluding the cease-fire without consulting the army Bismarck managed to assert the supremacy of the civil government over the army, but the clashes between him and Moltke had disastrous consequences. Moltke demanded the exclusion of politics from the conduct of war once hostilities had begun. War had become too serious a matter for soldiers to be able to tolerate interference from civilians. This lesson Moltke passed down to later generations of General Staff officers, with unfortunate results; for Moltke's theoretical writings on the subject gave authoritative backing to the army's inborn distrust of politicians and diplomatists, and served to widen the gap between the army and the civilians.

Popular enthusiasm for the army in 1871 meant that there was a genuine opportunity of ending the Prussian dualism between the military and civilians. But no such attempt was made. Officer selection was made more rigidly aristocratic and the autonomy of the Officer Corps was strengthened. Bismarck resisted Roon's attempts to establish an Imperial War Ministry, rather than a Prussian one, in the fear that this might make the army too influential; but the distinction was largely academic, since the Prussian War Minister answered questions in the Reichstag, and his position was further enhanced by the military dominance of Prussia.

With Bismarck as Chancellor and with political uncertainties both at home and abroad, military affairs tended to retire into the background, but the basic problems of the army and its relations with the nation were not solved. William II, whose admiration for his grandfather was unbounded, and who dreamt of emulating his military exploits, was equally determined to resist any change in the fundamental structure and influence of the Officer Corps. At the same time the democratic mass parties, particularly the Social Democrats, increased rapidly and were clamouring for reform. Germany had moved into the industrial age with its concomitant liberalism and socialism, and the army was determined to resist any attempts by these forces to shake Junker and conservative domination. As in 1815 and in 1848 it was determined to fight against the forces of change, and to entrench itself in an inflexibly conservative position.

The isolation of the Officer Corps from the rest of society became all the more anomalous as Germany underwent fundamental economic and social changes. The rapid industrialization of Germany was helped by the crisis of the 1870s, which led to the failure of many smaller banks and industrial concerns. The resulting trend towards the concentration of bank capital and the formation of industrial cartels was further accelerated by Bismarck's protective tariffs of 1879. The great new industries, particularly the chemical and electrical industries, were in the hands of a few giant concerns which were not slow to form cartels, or even to unite to form monopolies such as I. G. Farben in 1916. The German cartels were stronger than those of any other European country; they enabled the rational exploitation of the country's natural resources, they obviated the need to duplicate expensive plant, and they were attractive to the investor. The cartels gave German industry its characteristic efficiency, but they were also highly aggressive, and this aggressiveness was soon to be reflected in German policy. The search for more and cheaper raw materials, for larger and more profitable markets, was to bring the Germans face to face with others on similar quests, hence the strains and stresses of *Weltpolitik*.

This mushroom growth of German industry led to rapid changes in German society. A steady flight from the land meant that Germany was no longer predominantly an agricultural country. Men left the country districts to earn higher wages in industry, girls left to find work as maids in *bourgeois* households. Craftsmen were no longer able to compete with cheap mass-produced goods, and were often obliged to work in the factories. This change to an industrial society had profound political effects. The growth of an urban proletariat meant an increase in the number of votes cast for the Social Democrats. Industrialization meant the rise of a wealthy and politically powerful capitalist class, and the industrial magnates from Western Germany were to challenge the hegemony of the East Elbian landed aristocracy. The whole structure of the Bismarckian Reich began to topple. The authoritarian monarchical state which carefully preserved the dominance of the Prussian Junker no longer reflected the social and economic realities of the Germany of the industrial age.

Since the Reichstag had no control over government policy and had no say in the appointment of either the Chancellor or the ministers, the political parties were essentially interest groups, reflecting the increasingly widening divisions of German society. Eastern agrarians and western industrialists, northern protestants and southern catholics pursued their own interests, but at the same time they accepted the assumptions on which the Reich was based. Two parties stood apart from the rest. The left liberals and the Social Democrats demanded fundamental changes. The Reich, they demanded, should become a constitutional monarchy, or even a republic.

If on the one hand the differences between these conflicting interest groups became increasingly hard to reconcile, the challenge from the left held them together in an uneasy and erratic coalition. This desperate attempt to reconcile conflicting interests goes some of the way to explain the vagaries of German

policy in the Wilhelmine period. The agrarian conservatives
were determined to resist the influx of cheap wheat, particularly
from Russia, and demanded high protective tariffs. An anti-
Russian policy was therefore the price the government had to
pay for conservative support. On the other hand the industrialists with their aggressive commercial policies antagonized
the British. This combination of *Weltpolitik* and agrarian conservatism was to lead to the diplomatic isolation of Germany.
The alliance was fragile, but the agrarians, although lukewarm
in their enthusiasm for the fleet, and appalled by the demagogic
agitation of the Navy League (*Flottenverein*), had little affection
for Britain, which represented to them all that was worst in the
modern capitalist and materialist world. Their support for
Weltpolitik could be bought with suitable tariff adjustments and
guarantees for their continued exaggerated influence in the
affairs of the Reich. Similarly the industrialists had their
reservations about William II, but he was an enthusiast for
Weltpolitik and for modern industry. Expensive bread for their
workers seemed a reasonable price to pay for the prospect of
a larger share in the world's markets.

The formation of powerful interest groups also began in the
1870s with the *Zentralverband deutscher Industrieller*, which agitated for protective tariffs. With the industrialists calling for
tariff reform to protect a nascent industry against foreign
competition, the way was open for the alliance between industrialists and agrarians that was to form the basis of both domestic and foreign policy in Wilhelmine Germany. The instability
of this alliance soon became apparent in the Caprivi era.
Caprivi was faced with the problem that Germany, although
in the midst of rapid industrial expansion, was not exporting
enough. Stock-piling at home, coupled with the high price of
bread, due to the protective tariffs, was causing a rapid infla-
tion. Hardship and discontent with government policy were
reflected in a wave of strikes in 1890. Caprivi coined the phrase
'either we export goods, or we export people', and argued that
free trade, and if possible a European customs union, was the
only possible answer to Germany's economic ills. The tariff
policy of the New Course was anathema to the agrarian conservatives who saw it as a direct threat to their privileged position in the state. The arguments of the agrarians were

strengthened by the fact that the economic boom of 1889 had collapsed by December 1891 when the new agreements were first discussed in the Reichstag. Now the old protective conservative cry of 'the Fatherland in danger' was heard once again.

William II was incensed by the attitude of the agrarians. An open attack on the government by those who were traditionally its most loyal supporters seemed to him to border on treason. In characteristic tones he claimed that his vassals had broken their feudal oath of allegiance. Thus, in spite of the slogan of full steam ahead, it seemed that the New Course was in danger of grinding to a halt. The conservatives were in opposition, the Catholic Centre party remained as opportunistic as ever, interested only in getting the maximum political advantage out of any given situation, and the left liberals and socialists were openly critical of existing society. In the upheaval over tariff reform a curious reversal had taken place with the Social Democrats and left liberals voting with the government. Their votes had been welcome, but this marriage of convenience was an embarrassment to the government and had no chance of survival.

The agrarians were determined to organize themselves for the fight for their own interests which they saw threatened by the New Course. In 1893 the Farmers' League (*Bund der Landwirte*) was formed, and the Conservative Party ceased to represent a political ideal with appeal beyond the sectarian interests of the landowners of the East, and became indistinguishable from the *Bund der Landwirte*. Thus although the conservatives fought ferociously for the established order their attitude to the government was determined by purely economic considerations. William II could thus no longer automatically rely on conservative support.

In the face of these radical changes in German political and social life the Kaiser began to think in terms of a drastic solution to the problems that beset him. Like the Queen of Hearts in *Alice in Wonderland* he was only too apt to call for precipitate action without stopping to consider the consequences, and with little real intention of carrying it out. At times it seemed to him that the only possible cure for present ills was a *coup d'état* from above, the *Staatsstreich*. Bismarck had thought along these lines when he saw his policies frustrated by changes in German political life that he could do nothing to control. This is one of the main reasons why a *Staatsstreich* had little chance of being implemented. The whole idea was too closely associated with Bismarck. There were many, particularly in the Foreign Office, and among them noticeably Holstein, who feared that a *Staatsstreich* would mean the return of Bismarck as Chancellor, a prospect which filled them with horror. William, who in spite of his drastic pronouncements was not entirely convinced of the wisdom of such a course of action, was easily persuaded against it.

If the idea of a *Staatsstreich* was abandoned there still remained a more limited alternative, the reintroduction of the anti-socialist laws which had not been renewed in 1890. Since it no longer seemed possible, or even desirable, to overthrow the constitutional framework of the Reich, then at least legislation could be brought in against those who seemed determined to overthrow the existing state. William had tried to win over the workers by continuing Bismarck's social legislation. This programme had been launched with all the bombast of which he was such a master, but once again in spite of all the high-flown words there was little concrete achievement. The workers remained unimpressed, and the Social Democrat vote continued to rise. Once again William was frustrated. Such monstrous ingratitude on the part of the workers seemed to him to be proof of a fundamental perfidy on their part that could only be rooted out by severe measures.

The difficulty of getting the Reichstag to accept such anti-socialist legislation was even more acute than it had been at the time of Bismarck's first attempt in 1875. Many parties, among them the National Liberals, feared that such legislation could easily be used against them. Caprivi argued that the laws, the *Umsturzvorlage* (anti-subversion bill), could not be passed without dissolving the Reichstag and thus running the risk that the Social Democrats might use the crisis to their own advantage and increase their share of the vote. Caprivi was faced with the determined opposition of Botho von Eulenburg, the Prussian Minister President and champion of the *Umsturzvorlage*, who had powerful conservative support. The resulting deadlock obliged the Kaiser to dismiss both Caprivi and Eulenburg and to appoint Hohenlohe to the traditional dual role of Chancellor and Minister President of Prussia. After this upheaval there was even less likelihood of the bill passing the Reichstag. Only the conservatives gave unconditional support to the bill, although the backing of the Centre party had been won by introducing into the bill legislation against atheistic and blasphemous behaviour. In May 1894 the bill was rejected by the Reichstag.

The failure of the *Umsturzvorlage* was followed by attempts to introduce anti-socialist legislation in the individual states. This tactic also met with little success. In 1896 Saxony introduced the three class vote, on the Prussian model, thus ending Social Democratic representation in the Saxon chamber. An attempt to bring in anti-socialist legislation in Prussia met with similar objections to those voiced in the Reichstag. The only result was the Lex Aron of 1898 which banned Social Democrats from teaching in the Universities.

One further attempt was made to pass anti-socialist legislation in the Reichstag. In 1898 the *Zuchthausvorlage* (Penitentiary Bill) was debated. The bill was designed to introduce the notion of class justice, and to enable particularly severe measures to be taken against workers. The philosophy behind the bill was such an affront to the idea of equality before the law that all parties, except the conservatives, voted against it.

Once again the pendulum swung away from repression to a renewed attempt to win over the workers by a programme of social reform. This programme, associated with Posadowsky, the State Secretary in the Imperial Home Office (*Reichsamt des Innern*), won the qualified support of the Social Democrats, and resulted in an improvement of insurance benefits, in legislation against child labour, and the subsidized building of workers' homes. The programme came to an abrupt end in 1906 when the Centre and the Social Democrats voted against Bülow's colonial policy. The Chancellor dissolved the Reichstag and announced his determination to fight against the Centre and the Social Democrats. The resulting anti-Centre and anti-Social Democrat coalition, known as the Bülow Block, was to survive uneasily until 1909 when the Block disintegrated owing to conservative opposition to the introduction of new taxes.

Bethmann Hollweg, who succeeded Bülow as Chancellor in 1909, was in favour of moderate reform, but after his failure to achieve any change in the Prussian electoral law in 1910 he lost heart. Bethmann was faced with a dilemma that was becoming increasingly acute. He knew that reform was needed, but realized that it would mean a break with the conservatives, and would be met with the resolute opposition of those circles that supported them, particularly the higher civil servants and the Officer Corps. Although the majority of the Social Democrats now accepted the basic principles of revisionism, and were even prepared to accept the idea of a constitutional monarchy, Bethmann was unwilling to risk any radical change of parliamentary alliances. Such a course would have been extremely difficult. Without reform of the Prussian electoral system, which would have ended conservative domination in Prussia, the dichotomy between Prussia and the Reich would have been so acute as to make an effective reform programme exceedingly difficult. Bethmann was unable to break the resolute opposition of the conservatives to any reform of the Prussian franchise.

Thus neither the idea of a *coup d'état*, nor that of anti-socialist legislation, nor attempts at social reform had done anything to bridge the gulf betweeen society and government. Similarly the idea of an anti-socialist parliamentary coalition determined to uphold the status quo was unable to withstand the clash of interests between the parties concerned. The idea, based on the parliamentary alignments of the 1870s, was taken up by Miquel, the Prussian Finance Minister from 1890 to 1901. Miquel had favoured the idea of a *coup d'état* in 1890 after the success of the Social Democrats in the election of that year, but, aware of resistance to such a policy, he became the architect of *Sammlungspolitik*, the alliance of the bourgeois parties for the defence of the existing order, and an attempt to heal the wounds left by Caprivi's tariff policy. This parliamentary alliance formed the basis of domestic politics in the Wilhelmine era, but it could not reconcile the conflicting interests of the parties, and was greatly weakened with the collapse of the Bülow Block.

In addition to this fundamental failure to achieve either a concerted effort for the preservation of the *status quo*, or to reform the Reich to reflect the profound sociological and economic changes that had taken place since 1871, was the problem of the power structure of the Reich. The question 'who rules in Berlin' can be asked at any time after 1890 with very little chance of a clear answer. The dismissal of the strong man showed up only too clearly the structural weaknesses of the Empire he had created. William II was in many ways a man who personified the age in which he lived, but in spite of his constant interference with the government he did not form his times to the extent that Bismarck did. With his short-lived enthusiasms he was unable to apply himself to the hard task of ruling on his own, but he was also unable to find ministers who would do the job effectively for him. The power of the Reichstag was increasing, but was still severely limited. The government could not ignore the need for a parliamentary majority, but at the same time was not responsible to the Reichstag. The result of this fragmentation of political power was confusion and lack of consistency both in domestic and foreign policy, which became all the more acute and all the more dangerous as Germany became rapidly more prosperous and more powerful.

Amid this growing confusion William II stressed the divine right of the monarchy, and the obligation of his subjects to obey him implicitly. If all else failed then the loyalty of subject to monarch would ensure that the worst would not happen. Ultimate authority rested with the Kaiser, and he was determined that nothing should be allowed to undermine that authority. Here the position of the army, and of the Kaiser's power of command, was vitally important. The army took an oath of personal allegiance to the king and was beyond parliamentary control or ministerial responsibility. Thus the army, in the troubled and confusing times of Wilhelmine Germany, was virtually unaffected by the changes taking place around it. Its role was to preserve the established order, to uphold the authority of the Kaiser against any demands for democratization, and as 'School of the Nation' to educate the German people to be loyal subjects of an authoritarian monarchical state. One of the most extreme examples of this attitude was voiced in a speech in the Reichstag by the conservative Oldenburg-Januschau in 1910, when he said that the Kaiser should be able at any time to order a lieutenant to take ten men and close the Reichstag.

The army stood removed from the political struggle, its position greatly strengthened as the pillar of the old order as even those groups most deeply committed to the preservation of monarchical authority were unable to shelve their differences, even in the face of great changes that all of them abhorred. At the same time Bismarck's successors were unable or unwilling to challenge the army's determination to conduct its own affairs without due consultation with the civilian government.

If on the one hand the increasing complexity of warfare enabled the army to claim with some justification that civilians were unable to understand military problems, equally the need for mass armies with a technically trained Officer Corps meant that the exclusiveness of the Officer Corps could not be maintained without damaging military efficiency. This was the fundamental problem of the army in the period of William II. On the one hand a determination to maintain the Officer Corps as a conservative stronghold against the forces of change, and on the other hand the necessity of recruiting technically competent bourgeois officers. At the same time the lack of firm control by the government only increased the army's tendency to disregard political considerations in its military planning. The army's desire to turn back the clock, the attempt to return to a situation that was basically anachronistic even in the days of Frederick the Great, inflamed the antagonisms of the civilians towards the army, and further frustrated the Officer Corps, forcing it into a position which, in the long run, it was unable to defend.

I

THE KAISER, THE ARMY, AND ITS ORGANIZATION

THE Reich had neither a unified national army nor a unified military command. The Prussian army exercised an indisputable predominance over the armies of Bavaria, Saxony, and Württemberg, whatever the theoretical independence of the other armies, but within the Prussian army the position of General Staff, Military Cabinet, and War Ministry, and their relations with Kaiser, Chancellor, and the government departments were highly complex.

The General Staff had become increasingly powerful after the wars with Austria and France. However much the military qualities of the elder Moltke were the subject of passionate debate, there could be no doubt that he was an almost godlike figure to the army, and certain officers of the General Staff, above all Waldersee, stimulated the Moltke cult in order to strengthen the authority of the General Staff over that of the War Ministry. Although Moltke's immense prestige had given to the General Staff a predominant position within the army, it was not in fact until 1883 that the Chief of the General Staff was officially given the right of direct access to the Kaiser, without the War Minister having to be present. This was largely the result of Waldersee's efforts to remove the army, and particularly the General Staff, from anything remotely like parliamentary control.[1] In 1883 the War Minister, Kameke, had been the butt of particularly violent attacks in the Reichstag, and Waldersee had skilfully used the ensuing crisis, which led to Kameke's fall from office, to secure greater independence for the General Staff. This was achieved in an agreement between War Ministry, Military Cabinet, and General Staff on 24 May 1883.[2]

[1] See Chapter IV.
[2] Ernst Rudolph Huber, *Heer und Staat in der deutschen Geschichte* (Hamburg, 1938), p. 347.

The Cabinet Order of 1883 was in fact a recognition of an already existing practice. Moltke had paid but scant notice of the stipulation that the General Staff was under the control of the War Ministry, and had seldom troubled to inform the War Minister when discussing military problems with the Kaiser.[1] For Waldersee, however, the order was a further encouragement to strengthen the autonomy of the General Staff, and a spur to his political ambitions.

The period between 1888 and 1891 when Waldersee was chief of the General Staff was also the period of its greatest political influence. Through the military attachés the General Staff exercised a considerable, and almost exclusively harmful, influence on foreign policy. Furthermore Waldersee's own political ambitions and his feud with Bismarck brought the General Staff into the very centre of the political arena.

Caprivi's decisive victory over the military attachés and over Waldersee himself, coupled with the character of Waldersee's successor, Schlieffen, marked the end of the active political influence of the General Staff. Caprivi and the War Minister Bronsart II (1893–6) watched Schlieffen carefully, and tried to prevent him from having anything to do with matters that smacked of politics.[2] Schlieffen himself harboured no political ambitions. The classic type of military 'technician', he confined his attention to strategic planning, and his own reserved nature resulted in the General Staff itself becoming increasingly remote from the rest of the army, and more and more the prey of what Engels described as 'sword-bearing scholasticism'. Schlieffen continued to send regular reports on the military situation in various foreign countries to the government, but they were no longer spiced with outspoken criticisms of the Foreign Office or of official German policy as they had been under Waldersee.

This growing isolation of the General Staff from politics had in many ways as disastrous an effect as the political meddling of the Waldersee era. The famous Schlieffen plan itself is a case in point. Conceived and worked out to the finest detail by the hardworking and in many ways highly capable officers of the General Staff it was, through lack of consideration for the political

[1] Wiegand Schmidt-Richberg, *Die Generalstäbe in Deutschland 1871–1945* (Stuttgart, 1962), p. 16.
[2] Huber, *Heer und Staat*, p. 349.

complexity of Germany's position in Europe, and through inadequate discussion with the government and the civil service, an
intellectual construction, a brilliant sand-table exercise; but it
was also in the last analysis appallingly inflexible and fettered
the government to the idea that a two-front war alone could
offer to the Reich a guarantee of military security in the future.
Here indeed was a crass example of the 'scholasticism' of the
General Staff. One critic of the old Imperial Army, himself a
general in command of a reserve corps, speaks of the 'undeniable
political and diplomatic seclusion (*Weltfremdheit*) of the General
Staff', and claims that, although the General Staff officers were
immensely hard-working, there were no truly creative or
brilliant figures among them.[1] The General Staff in fact was
unable to strike a happy balance between actively meddling
with politics and remaining in splendid and somewhat arrogant
isolation; and in the last resort this latter attitude had important
and unfortunate political results.

Schlieffen's undoubted qualities and his almost Olympian
remoteness earned him a considerable reputation in the army
which believed him to possess the infallible recipe for fighting
a victorious war, a belief which he shared himself. His successor
Moltke had none of these qualities, and was considered by
many to be unsuitable for the post. Schlieffen had been strongly
critical of Moltke, who had dared, when Schlieffen was away
on sick leave, to issue an order stressing the importance of
frontal attack, a complete negation of Schlieffen's obsession
with outflanking movements.[2] Schlieffen then associated himself with a group which included Hülfen-Haeseler and Bernhardi who tried to get Beseler appointed as Schlieffen's successor, and Moltke himself said that he would much prefer
Beseler's appointment to his own as he feared that he might let
down the name of his glorious ancestor.[3] Baroness Spitzemberg
in her diary echoed the disappointment in Conservative circles.
'It is depressing that Schlieffen, who is very highly regarded by
the officers, should just at this moment resign, somewhat against

---

[1] Otto Moser, *Ernsthafte Plaudereien über den Weltkrieg* (Stuttgart, 1925), pp. 33–35.
[2] Friedrich von Boetticher, *Schlieffen* (Göttingen, 1957), pp. 78–79.
[3] Werner Conze, *Polnische Nation und deutsche Politik im Ersten Weltkrieg* (Cologne, 1958), p. 110; Friedrich von Bernhardi, *Denkwürdigkeiten aus meinem Leben* (Berlin, 1927), p. 255.

his will, and that H. Moltke has been appointed his successor.'[1] Moltke's own career was also not calculated to inspire confidence among the 'technicians' of the General Staff. His career was typical for a highly placed member of the military aristocracy. He had served for eight years as adjutant to his illustrious uncle, and for five years as aide-de-camp to the Kaiser. He had commanded a guards regiment, a guards brigade, and finally a guards division. He had only been attached to the General Staff for one year.[2] His appointment, like most of the other steps in his career, was almost entirely the work of William II, who said of the other two candidates whose names had been suggested that he did not know Beseler and would not accept Goltz.[3] Moltke was highly reluctant to take on the job, and was constantly plagued by the suspicion that he was likely to fail when it came to the test: a suspicion that was entirely justified.

Curiously enough Moltke, although lacking in determination, and without the uncritical support of the army in general, played a vital role in foreign policy. Schlieffen, who paid scant regard to anything that happened outside the four walls of his office, had treated his Austrian allies with something approaching contempt, and the relations between the two General Staffs had become exceedingly strained. Moltke quite rightly realized that the Schlieffen plan needed the active support and co-operation of the Austrians to hold the Eastern front whilst the German army was tied down in France. This led to military talks with Conrad von Hötzendorf, the Austrian Chief of the General Staff, and to the guarantee of German support for Austrian ambitions in the Balkans. Moltke soon became an advocate of preventive war, whether as a result of the growing belligerence of the army, or through a desire to prove to himself that he was capable of leading the army to victory, we cannot tell.

In one important respect Moltke was an improvement on Schlieffen. Schlieffen, in spite of his imperious ways, was extremely subservient to the Kaiser, and was incapable of standing

---

[1] Baronin Spitzemberg, *Tagebuch* (Göttingen, 1961), 1-1-1906.

[2] Boetticher, *Schlieffen*, p. 72.

[3] Generaloberst Helmuth von Moltke, *Erinnerungen—Briefe—Dokumente 1877–1916*, ed. Eliza von Moltke (Stuttgart, 1922), p. 306.

up to his interference with the army. This was particularly true of manoeuvres when Schlieffen went out of his way to show up the Kaiser in a good light. This attitude, which may partly have been dictated by Schlieffen's desire to placate the Kaiser in order to be left in peace afterwards, was not shared by Moltke, who as a friend of William, and well schooled in the arts of court intrigue, was able to stand up to him, with the result that manoeuvres and exercises improved greatly.[1] Although this was an undoubted achievement, many people agreed with Eckardstein's comment on Moltke: 'he belongs to the category of the correct and limited.'[2]

The General Staff was divided into four main divisions, the first three of which were under the three 'Over-Quartermasters'. The first division was responsible for overall strategic planning and for the details of the mobilization. This division was also responsible for the fortifications, armaments, and the military use of the railways. The second division supervised the training and manoeuvres of the army, the collection of information on other countries, and the co-ordination of the plans made by the first division. The third division was responsible for collecting information about Russia and France and assessing their war potential. The fourth division was divided into the trigono-metrical section, the topographical section, and the carto-graphical section, and was responsible for drawing up highly detailed military maps. Apart from the four main divisions there were a number of smaller sections which came under the direct control of the Chief of the General Staff. These included the central section, which dealt with the organization and administration of the General Staff itself, the military history section, the Staff archives and library, and a further section for topography.

In 1888 there were 239 officers on the General Staff of whom 197 were Prussians, 25 from Bavaria, 10 from Saxony, and 7 from Württemberg. This number included the General Staff officers attached to the corps, the army inspectorate, and the military attachés. By 1914, however, this number was increased to 625, a reflection not only of the vast increases in the size of the army, but also of the increased complexity and technical

---

[1] Ludendorff, E. *Mein militärischer Werdegang* (Munich, 1933), p. 42.
[2] Hermann von Eckardstein, *Die Isolierung Deutschlands* (Leipzig, 1921), p. 186.

advances in modern warfare. These factors were also reflected in changes of organization within the Staff. The various sections within the divisions became increasingly independent. There were now six Quartermasters responsible for nine principal sections. These sections were: 1. Russia, including the Balkans and the Far East. 2. Deployment and mobilization. 3. France and the West. 4. Foreign armies. 5. Training and the War Academy. 6. Manoeuvres. 7. Sub-section of section 4. 8. Sub-section of section 5. 9. Austria. Further there were two sections for military history and one for map-making. The General Staff was never short of funds. 350,000 marks were provided for espionage alone, most of which was spent on spies in France and Russia. This sum was increased in 1913.

The General Staff in the Corps, the '*Truppengeneralstab*', which was usually under the command of a colonel, was responsible for the mobilization plans in the corps, for manoeuvres, firing practice, and other exercises. The *Truppengeneralstab* was directly responsible to the General Staff in Berlin, and therefore had a marked tendency to work behind the backs of their own corps commanders. It needed an energetic general to keep a close eye on the activities of his General Staff officers, and since many generals were of an advanced age this was very rarely the case, thus causing a serious breakdown in the unity of command at corps level.[1]

The General Staff was a small and highly influential military clique, and membership of the Staff was an almost essential prerequisite for a successful military career. The examination for entrance to the War Academy, the first step on the way to the General Staff, was by no means easy. The competition was particularly severe for candidates from infantry regiments, because the number of applications from them was far greater than from the cavalry who, being largely dominated by the aristocracy, were not so career-minded.[2] Although it was difficult for young officers to find the time for study, between their many social engagements, to say nothing of long hours spent

---

[1] See: Max Van den Bergh, *Das deutsche Heer vor dem Weltkriege* (Berlin, 1934); Schmidt-Richberg, *Die Generalstäbe in Deutschland*; Georg von Alten, *Handbuch für Heer und Flotte* (Berlin, 1909); A. S. Jerussalimski, *Die Aussenpolitik und Diplomatie des Deutschen Imperialismus* (Stuttgart, 1954).

[2] Ludwig Renn, *Adel im Untergang* (Berlin, 1948), p. 340.

on the barrack square or on the manoeuvre grounds, the rewards were great. Membership of the General Staff was estimated to put an average of eight years on to an officer's seniority.[1] Although the General Staff was preponderantly aristocratic, blue blood alone was not sufficient for appointment to the Staff. Bernhardi for example refused to allow the son of his friend General von Schlichting to sit for the examinations for the War Academy saying that he was not good enough for the General Staff, and the father, though somewhat shattered, accepted Bernhardi's criticisms.[2] Among the General Staff were also many who owed their careers entirely to their own military capabilities, such as Groener and Ludendorff, examples of the 'technicians' who increasingly set the tone in the Staff.

If the General Staff was to some extent prepared to make concessions to a new spirit which put attainment above birth, the Military Cabinet remained an aristocratic preserve. The reforms of 1883 had strengthened the Military Cabinet at the expense of the War Ministry, the personnel section of the War Ministry being abolished, and the Military Cabinet given control over matters of personnel. Albedyll, the chief of the Military Cabinet from 1871 to 1888, was a highly energetic officer who did much to increase its influence.[3] The Military Cabinet had the advantage of being in constant touch with the Kaiser, not only in Berlin but also on his frequent journeys when the Chief of the Military Cabinet, or one of his subordinates, usually accompanied him. This placed it in a considerably more advantageous position than either the General Staff or the War Ministry.[4]

The power and authority of the Military Cabinet, in the absence of any clear-cut definition of its position, depended to a large extent on the personality of its chief. None of Albedyll's successors had his qualities. Von Hahnke, who followed him, played an important part in the intrigues over the long-overdue reform of military law which began in 1894, but although this led to the fall of the Foreign Minister Marschall, the Minister

[1] Van der Bergh, *Heer vor dem Weltkriege*, p. 115.

[2] Bernhardi, *Denkwürdigkeiten*, p. 185.

[3] Huber, *Heer und Staat*, p. 327.

[4] Friedrich Hossbach, *Die Entwicklung des Oberbefehls über das Heer in Brandenburg, Preussen und im Deutschen Reich von 1655–1945* (Würzburg, 1964), p. 220.

of the Interior Boetticher, and the War Minister Bronsart, in the last resort the Military Cabinet and the Kaiser had to give way to the justified demands of the Reichstag.[1] Hahnke was followed in 1901 by Graf von Hülfen-Haeseler, who was soon to realize that the Military Cabinet's control of appointments did not apply to the higher positions in the army which were controlled by the Kaiser. Hülfen-Haeseler lamely tried to stop Moltke's appointment as Chief of the General Staff, but realized there was nothing he could do about it.[2] The unfortunate count's military career ended abruptly with a heart attack which he suffered while dancing in front of the Kaiser dressed up as a ballerina.

Lyncker, who succeeded Hülfen-Haeseler in 1908, was equally subservient to the Kaiser's wishes, but this did not imply any real decline in the importance of the Military Cabinet. The War Ministry showed no wish to win back any of the authority it had lost to the Military Cabinet in 1883, and neither Bülow nor Bethmann showed any real interest in military affairs, believing that humble politicians were unable to grasp such technical problems. The Military Cabinet was, however, constantly attacked by the opposition in the Reichstag as being unconstitutional, thereby raising a difficult problem of constitutional law.[3] Criticism of the Military Cabinet reached a new peak after the *Daily Telegraph* affair, which was thought to be a further example of the Kaiser's desire to rule alone, unhampered by the restrictions placed upon him by the Reichstag. A strong movement arose to place the Military Cabinet under the control of the Reichstag, for the War Minister seemed increasingly to be a mere puppet unaware of what was happening in the army, thus making nonsense of any idea of ministerial responsibility.[4] Neither the army nor the War Ministry had any intention of weakening the Military Cabinet, for there was nothing they feared more than that the Reichstag might be able to strengthen its grip on military affairs. Quite apart from these considerations the army was unlikely to criticize an

---

[1] See Gordon Craig. *Politics of the Prussian Army 1640–1945* (Oxford, 1955), pp. 246–51.

[2] Rudolf Schmidt-Bückeburg, *Das Militärkabinett der preussischen Könige und deutschen Kaiser* (Berlin, 1933), p. 230.

[3] Huber, *Heer und Staat*, p. 333.

[4] Rudolf Schmidt-Bückeburg, *Das Militärkabinett*, p. 238.

institution which was directly concerned with promotion and postings, and which held the personal papers of the officers. An officer would be loath to risk his chances of a career by criticizing the Military Cabinet.

The War Ministry, which had been described by Bismarck as a 'difficult and unfinished constitutional construction', had lost much of the authority it had had in the days of Roon. This was due in part to the determination of the army to reduce the power of the War Ministry, which it believed to be a dangerous compromise with parliamentarianism, but equally important was the fact that for many years the office of War Minister was held by men who were either unable or unwilling to assert what authority was left to them. Walter Bronsart von Schellendorf,[1] who was War Minister from 1893 to 1896, was determined to restore some of the authority of his office, and was convinced that the army should make at least some concessions to the demands of the Reichstag in the interests of creating a more satisfactory balance between the army and society. Inevitably these heretical views brought him into direct conflict with the Kaiser and his conservative military entourage. The Kaiser was determined to preserve his rights over the army, and was horrified at Bronsart's suggestion that the War Minister should have the right to counter-sign his orders to the army. Although Hohenlohe agreed with Bronsart that the army should not be allowed to remain in such an isolated position, he was too old and feeble to give the War Minister adequate support. Thus Bronsart fell on the issue of military law reform, a measure to which he had given energetic support, in the belief that it was well calculated to bridge the gap between the army and the Reichstag without seriously damaging the independence of the army.[2] The two last ministers before the war, von Heeringen and von Falkenhayn, did something to reassert the remaining

[1] Lieutenant General Walter Bronsart von Schellendorf came from an old Prussian aristocratic family, and was the younger brother of Paul Bronsart von Schellendorf who had been War Minister from 1883 to 1889. Paul, unlike his younger brother, had been a fierce opponent of any parliamentary influence over the army and of any restriction of the Kaiser's power of command. The Schellendorfs' mother was Ingeborg Stark, a well known pianist and pupil of Liszt. Another Schellendorf brother was the composer, among other works, of the now long-forgotten Spring Symphony 'In den Alpen'.

[2] Bogdan Graf von Hutten-Czapski, *Sechzig Jahre Politik und Gesellschaft* (Berlin 1936), p. 244.

powers of the War Ministry over other military departments. Heeringen for example sent a strongly worded note to Moltke in December 1912 protesting against Moltke's habit of dealing directly with the Chancellor, and omitting to inform the War Ministry which was responsible for military affairs within the government.[1] In 1883 the War Ministry had lost not only its personnel section but also the right of military command. It became in fact an almost purely administrative organization. The Ministry was divided into four departments. The Central Department (ZD) was responsible for matters dealing with the Reichstag and the press, as well as for the organization of the Ministry itself. The General War Department (AD) was for purely military affairs, and was divided into 7 sections (A1–A7) dealing with the various branches of the army. The Army Administration Department (BD) dealt with general administrative problems and the Justice Department (CD) was responsible for granting pensions and compensation in addition to general legal matters.[2] Although the War Ministry had lost much of its power and authority it was not, as many contemporaries believed, reduced to complete impotence. In the army the War Minister was known as the 'parliamentary whipping boy', a term which suggests that to many soldiers it was now little more than a concession to the demands of the Reichstag, devoid of any real usefulness in military terms. The Reichstag was annoyed that the army was so weakly represented, a clear demonstration, to the liberals and the left, that the army was determined to avoid any sort of parliamentary control. This view was voiced by one Dr Wiemer in the Reichstag in 1909 who said that: 'The War Ministry today is only a purely administrative organization, and the War Minister has "*nix to seggen*" in all matters of command, although he must be responsible for them to the Reichstag. This causes all kinds of frictions.'[3] The War Ministry was in fact perfectly content with the situation, for it did not wish to allow the Reichstag any control over the army, particularly in matters of command, and often found it a useful excuse against the more virulent attacks to

---

[1] Rüdt von Collenberg, *Wissen und Wehr*, Heft 5 (1927).
[2] Generaloberst von Einem, *Erinnerungen eines Soldaten* (Leipzig, 1933), p. 49.
[3] *Stenographische Berichte über die Verhandlungen des Deutschen Reichstages*, 7-12-1909.

state that the question involved did not fall within its sphere of influence.

Its weakened position in terms of responsibility for the army in the Reichstag did not automatically mean a loss of authority in other fields. The Prussian War Minister represented the point of view of the army at ministerial meetings, and was thus the most important link between the army and the government. It was neither utterly removed from the day-to-day affairs of the Reich as was the General Staff, nor was it slavishly subject to the whims of the Kaiser as was the Military Cabinet, but was directly involved in discussions at governmental level. Further as an essentially administrative body it had much to do with the links between the Prussian army and the other armies of the Reich, and was thus an important organ of Prussian military domination. Lastly, and perhaps most important, it used the fact that it had to represent the army in the Reichstag as a stick with which to beat the General Staff and the Military Cabinet, should it be at odds with either of them. Thus it was that the War Ministry was able to reduce drastically the demands of the General Staff for increases in the size of the army, by insisting that the Reichstag would under no circumstances accept such increases, although this argument was fallacious and the real reason was that the War Ministry wished to preserve the small, aristocratic, 'reliable' Officer Corps.

Thus although the War Ministry had lost much of its former authority as a result of the reforms of 1883 its importance should not be underestimated. The War Minister was responsible for representing the views of the army in the Reichstag, the Bundesrat, and the Prussian Landtag, and thus had important connexions with the conservative parties, quite apart from his attendance at ministerial meetings. This position could be used by a determined War Minister to win back much that had been lost. For the General Staff and even for the Military Cabinet the War Minister was a great deal more than a 'parliamentary whipping boy', he was a force to be reckoned with.

Although the German army was divided into four separate armies few disputed the dominant role of the Prussian army, and the officers of the different armies feared nothing more than to be branded as separatists. The army was seen as the embodiment of the idea of the Reich, where local pride and loyalties were submerged in loyalty to the German Emperor as supreme warlord. As one journalist remarked of the Bavarian army: 'The Bavarian Officer Corps is the bearer of the idea of the Reich in Bavaria; in this Corps there is no room for anti-imperial feelings.'[1] The armies of Bavaria, Württemberg, and Saxony were often criticized by local patriots as being the slavish imitators of the Prussians, unmindful of the needs of their own states, and traitors to the ideal of historical and ethnic independence. In Württemberg, for example, the War Minister continually defended the Prussian army against the attacks of the Swabian patriots, and insisted on the necessity of a firm and unequivocal lead in military matters from the Prussian army.[2] The army saw it as part of its duty to support the notion of the Reich and to fight against particularist ideas within the different Officer Corps, and to convince those officers who entertained outmoded notions of the individual rights of the various German states of the folly of their ways. Many officers were well aware of the important role they had to play in forging the unity of the Reich. As one of them wrote: 'It is the most sacred duty of the commanders to watch over the loyalty of their officers, to stamp out particularist ideas and to eliminate any disloyal elements.'[3]

Coupled with this determination to use the army as a breeding ground for true sons of the Reich was an almost unqualified admiration for the Prussian army. Thus although a complex series of military treaties between the various states of the Reich endowed the War Ministries of the different armies with a certain formal independence, in practice the Prussian War Ministry and General Staff took little notice of the opinions and requirements of the other armies, and were able to count on the meek submission of such lesser beings. Even in Bavaria, whose army only came under the command of the Kaiser in time of war, independence from Prussia in any real sense of the word was neither practically possible, nor, on the Bavarian side, even desired.

The allied armies lost many of their most promising officers

---

[1] Heeresarchiv Stuttgart: Persönliche Angelegenheiten des WKM, Band 25.
[2] Ibid., Band 19.
[3] Heeresarchiv Stuttgart: Nachlass von Gleich; Reprint of a speech by General von Alvensleben, 'Über Offiziere und Demokratie 1890'.

to the Prussian army, but on the whole they regarded this as a compliment rather than a drain on manpower. The Prussian War Ministry would ask the different armies for officers to fill certain posts, the choice of the candidate being left to the individual army. It is clear, however, that great trouble was taken to choose a well qualified officer so that the Prussians could see that they did not have a monopoly of good soldiers. There were some complaints that such officers were not treated as equals by the Prussians, and that important information was often withheld from them. A memorandum of the Bavarian War Minister of January 1914 stressed this point: 'A reconsideration of the agreement seems necessary to increase Bavaria's influence in the wartime leadership of the army.' The Minister suggested that a Bavarian General be attached to the Prussian General Staff.[1] The Prussians did not find it necessary to make any substantial concessions to such demands for equality of rights; confident of their dominating position, they could shrug off such claims as being merely separatist in character and contrary to the spirit of the Reich.

Individual officers often applied for transfers to another army. Many officers who felt that they had unjustly failed to be given promotion tried to get transfers in the hope that in another army promotion might be more speedy. Also officers who were guilty of breaches of military law tried to obtain commissions in other armies in order to start their military careers again from scratch; thus a captain from a Hessian regiment who had gone A.W.O.L. to fight with the British Army in South Africa, thereby coming up against the Prussian military authorities, applied for a transfer to Bavaria, but the gallant captain's request was turned down, he was sent back to his unit and then dismissed from the army. Other reasons given for transfers were usually from officers who wished to live nearer their parents or their estates. In order to stop such transfers it was agreed that an officer should only be allowed to transfer with the express permission and sanction of his War Ministry, a measure which helped to reduce the number of undesirables seeking their luck elsewhere.[2]

The Prussian army was less scrupulous in its use of transfers, and would use the system to get rid of some of its black sheep.

---

[1] Bayr.HSA, Abt. IV, KA, M.Kr.2114.   [2] Ibid., 1944.

Thus one Freiherr von Thüngen was transferred to the Bavarian army when it transpired that his parents had married some time after his birth.[1] Another officer, Lieutenant Senger, was transferred to Bavaria when he became engaged to the divorced wife of another officer in his regiment. Although the lady's honour was unquestioned it was felt that such a match was undesirable within the Prussian Officer Corps.[2]

In spite of such cases the number of formal transfers between the different armies was not very large. Applications were carefully considered, and the transfer involved an immense amount of paper work which the ministries no doubt wished to avoid. From the surviving records of the Bavarian army it would seem that an average of between four and five officers were transferred from the Bavarian army yearly, and the number in Saxony and Württemberg is unlikely to have been any greater.[3]

The number of officers attached to other armies, without actually being transferred to a different Officer Corps, was much higher. These postings were almost the same as actual transfers in that the officer wore the uniform of the Officer Corps to which he was attached. Thus in 1914 6 generals, 24 staff officers, 28 captains, and 20 lieutenants were posted from Württemberg to Prussia, and 3 generals, 15 staff officers, and 19 captains were transferred to Württemberg from Prussia. Such postings were an inevitable result of the military convention between Prussia and Württemberg, the 'Bebenhausener Konvention', which guaranteed equal opportunities of promotion in the two armies. This was not possible within a small army such as that of Württemberg, and officers due for promotion had often to be transferred to the Prussian army where the openings were greater. Transfers from Prussia on the other hand were dictated by Prussia's desire to have as many Prussian officers as possible serving in important posts in other armies, so as to guarantee a high degree of subservience to their requirements. Figures taken at random from the number of Prussian and Württemberg officers in military positions classified as 'important' in an official report on the Württemberg army give the following picture: 1890, 14 Württemberg and 11 Prussian; 1893, 12 Württemberg and 13 Prussian; 1900, 18 Württemberg

---

[1] Bayr.HSA, Abt. IV, KA, M.Kr.2114, 1945 (Pr. Mil.Kab., 12-10-1913).
[2] Ibid.   [3] Ibid., 1947.

and 12 Prussian. In such circumstances it is difficult to claim any high degree of independence from the Prussian army.[1] Such a situation was justified by the Württemberg War Minister to the Württemberg Chamber of Deputies in the following terms: 'The safety of a small contingent is guaranteed through co-operation with the life and activities of a large army, so that it will always remain master of any situation.' Although attacked by the local patriots the Württemberg army was determined not to be branded by their Prussian brothers-in-arms as separatist.[2]

The division of the German army into four separate armies was thus much less of a hindrance to effective military unity than might at first be assumed. In spite of paper concessions to other armies the Prussian army remained supreme and unchallenged; the idea of the Reich, the need for a common strategic plan, and the position of the Kaiser as supreme commander in time of war proved far stronger in the army than any local sentiment. Patriotic toasts and anti-Prussian jokes enlivened many an evening in the mess, but in purely military matters the Prussian army was an ideal that, however grudgingly, was admired and emulated.

The fundamental weakness of the German army was not this division into four separate armies, but rather the confusion, and indeed chaos, that ruled at the top of the Prussian army. The duties and the activities, to say nothing of the constitutional positions, of War Minister, General Staff, and Military Cabinet were never properly defined, and the division of effective command into the hands of three jealous rivals had disastrous consequences. The reforms of 1883 might have helped the army to remain free from any sort of parliamentary control, but the army's efforts to reduce the authority of the War Minister put an end to any notion of unity of command. This unity could never have been provided by the Chancellor, for he had little authority over the army, and in any case none of Bismarck's successors made the slightest attempt to meddle in the affairs of the army. The only possible lead could have come from the Kaiser.

---

[1] Heeresarchiv Stuttgart. Persönliche Angelegenheiten der WKM, Band 2.

[2] *Verhandlungen der Württembergische Kammer der Abgeordneten 1899/1900* (Stuttgart, 1900; 30-10-1900).

William II was greeted with enthusiasm by the army, and only a few officers considered the fact that he appeared for his first official engagement in naval uniform an ominous portent. The army had as little love for Frederick William as had his own son, and was on the whole relieved at his early demise, regarding him, for reasons which are somewhat obscure to members of a later generation, as a dangerous liberal. William began his reign with a period of frenetic energy in military affairs, aged generals were swiftly pensioned off, and the Officer Corps was rendered somewhat more youthful, a measure which was long overdue. The army, delighted at the sudden prospect of quicker promotion, and excited by the Kaiser's swash-buckling utterances, stood solidly behind him. The military attaché in Vienna, von Deines, was thrilled, and said of the Kaiser: 'A real man—he is bound to fight!'[1] One officer recalled in his memoirs: 'Under the young Kaiser a breath of fresh air went through the army—many elderly officers were retired, and the higher ranks from regimental commander upwards were on the whole given to younger men. The Kaiser was very active, took part in many inspections and was everywhere stimulating and enlivening.'[2] This description of the atmos-phere of the time is in agreement with that of the later War Minister, von Einem, who stresses the popularity of the Kaiser in the army on account of these measures.[3] Baroness Spitzem-berg noted in her diary: 'Yes, the young Kaiser really chases his people around, particularly the military.... The tempo of an impetuous, ambitious and energetic young man.'[4] The emphasis which the Kaiser placed on military affairs can be seen in his weekly time-table which foresaw seven interviews per week for the army, one for the navy, and only two for the civil cabinet.[5] Further the Kaiser spent much of his time inspecting military units, often at short notice in the middle of the night, or drinking with his friends in the Potsdam guards regiments. His speeches were full of references to the splendid traditions of the army, stressing the intimate and sacred links between Kaiser and army, and of vivid promises of a blood-stained future, whether

[1] E. von Witzleben, *Adolf von Deines, Lebensbild 1845–1911* (Berlin, 1913), p. 176.
[2] BA Militärarchiv: 1108-58/1 Nachlass von der Schulenburg-Tressow.
[3] Von Einem, *Erinnerungen eines Soldaten*, p. 39.
[4] Spitzemberg, *Tagebuch*, 19-8-1888.
[5] Rudolf Schmidt-Bückeburg, *Das Militärkabinett*, p. 178.

fighting against Germany's enemies abroad, or against the Social Democrats at home.

The army's admiration for the Kaiser did not last long. The elder Moltke was one of the first to realize that William had militarily and politically the maturity of a lieutenant.[1] Slowly but surely many officers who knew William well enough came to much the same conclusion. The Kaiser had not only an inadequate and superficial knowledge of military affairs but also an inability to accept any sort of criticism from his military advisers. Pomp and circumstance and immaculate drill were of more importance to him than the more technical problems of modern warfare, a fact which often tried the patience of his long-suffering but nevertheless loyal generals. The Officer Corps gradually realized that behind the dramatic and threatening words of William's speeches to the army there was little more than a passion for the dramas of the manoeuvre ground and the splendour of the uniforms to which the Kaiser paid such close and loving attention. The Kaiser, it was feared, was essentially a peace-loving man, prepared to compromise with Germany's enemies. It is hardly surprising therefore that the annual display of German military strength, the Kaiser manoeuvres, was very much to William II's histrionic taste. This was his show, a demonstration to all the world of the fine qualities of the army, and above all of his own remarkable abilities as a commander. The world was to know that the German army was second to none, and that in Kaiser William II it had a war lord who was certain to take his place in military history.

William II's love of the army and for things military was here given full rein. Here was his chance to show military experts from the whole world that the extravagant claims he made for himself were justified. His allies were to feel confidence in his leadership and his enemies fear of his wrath. That William II put such emphasis on the importance of the manoeuvres for German prestige, coupled with the fact that as a military leader he was not endowed with any exceptional qualities, meant that the General Staff had to devise ingenious methods of allowing the *Oberste Kriegsherr* to win his battles on the manoeuvre ground. The Kaiser's side in the manoeuvres had to win, come what

[1] Rudolf Stadelmann, *Moltke und der Staat* (Krefeld, 1950), p. 330.

may, otherwise he would be made to look ridiculous in the eyes of foreign observers, and the prestige of the Reich would suffer. This view was endorsed by the General Staff.[1] The fact that the General Staff went to endless trouble to disguise the fact that the whole manoeuvre was designed for the Kaiser to win, led him to believe that he was in fact a military leader of quality. Baroness Spitzemberg describes the Kaiser's attitude at manoeuvres as 'Caesarean mania'.[2] The fact that the Kaiser was often able to make a pointed appreciation of a military problem, only helped to confuse the issue. Baroness Spitzemberg notes, 'I should like to add that Axel (a relative of the writer's) stressed that the Kaiser's military criticisms are often excellent, that he can appraise and judge a battle, for example, clearly and correctly and then he will give orders for an attack that is so absurd that one would think that one was in the presence of an utterly incompetent officer.'[3]

A particularly unattractive aspect of the manoeuvres was that they were often used as a means of getting rid of unwanted officers. The method was simple. The officer, usually an elderly officer who was otherwise due for promotion, was set an extremely difficult problem, usually one to which several answers could be given. At the criticism of the manoeuvres, which was usually given before a large group of officers, the solution given by the unfortunate victim was then torn to pieces, thus humiliating him in the face of his brother officers. A passionate apologist of the Wilhelmine army describes this unattractive practice as 'one of the few dark spots in the old army'.[4] Equally, criticism of the Kaiser's leadership could seriously harm an officer's career. Waldersee's criticisms of the Kaiser at the manoeuvre in 1890, when he was Chief of the General Staff, was one of the causes of his dismissal in the following year.[5] Similarly in 1908 Hindenburg, who was commanding the 4th Army Corps, allowed the Kaiser's corps to

---

[1] Freiherr von Freytag-Loringhoven, *Menschen und Dinge wie ich sie in meinem Leben sah* (Berlin, 1923), p. 106.

[2] Spitzemberg, *Tagebuch*, 3-11-1900.

[3] Ibid., 7-12-1913.

[4] Van den Bergh, *Das deutsche Heer vor dem Weltkriege*, p. 112; also R von Rijn, *Individualismus und Schablone im deutschen Heere* (Berlin, 1892).

[5] Generalfeldmarschall Alfred Graf von Waldersee, *Denkwürdigkeiten*. H. O. Meisner (Stuttgart, 1925).

lose the battle. This led to a lot of bad feeling between the two, and may well have been the decisive factor which led to Hindenburg's resignation in 1911.[1]

Naturally enough many officers were severely critical of the whole idea of the Kaiser manoeuvres. That so much money and planning should be wasted on such an empty show was, for serious soldiers, a scandal. The British military attaché in Berlin was at first impressed by the manoeuvres, and wrote in his report on the manoeuvre in 1897 that 'the Emperor is probably the best cavalry leader in the German Army'.[2] But it did not take him long to see through the outward dash and splendour. Two years later he wrote, 'the theory of *toujours l'audace* and of a bold offensive carried out with great energy and regardless of losses is all very well and reads very well on paper. But it may be carried too far.' It seemed as if 'the minds that put the theories into practice were unbalanced'.[3] The younger Moltke considered that the manoeuvres were a complete waste of time as the Kaiser always won.[4] Bernhardi wrote in his memoirs, 'these Kaiser manoeuvres were pure torture for me. They were no longer military exercises which could be taken seriously and none of us thought of them as such. They were exhibitions, designed more for the general public than for serious soldiers.'[5] But he found some encouragement in Schlieffen's last manoeuvre. In 1906 he wrote, 'he has . . . really got his own way, and the Kaiser no longer commanded the last Kaiser manoeuvre. One must take off one's hat to him.'[6] But the possibility of keeping the Kaiser away from his manoeuvres was very small, and Moltke had to use roundabout methods to reduce his influence on the exercises, a course which did not appreciably increase their effectiveness.

The manoeuvres had a number of important results. They confirmed many of William's exaggerated ideas as to his military genius. They led many foreign observers to underestimate the real qualities of the German army. But probably most important of all, they convinced the vast majority of the

[1] John Wheeler-Bennett, *Hindenburg, The Wooden Titan*, (London, 1936), p. 5.
[2] D. S. Macdiarmid, *The Life of Lt. Gen. Sir James Moncrieff Grierson* (London, 1923), p. 129.
[3] Ibid., p. 141.   [4] Moltke, *Erinnerungen*, p. 308.
[5] Bernhardi, *Denkwürdigkeiten*, p. 215.   [6] Ibid., p. 272.

generals that the Kaiser was not capable of playing a decisive part in any future war. When war broke out they knew that it was too serious a matter to be left to emperors, and hence the intimate links between the crown and the army began to break. On the administrative level William appointed a Royal Headquarters, an institution which previously had only existed in time of war. It included the personal military aides many of whom were also military attachés, and the generals *à la suite*, the whole coming under the command of the Commandant of the Headquarters. The Royal Headquarters caused further confusion in an army whose command had been divided, and the lack of definition between Military Cabinet and Royal Headquarters was the source of some friction.[1] It was through the Royal Headquarters that William tried to conduct his policy independently from the civil administration, an attempt which was not only doomed to failure by the determination of the civilians not to be by-passed, but also through the fact that the Royal Headquarters could never speak for the army as a whole. The divisions within the army made it virtually impossible to use the army as an instrument of the 'personal regiment' without fundamental reforms at the top, and William was not the man to undertake such a wearisome task.

That the army gave the impression of being a united whole was largely due to the reverence paid by all officers to the Kaiser. In the presence of the supreme warlord criticism was stilled and an obsequious subservience took its place. Although in private and on the pages of their diaries many leading generals expressed their dissatisfaction and even contempt for William, to his face they presented a united front of respectful obedience. William's Controller of the Household, who had ample opportunity to watch the Kaiser and the leading officers, wrote of a meeting between the Kaiser and some high-ranking officers in 1904 that 'not one present dared to speak dispassionately, objectively, and from expert knowledge, about the causes of so many obvious abuses'.[2] Philip Eulenburg, 'the Kaiser's friend', said of William's military advisers: 'the Maison Militaire—which, in the hard-bitten "German" style HM has

[1] Gordon Craig, *Politics of the Prussian Army*, p. 240.
[2] Count RobertZ edlitz-Trützschler, *Twelve Years at the Imperial German Court* (London, 1924), p. 56.

re-named Head Quarters!—has been pompously inaugurated with Plessen in charge, who talks of nothing but gunfire. My God, if only Bismarck were here to keep *that* crew under his coarse thumb!'[1] Although the confusion in the upper echelons of the army gave hot-heads like Plessen the opportunity of expounding their drastic views to an appreciative Kaiser, it had the converse effect that the extremists did not have the means of putting their dreams into practice. It was not until July 1914 that the exhilarating prospect of a European war at last brought a sense of unity to the army, and the divisions and squabbles of the peace-time era were forgotten.

[1] Johannes Haller, *Philip Eulenburg: The Kaiser's Friend* (London, 1930), p. 163.

II

THE SOCIAL STRUCTURE OF THE
OFFICER CORPS AND THE ISSUE
OF ANTI-SEMITISM

THE fundamental changes in German society under
William II naturally led to changes in the social composition of the German Officer Corps. Throughout the period
the old landed aristocracy was losing ground to the industrialists, and the rear-guard actions of the East Elbian Junkers
were insufficient to halt the march of industrialization, and
with it the growing social and political influence of the capitalist
bourgeoisie. Understandably there were many links between
the aristocrats and the capitalists. Aristocrats were often eager
to emulate the ways of the successful capitalist concerns, and
entered industry with enthusiasm and often with success. Pless,
Henckel von Donnersmarck, Schaffgotsch, and Ballestrem
were among the most powerful coal magnates in Silesia. The
King of Württemberg, the Grand-duke of Sachsen-Weimar, the
Duke of Sachsen-Koburg and Gotha, and Prince Reuss were
all involved in colonial enterprises. On the other hand many
successful industrialists and merchants bought up country
estates, and led the life of country gentlemen. Inter-marriage
between the two groups was also common. Krupp's heiress, for
example, married the aristocrat von Bohlen und Halbach, and
Stumm's granddaughter the ambassador von Kühlmann.[1]

These changes were reflected in the Officer Corps. In 1860
65 per cent. of the officers in the Prussian army were aristocrats.
By 1913 the number of aristocrats had declined to 30 per cent.[2]

The decreasing percentage of aristocrats in the Officer Corps,
caused as much by the enormous increases in the size of the

[1] A. S. Jerussalimski, *Die Aussenpolitik und die Diplomatie des deutschen Imperialismus*,
pp. 78–79.
[2] Karl Demeter, *Das Deutsche Offizierkorps in Gesellschaft und Staat, 1650–1945*
(Frankfurt-am-Main, 1962), p. 26.

army, as by the weakened position of the aristocracy in German society, was a matter of concern for the army. The traditional image of the German officer had always been aristocratic, and many officers believed that any change in the social structure of the Officer Corps would be a change for the worse. Nearly all the military writers of the day believed that a weakening of the aristocratic element in the Officer Corps would reduce the military effectiveness of the army. The importance of family tradition was stressed: 'When sons follow the profession their fathers have practised for generations it is obvious that from childhood they are accustomed to the ins and outs of it, that they cherish and emulate the inheritance of their fathers' deeds.'[1] Von der Goltz in his influential work, *The Nation in Arms*, argued on much the same lines, claiming that an aristocratic background gave a young man the habit of commanding others, and thus suited him particularly for a military profession.[2] Another writer described the privileges of the aristocracy in the army as an 'historical necessity'.[3] A weakening of the aristocratic element in the army, it was argued, would reduce the distinctions between officers and men, and thus undermine military discipline. 'Such a democratization of the Officer Corps, would mean that the distinction between officers and N.C.O.'s would soon cease to exist. Precisely in the unique present day position of the German officer lies his strength and his military efficiency.'[4] The military theorist Freiherr von Freytag-Loringhoven was another apologist for the aristocracy. 'This aristocratic composition of the German Officer Corps and its direct relationship with the supreme warlord gives our army stability, and should be preserved at all costs.'[5]

Although the army increased rapidly, and many aristocratic families died out, the fear that the aristocracy would lose its preponderant position in the army was only partly justified. The percentage of aristocratic officers was in no proper proportion to the number of aristocrats in the Reich. Aristocrats had

---

[1] A. von Boguslawski, *Deutschland, Das Heer* (Berlin, 1904), p. 125.
[2] Generalfeldmarschall Colmar von der Goltz, *The Nation in Arms* (London, 1906), p. 83.
[3] Van den Bergh, *Heer vor dem Weltkriege*, p. 99.
[4] E. A. Selbach, *Der Einjährige muss bleiben!* (Dusseldorf, 1895).
[5] Freiherr von Freytag-Loringhoven, *Krieg und Politik in der Neuzeit* (Berlin, 1911), p. 275.

far better chances of promotion and had the best positions in the army. In 1900 60 per cent. of the officers of the rank of colonel and above were aristocrats, and even by 1913 the percentage had only dropped to 53.[1] In 1909 of 190 infantry generals only 39 were from bourgeois families, and nearly 50 per cent. of the majors were aristocrats.[2] The aristocrats naturally tended to be concentrated in certain regiments, and these regiments set the tone for the rest of the army. In 1913 61·5 per cent. of the regiments in the Prussian army had more than 50 per cent. aristocratic officers. 16 regiments were exclusively aristocratic.[3] Particularly favoured were the cavalry regiments. In the Württemberg army in 1908 57 per cent. of the cavalry officers were aristocrats, although the total average of aristocrats in the Württemberg army was well below that of the Prussian army. All colonels in the cavalry were aristocrats.[4] The percentages remained very much the same till the outbreak of the war. Equally attractive for aristocrats were the various guards regiments. In Prussia in 1908 there were only 4 *bourgeois* officers in the guards. By 1913 there were 59.[5] In comparing these figures it should be remembered that the foot artillery regiments of the guards which had been strengthened were almost exclusively *bourgeois*, for the artillery was considered a technical, and therefore socially suspect, arm.

The General Staff also remained predominantly aristocratic. In 1906 60 per cent. of the officers at the General Staff were aristocrats.[6] Becoming a staff officer was essential for a successful military career, and nearly all senior officers had passed through the war academy. Here again the percentage of aristocratic to *bourgeois* was disproportionate. By 1909 four times more aristocrats passed into the Staff than *bourgeois* officers.[7] Thus the General Staff was becoming more aristocratic in composition.

The percentage of aristocratic officers also depended on the garrison in which the regiment was stationed. The percentage

[1] Demeter, *Das Deutsche Offizierkorps*, p. 26.
[2] *Berliner Tageblatt*, 11-2-1909.
[3] *Frankfurter Zeitung*, 7-12-1913.
[4] Heeresarchiv Stuttgart: Denkschriften Sammlung, Band 3.
[5] Demeter, *Das Deutsche Offizierkorps*, p. 29.
[6] Demeter, *Das Deutsche Offizierkorps*, p. 26.
[7] *Berliner Tageblatt*, 11-2-1909.

of aristocratic officers was considerably higher in regiments stationed in a social centre, in the large towns or near a ducal palace, than in regiments in the smaller garrison towns, and particularly on the frontiers. Thus the 3rd Regiment of Foot Guards in Berlin had 67 aristocratic officers, but no *bourgeois*. The 31st Infantry Regiment in Altona had 47 aristocratic officers and only 6 *bourgeois*. The 92nd Infantry Regiment in Brunswick had 44 aristocrats and 10 *bourgeois*. By contrast the 97th Infantry Regiment in Saarburg had 4 aristocratic and 48 *bourgeois* officers. The 45th Infantry Regiment in Insterburg-Darkehnen in the East had 2 aristocrats and 50 *bourgeois*. Even in the cavalry, which was particularly favoured by the aristocracy, the picture was much the same. Cavalry regiments in Potsdam, Münster, Oldenburg, Bonn, and Hanover can be found which were entirely aristocratic, whereas the 1st Dragoon Regiment in Tilsit had only 3 aristocrats and 24 *bourgeois*. In the field artillery the 6th Regiment in Breslau had 29 aristocrats and 6 *bourgeois*, and the 10th Regiment in Hanover 32 aristocrats and 11 *bourgeois*; whereas in Metz the 70th Regiment had only 2 aristocrats and 28 *bourgeois*, and in the East the 1st Regiment in Gumbinnen-Insterburg had 3 aristocrats and 40 *bourgeois*. The foot artillery which was essentially a *bourgeois* weapon had a low percentage of aristocrats even in the guards in good garrisons. Thus the foot guard artillery in Spandau had only 10 aristocrats and 37 *bourgeois*, and in Metz the 18th Foot Artillery Regiment had no aristocrats. The same applied to the pioneers. The pioneer guards in Berlin had 7 aristocrats and 18 *bourgeois*, whereas pioneer battalions in Königsberg and Cologne, even though both garrisons can be classified as good, had only *bourgeois* officers.[1] A regiment which moved from a good garrison to a poor one could very well lose a number of its aristocratic officers. Thus the 15th Uhlan Regiment when in Strasburg had 25 aristocrats and 3 *bourgeois*, but when it moved to Saarburg on the frontier only 7 aristocrats remained and the regiment then had 17 *bourgeois* officers.[2]

Although the aristocracy had managed to retain much of its favoured position in the army it was slowly losing ground. Many sons of aristocratic and traditionally military families

[1] Franz Carl Endres, *Archiv für Sozialwissenschaft und Sozialpolitik* (1927), lviii. 296.
[2] *Der Beobachter* (Stuttgart), 24-3-1909.

were entering industry and trade where the financial rewards were greater, and which no longer had the same social stigma in an age of industrialization. In 1902 the Military Cabinet pointed out that of the ensigns (*Fahnenjunker*) 'about half belong to professional groups, from which previously the Officer Corps was not usually drawn, and in the infantry particularly sons of officers and of the landed aristocracy are less numerous from year to year'.[1] These developments filled the army with concern, and many officers feared that the changing social structure of the Officer Corps would prejudice military discipline and lower the prestige of the army. Bernhardi complained to the War Minister, von Einem, that 'sons of our old officer families do not wish to serve any longer, they want to earn money, on the other hand sons of rich parvenus want to become officers, usually from vanity'.[2] Waldersee also complained that standards in the Officer Corps were declining.

Unfortunately it is a fact that many old officers, even officers who are still serving, find other professions for their sons. If the situation in the army was healthy it would be self-perpetuating, but this is certainly no longer the case. Sons of minor civil servants and businessmen etc. will soon be in a majority among officers joining the infantry. In the cavalry sons of industrialists who have got rich quickly are pushing their way in, and are ruining its simple customs.[3]

Against these arguments that the influx of middle-class officers was undermining the morale of the Officer Corps, and that the German army should be a self-perpetuating clique, it was argued that the army could not do without the technically qualified middle-class officer, and that in any case an expanding army would have to draw its officers from an ever widening section of the community. In March 1890 the Kaiser spoke out in favour of increasing the middle-class element in the army.

The increased standards of education of our people makes it possible to widen the circle of those who could be considered as recruits for our Officer Corps. The aristocracy of birth alone can no longer, as it did before, claim privileges for itself in providing officers for the army. The aristocracy of character, which has always inspired the Officer Corps, must be preserved unchanged within it.

---

[1] Demeter, *Das Deutsche Offizierkorps*, p. 23; Militär-Kabinett to K.M., 15-2-1902.
[2] Bernhardi, *Denkwürdigkeiten*, p. 263.
[3] Waldersee, *Denkwürdigkeiten*, iii. 226.

That is only possible when potential officers are drawn from circles where the aristocracy of character is to be found. I look for the men who will build the future of the army not only among the offspring of the aristocratic families of the country and the sons of my gallant officers and civil servants who traditionally have formed the keystone of the Officer Corps but also among the sons of honourable bourgeois houses in which a love for King and Country and a heartfelt devotion to the profession of arms and to christian culture are planted and cherished.[1]

William later told Wedel that he was making concessions to the middle-class in the army in order to create a united front against the Social Democrats.[2] The older Moltke had also thought in similar terms. He argued that the aristocracy needed the support of a strong *bourgeoisie* if it was to survive, and was prepared to make concessions to the middle-class in the army in order to achieve this aim. But he was also anxious, as was William later, that this process should not too go far. To Bernhardi he wrote that many *bourgeois* potential officers had been refused commissions either because they did not have suitable military qualifications, or because they did not have the right attitude of mind to become officers. This he endorsed, insisting that the highest standards should be set.[3]

The rising influx of middle-class officers did not mean that the Officer Corps became more liberal in outlook. *Bourgeois* officers were expected to accept uncritically the attitudes and characteristics of their aristocratic brothers-in-arms. The aristocratic officer remained the ideal. A book published in 1886 which suggested, in most moderate terms, that the army placed too much emphasis on the aristocratic background of its officers, instead of trying to form an Officer Corps which would act as a link between aristocracy and *bourgeoisie*, was severely criticized by the chief of the Military Cabinet, Albedyll.[4] In the novel *Jena oder Sedan*, a work which criticized the army and gained immense popularity, the author argued that: 'it is of immense importance that the corps of German officers should be strengthened by the infusion of fresh blood from the middle- and lower-middle classes, whose members, having been brought up and educated

[1] Demeter, *Das Deutsche Offizierkorps*, p. 21; (WII, 29-3-1890).
[2] Carl Graf von Wedel, *Zwischen Kaiser und Kanzler* (Leipzig, 1943), p. 92.
[3] Rudolf Stadelmann, *Moltke und der Staat*, p. 407.
[4] 'K. von R.', *Der nächste Krieg* (Berlin, 1886).

according to modern ideas, are of great service to the other officers in enlarging their range of view'. Yet at the same time the author reiterated the traditional view that 'the best material to draw from is the so-called "army nobility"'.[1]

For young middle-class officers who accepted uncritically the traditional attitudes of an aristocratic Officer Corps there were few problems, and they were soon assimilated and accepted in their new surroundings. The problem, however, was acute for young academics who served with the army as officers. Their particular technical knowledge was often resented by their fellow officers who mistrusted a scientific and critical spirit in their midst. Often they would assume the anomalous position of 'civilian in uniform'.[2] This was particularly true of doctors, veterinary surgeons, and the like. In an official work which appeared after the first World War, and examined the reasons for the failure of the German army to win the war, the social composition of the Officer Corps was taken as one contributory cause. Speaking of the Officer Corps before the war it says: 'The Officer Corps was in its whole attitude aristocratic. The aristocracy formed its nucleus, it found its recruits principally among the sons of officers and civil servants. It is true that in the years before the war members of other *bourgeois* groups were accepted, but its fundamental character was in no way changed by this fact.'[3]

The emphasis on aristocracy, and the distrust of the *bourgeoisie*, particularly the academically trained and the technically equipped, was part of a deliberate attempt to create out of the Officer Corps an hermetically sealed and autonomous body, removed not only from the daily political struggle of class and and party but also from many of the intellectual movements of the day. Zedlitz-Trützschler wrote: 'it was never even mentioned that the officers, by their exclusiveness and their one-sided views of life, had not merely failed to keep pace with the moral progress of the nation, but were facing the daily increasing risk of complete estrangement'.[4]

[1] Franz Adam Beyerlein, *Jena or Sedan* (London, 1904), p. 267.
[2] Gerhardt Papke, 'Offizierkorps und Anciennität,' *Beitrage zur Militär—und Kriegsgeschichte* (Stuttgart, 1962), iv. 196.
[3] *Die Ursachen des deutschen Zusammenbruchs im Jahre 1918.* (Berlin, 1929), eds. Volkmann and Hobohm, 4th Series, ix. 14.
[4] Zedlitz-Trützschler, *Twelve Years*, p. 57.

This estrangement of the Officer Corps from the realities of civilian life was reflected in the selection of officers. A university student, although armed with a number of exemplary references, was turned down by a number of regiments to which he had applied for a commission, on the grounds that his father, who earned a comfortable living from a shoe factory, had started his career as a cobbler. He appealed to the Bavarian War Ministry which replied that it was a matter for the individual regiments and that the War Ministry was unable to intervene. The archives contain numerous examples of such cases, usually of the sons of industrialists, who, although in many ways suitable for commissions, were refused because of their social background.[1] The system whereby officers were elected by the officers of the individual regiments meant that the prejudices of the Officer Corps were given ample opportunity for expression in the selection of new officers.

Mounting criticism of the army's attitude towards the aristocracy could not be ignored, and the Military Cabinet, which was responsible for appointments and postings within the army, encouraged regiments which had previously been exclusively aristocratic to accept *bourgeois* officers. Some such regiments agreed to these proposals, and the army then tried to answer its critics by claiming that since very few regiments were exclusively aristocratic there were no grounds for criticism. *Bourgeois* officers who now served in what had previously been aristocratic regiments were known in Prussia as 'Compromise Joes' ('*Kompromisschulzen*') and their position was often uncomfortable.[2] The middle-class officer in such surroundings was regarded as the representative of a more liberal world than that of the military aristocracy, and his presence was seen as a further step towards the removal of the privileges of the aristocracy within the army. Small wonder then that the middle-class element in many regiments was despised by the senior officers, who rejected out of hand any such changes in the structure of the Officer Corps.[3] A *bourgeois* officer who served with the Württemberg army in a regiment of dragoons describes in his memoirs the problems of a middle-class officer. His regiment became

[1] Bayr.HSA, Abt. IV, KA, M.Kr.2048.
[2] F. C. Endres, *Archiv für Sozialwissenschaften*, p. 295.
[3] See F. A. Beyerlein, *Jena or Sedan*.

increasingly aristocratic in composition, all new officers who joined the regiment were aristocrats. The commanding officer was an outspoken opponent of the *bourgeoisie* and made his life difficult. He was also unable to take his wife, who was the daughter of the Berlin publisher Langenscheidt, to any balls or receptions as she was also from a bourgeois family. Although the '*Kompromisschulzen*' wore the glamorous uniforms of the most splendid regiments of the German army, life in the mess was hard for them, and they were seldom accepted as equals by their fellow officers.[1]

The army leaders were determined to reduce the influx of the *bourgeoisie* into the Officer Corps as far as possible. To this end they developed an ingenious theory, which found many influential supporters, that character mattered more to an officer than intellect. Character was of course an essentially aristocratic virtue, whereas intellect was the mark of the *bourgeois*. Goltz in his book *The Nation in Arms* stressed that too much intelligence was a bad thing for an officer, because it could lead to doubt and hesitation in giving an order. Heart and character should be decisive in selecting officers, not intellect and scientific attainment.[2] In January 1904 the Kaiser complained that too little emphasis was being placed on character in the Officer Corps, and insisted that in a period of such rapid social change the preservation of the traditional attitudes of the officers was essential for the stability of the Reich.[3] In 1909 the General Inspectorate of the Militär-Erziehungs- und Bildungswesen complained to the Military Cabinet that the educational standards of the Officer Corps were far too low, and that this was giving the German army a bad reputation in other countries. The Military Cabinet replied: 'How many people are there whose strength lies more in practice than in theory, but who as soldiers really prove their worth!'[4]

Throughout the pre-war years the German army continued to distrust the educated *bourgeois;* this was the natural consequence of an attempt to preserve the traditional aristocratic image of the Officer Corps and to avoid any risk of making it

---

[1] Heeresarchiv Stuttgart: Nachlass Lauffer, Lebenslauf 1939, Nr. 1.
[2] Goltz, *The Nation in Arms*, p. 51.
[3] Demeter, *Das Deutsche Offizierkorps*, p. 156.
[4] Ibid., p. 250.

more liberal or democratic. But the army was fighting a losing battle. The growing complexity of modern warfare made it essential to have officers from just that section of society which ideologically it distrusted; and thus the 'technicians' were always at an immense disadvantage. Ludendorff's career in the General Staff is a case in point.

The generally accepted theories as to the ideal social composition of the Officer Corps had a decisive effect in limiting the expansion of the army. The view, frequently put forward by generals and politicians after the failure of the German army to win the first World War, that Germany lost the war because the Reichstag refused to grant the necessary increases in the strength of the army, does not stand up to critical examination. The size of the army was not dictated by the Reichstag, but was much more the result of the army's desire to keep the army small so as to halt the influx of *bourgeois* and liberal officers into an essentially aristocratic and reactionary Officer Corps. The army was to be kept politically safe at all costs, the reliable pillar of a conservative state.[1]

The constitutional problem of the Reichstag's control over the budget of the army was a hotly debated point. Since universal military service was written into the constitution, it was argued that any attempt by the Reichstag to control the size of the army was automatically unconstitutional.[2] Only once under William II did the Reichstag assert its rights over the army, but the elections of 1893 settled the matter in favour of the government. In any case the Reichstag had only been encouraged to take a firm stand because it knew full well that the army was only lukewarm in its enthusiasm for the estimates.[3] Throughout the rest of William's reign the Reichstag was on the whole exceedingly co-operative, and the army would have had little difficulty in pushing through far greater increases than were in fact demanded.

It was Schlieffen at the General Staff who was the main advocate of a larger army. In a letter to his sister in November 1892 he argued that it was absurd to claim that a small well-

[1] Eckart Kehr, *Die Gesellschaft* (1928), ii. p. 492.
[2] Ernst Rudolf Huber, *Heer und Staat*, p. 257.
[3] J. Alden Nichols, *Germany after Bismarck. The Caprivi Era 1890–1894* (Cambridge, Mass., 1958), p. 226.

trained and reliable army was better than a larger one when modern weapons were of much the same quality throughout Europe and were reducing the importance of actual human qualities as the individual became subordinated to mass technical armies. The number of guns mattered most, and guns had to be manned. He summarized his views as follows: 'A general's art is defined in that he must be numerically stronger on the battle-field.'[1] Schlieffen was the classic example of the 'technician' to whom pre-conceived notions of the social structure of the Officer Corps took second place to purely military considerations, and as a 'technician' he had to face the opposition of the War Ministry.

In 1899 the War Minister, von Gossler, wrote to Schlieffen saying that the army was quite large enough, and that emphasis should be placed on increasing the quality and efficiency of the existing army before launching out on enormous increases which would inevitably lead to a reduction of the standards of the army. Schlieffen pointed out in his reply to this note that since the mobilization plans foresaw an attack on France the army would have to be increased. The only hope for success was that the German army would be considerably larger than the French, otherwise the whole strategic planning of the General Staff would be worthless.[2]

Schlieffen's exchange with Gossler was a foretaste of the growing struggles between War Ministry and General Staff. Gossler's successor, von Einem, was an outspoken opponent of the Chief of the General Staff. By 1903 Einem was writing testily that it was about time to decide once and for all whether it was really essential to follow Schlieffen's ideas for increasing the army, adding that Schlieffen himself was not immortal. There ensued a voluminous correspondence between Schlieffen and von Einem, the one reiterating his arguments in favour of a larger army, the other arguing the reverse.[3] Einem's position was strengthened by the backing he received from the Chancellor, Bülow. The Chancellor insisted that he had no fears about foreign policy and told Einem that there was thus no need

[1] Generalfeldmarschall Graf Alfred von Schlieffen, *Briefe*, Ed. Eberhard Kessel (Göttingen, 1958), 19-11-1892.

[2] Reichsarchiv, *Kriegsrüstung und Kriegswirtschaft*, Vol. ii. (Berlin, 1930). Gossler to Schlieffen, 8-7-1899; Schlieffen to Gossler, 10-11-1899.

[3] See. *Reichsarchiv*, Vol. ii.

to increase the army.[1] In 1904 von Einem told the Budgetary Committee: 'I regard the development of the army as far as the creation of new formations and the building of new units is concerned as on the whole completed. The question whether the number of our cadres for use in wartime is sufficient can, in general, be answered in the affirmative, and also the further question whether the effective strength of the army is sufficient for an adequate strength of the existing cadres.'[2] Einem failed to add that the Chief of the General Staff, who was responsible for the strategic planning and for the technical questions of military policy was of exactly the opposite opinion.

After the conference of Algeciras Bülow was no longer quite so confident in the success of his foreign policy and asked for considerable increases in the strength of the army to meet the eventuality of a war which he was no longer certain of being able to avoid. Once again it was Einem who dissuaded him from taking any further steps to increase the size of the army. The War Minister answered the Chancellor's memorandum with the arguments that a sudden increase in the army at this point would make it quite clear to the rest of the world that Germany had lost confidence in itself; that Tirpitz, the Kaiser, and the *Flottenverein* were such able propagandists for the navy that the army would be unable to secure sufficient funds; that the army was in any case in the middle of a five-year period of reorganization; and lastly that the Social Democrats would 'make a good feast' out of any bill for an increased army.[3] Einem also brought forward the inevitable argument that it was quality and not quantity that mattered in an army. Bülow tried to concoct a scheme for keeping any increases in the army secret, but Einem quite rightly pointed out that this would be impossible. By June 1906 Bülow had regained some of his old confidence, and wrote to the War Minister that he did not think that war would break out for some time yet, to which Einem promptly replied that in that case there was no need to increase the army.[4]

---

[1] See *Reichsarchiv*, Vol. i. p. 82, footnote.
[2] Rüdt von Collenberg, *Die deutsche Armee von 1871–1914* (Berlin, 1922), p. 64.
[3] Friedrich Thimme, *Front wider Bülow* (Munich, 1931) (articles by Einem and Collenberg).
[4] *Reichsarchiv*, ii. pp. 95–102. Bülow memo, 1-6-1906.

Moltke, although perhaps not so definite in his views, shared Schlieffen's belief in the importance of a radical increase in the strength of the army. Einem, however, was as determined to resist Moltke's demands as he had been Schlieffen's. In a memorandum to Moltke in 1909 he wrote: 'My opinion is that an increase of the peace-time effective strength by 6,500–7,000 men, spread out over the next 5 years from 1 April 1911, is the absolute maximum which, under the present circumstances, can be demanded and which is at all possible to achieve.'[1]

The driving force behind Moltke's demands for a larger army was Ludendorff. Ludendorff realized that, although the Schlieffen plan was a remarkable piece of strategic planning, it would be useless unless the army was increased in size to give the Germans a real predominance over the French army. This not only involved an improvement in the artillery, small arms, and other equipment in the reserve divisions, but also a complete modernization of the armaments of the standing army along with an enormous increase in size.[2] These ideas were reflected in a memorandum by Moltke dated December 1911. Moltke argued that France could be roundly defeated on condition that the army was increased. 'Everyone is preparing himself for the Great War which they all expect sooner or later . . . I consider . . . an increase in our peace-time effective strength as a precondition of survival.'[3] The General Staff was now urging an increase of 300,000 men; but both the Kaiser and the War Ministry were against any such radical steps.[4]

The War Ministry was able to point out that the army was in any case short of officers. In March 1912 it was claimed that there were the following gaps in units which would have to play a vital role in the event of war: 81 Staff officers, and 557 captains in the infantry, and 60 Staff officers and 134 captains in the artilllery.[5] By the end of 1912 there were 1,200 lieutenants too few in the Prussian army.[6]

The debates between Chancellor, War Ministry, and General

---

[1] *Reichsarchiv*, i. p. 97, Einem to Moltke, 23-7-1909.
[2] See Ludendorff, *Mein militärischer Werdegang*.
[3] *Reichsarchiv*, i. p. 135, Moltke memo, 2-12-1911.
[4] Huber, *Heer und Staat*, p. 277.
[5] Hans Herzfeld, *Die deutsche Rüstungspolitik vor dem Weltkrieg* (Bonn, 1923), p. 154.
[6] Rüdt von Collenberg, *Die deutsche Armee 1871–1914*, p. 102.

Staff on the war estimates for 1913 revealed the fundamental differences between the ideas of the War Ministry and the General Staff. Heeringen argued in the memorandum of January 1913 that the proposed increases would mean that 'less suitable elements' would have to be allowed into the Officer Corps, which would lead to a dangerous 'democratization' of the army which must be avoided. 'An increase in the Prussian army of nearly one-sixth of its strength is so drastic a step that, I believe, it requires most careful consideration whether the fundamental character of the army, particularly so far as officers and N.C.O.s are concerned, might not suffer considerably in consequence.' Heeringen also pointed out his own difficulties with the Reichstag: 'A War Minister, who for three consecutive years presents a military estimate, cannot, without making himself ridiculous, claim that the present estimate will suffice for some time. No one will believe that, and rightly so, because it simply is not true. No mortal can tell what the future will bring.'[1] Bethmann, who feared that such an increase in the army might be too provocative to Germany's neighbours, and who also had second thoughts about the cost of such a project, tended to agree with Heeringen. Bethmann however clothed his objections in terms that he felt the army would be able to understand: 'We would not be able to meet these greatly increased requirements without lowering our standards by using men from unsuitable classes to increase the Officer Corps, and this, quite apart from other dangers, would expose the army to democratization.'[2] Moltke, however, refused to accept Heeringen's arguments, and insisted that the problem of finding enough suitable officers could be solved. Heeringen wrote angrily in the margin of Moltke's memorandum 'How?' The War Minister then appealed to the Kaiser for support in his struggle with the General Staff. On 23 January he wrote to Moltke in triumph, saying that the Kaiser backed his views against those of the General Staff. Moltke at once appealed to the Kaiser, and forced him to change his mind. On 25 January William wrote to Heeringen telling him to follow Moltke's lead. Heeringen still continued to

---

[1] For Heeringen memo, 20-1-1913, see Eckart Kehr, *Die Gesellschaft*, 1928; Hans Herzfeld, *Deutsche Rüstungspolitik;* and *Reichsarchiv*, Vol. ii.

[2] Hans Herzfeld, *Deutsche Rüstungspolitik*, p. 63.

raise objections, and Moltke appealed this time to the Chancellor, but Bethmann tended to agree with the War Minister's views. Although the effective war strength of the German army was increased by some 90,000 men between 1912 and the summer of 1914 this was a compromise solution. The General Staff had achieved less than one third of their original demands, and Ludendorff, who was the principal agitator for the increases in the army, was removed from the General Staff and posted to Düsseldorf as a regimental commander to keep him out of harm's way. On the other hand, the War Ministry had to accept increases that were far greater than it thought desirable. After the estimates had been passed through the Reichstag with very little difficulty, the new War Minister, von Falkenhayn, wrote to Bethmann: 'A further increase in the army would at this stage be equivalent to a dilution and deterioration.' The General Staff commented that this was merely 'an empty phrase which was also used by the previous War Minister'. Once again Moltke raised his objections to Falkenhayn's point of view and insisted in a letter to the Chancellor that the army would have to be increased at all costs.[1]

Some historians have been mystified by the fact that although the Reichstag was co-operative the War Ministers von Gossler, von Einem, and von Heeringen all told the Reichstag that the army was large enough and refused to take the opportunity to increase the army.[2] The answer would seem to be that the ministry feared that a large increase in the size of the army would automatically lead to a democratization of the Officer Corps, and to an influx of 'unreliable' *bourgeois* elements, thus weakening an institution whose self-appointed role was the preservation of a monarchical and conservative state.

The prevailing view as to the social composition of the army was thus of vital importance. Social questions were given priority over purely military ones, and the 'technicians' of the General Staff, who based their strategic planning on the assumption of German numerical superiority over her potential enemies, met the opposition of the War Ministry and those who put 'quality' before 'quantity'. Thus the army, by trying to put

---

[1] *Reichsarchiv*, ii. pp. 195–7.

[2] viz. Gerhard Ritter in *Deutschland und Europa*, ed. Werner Conze (Dusseldorf, 1951).

a brake on the wheel of social change, undermined its own military effectiveness, and made nonsense of its own strategic planning.

If the army was forced by sheer necessity to make at least some concessions to the middle class, it was certainly not prepared to make any to the Jews. In an inward-looking, self-perpetuating hierarchy such as the German Officer Corps, which closely reflected the treasured prejudices of the Prussian Junker, it is hardly surprising to find that anti-Semitism was a universally accepted creed. Such was the autonomy of the Officer Corps that it was possible, with very few exceptions, to exclude Jews altogether.

As the officer's ideology was broadly that of the Prussian Junker he was distrustful of anything that smacked of industry and trade. The Junker and the officer regarded themselves as forming the spearhead of the traditional landowning conservatives, and the Jew seemed to them the paradigm of the new industrial and financial forces which challenged their privileged class position.[1] Maximilian Harden formulated this characteristically.

> The liberal press, the only one that was then powerful, very quickly realized that the spirit which was fought under the name 'Jewry' was the spirit of the liberalism of the second epoch, the liberalism which no longer fought for political freedom and the rights of the people but for Saint Manchester and for the splendours of a shopkeeper's paradise.[2]

In the conservative Tivoli programme 8-12-1892 this was clearly formulated: 'We are fighting against the insistently obtrusive and ruinous influence of Jewry on the life of our people. We demand Christian authorities for a Christian people.'[3] For the more extreme elements in the Officer Corps there was the headier wine of Heinrich Class and the Alldeutsche, of Stoecker and the Christian Social movement.

The army never came out with anything like an anti-Semitic programme, indeed there was no need to do so, but it contented itself with crudely veiled anti-Semitic observations

---

[1] See Ludwig Haas, *Der deutsche Jude in der Armee* (Berlin, 1913).
[2] Maximilian Harden, *Köpfe*, Vol. I (Berlin, 1921), article on Stoecker.
[3] Graf Westarp, *Konservative Politik im letzten Jahrzehnt des Kaiserreiches* (Berlin, 1935) i. 298.

on the spiritual and physical attributes of Jews, culled from so-called specialists in the field. By far the most popular theory, widely accepted throughout the army, and used, although in somewhat modified forms by War Ministers in debates in the Reichstag, was that Jews were not physically fit to serve in positions of authority in the army. A crass expression of this attitude was found in a work published in 1879, which achieved a certain popularity in army circles.[1] The Jew, it argued, is descended from a different species of ape from that which had the honour to sire the Germanic race. This accounts for the well-known fact that Jews have flat feet, no muscles, bad teeth, weak bones, and sloping shoulders. This pseudo-scientific mélange of Darwin and Herder was used to demonstrate that a Jew was physically incapable of being a good soldier. Flat-footed he was unable to march, without muscle he was unable to stand up to the rigorous physical strains of modern warfare, and with sloping shoulders he was unlikely to cut a very imposing figure on the parade-ground. If the Jews of the Old Testament had performed military wonders it was because their religious and racial fanaticism had been strong enough to overcome even these formidable physical handicaps; but the German Jew had no such motivating force behind him, quite the reverse: 'he sneers with derision at the Goy who is *chamer* (ass) enough to allow himself to be put to the sword'.

Nordmann's attitude was an extreme one, but like so many extremist attitudes a lot of what he said stuck. Many were impressed by what seemed to unsophisticated minds to be a scientific justification for their own deep-rooted racial, class, and political prejudices. Thus it was that in the higher echelons of the army overtly anti-Semitic discrimination was justified by arguments that varied in degree, but not in content, from those of the extremists.

German Jewry was naturally concerned to counter these accusations. This was not only because a minority which had on the whole been successfully assimilated into German life felt wounded and insulted, its patriotism questioned, and achievements threatened, but also, and probably more important, because the Officer Corps played such a vital and central role in German society that exclusion from it could ruin a promising

[1] H. Nordmann, *Israel im Heere* (Berlin, 1879).

career, undermine the social standing of an established family, or discourage a young man from entering public service. 'Their exclusion from the Officer Corps, having finished their training, makes it difficult for them to join any of the many administrative departments and results indirectly in a lowering of their social status.'[1] The struggle against discrimination in the army was not only one of principle, but also of vital material interest.

Jewish spokesmen had no difficulty in showing that Jews had fought with distinction in all the wars that Prussia had fought in the 19th century.[2] In the face of such incontestable evidence the editor of the *Thüringer Volksboten*, who had accused the Jews of lacking bravery in the face of the enemy, vanished rather than face a libel suit brought in against him by the Committee against anti-Semitism in Berlin.[3] Although 60 Jewish officers had served in the Prussian army during the Franco-Prussian war, their sons were unable to get commissions.[4] By 1878 there was not one Jewish officer in the Prussian army.[5]

Claims that the Jews were by very nature physically deficient were likewise easy to dispute. Army statistics showed that town-dwellers tended to be slightly below the level of physical fitness of country-dwellers, and Jewish recruits came largely from the urban areas. Furthermore a higher percentage of Jews volunteered for one-year service, and the physical tests for these volunteers were more rigorous.[6] The statistics tended in any case to be weighted against the townsmen, for the army, with all the prejudices of the East-Elbian Junker, regarded them as fundamentally unreliable, poor soldiers, materialists, and worst of all, socialists. Here was indeed a further crime of the Jews in the eyes of the Officer Corps, for those who did not worship 'Saint Manchester' were, as apostles of Karl Marx, the

[1] Max J. Loewenthal, *Das jüdische Bekenntnis als Hinderungsgrund bei der Beförderung zum Preussischen Reserveoffizier* (Berlin, 1911).
[2] Misc., *Die Juden als Soldaten.*
[3] Ibid.
[4] Julius Kopsch., *Die Juden im deutschen Heer* (Berlin, 1910).
[5] Nordmann, *Israel im Heere.*
[6] Kopsch, *Die Juden im deutschen Heer.* The system of one-year volunteers was established by Boyen in 1814. Candidates had to have reached a certain educational standard, and to provide their own uniform. They were allowed certain privileges including the right to live in rooms outside the barracks and to wear civilian clothes when off duty.

capitalists' sworn enemy—enemies of a common foe, but certainly not allies! Social Democracy, the anathema of the army, was yet another Jewish plot.[1]

In 1910 there were no Jewish officers in the Prussian army, whereas in Austria-Hungary, Germany's closest military ally, there were 2,179 Jewish officers, including one field-marshal, in Italy there were 500, and in France, in spite of the Dreyfus case, 720.[2] Although religious toleration was guaranteed in article 12 of the constitution, the army trampled on this fundamental right. 'Since 1880 it has no longer been possible for a single one of the many thousand Jewish one-year volunteers to join the higher ranks of the army.'[3] This state of affairs was admitted by the Prussian War Minister, von Einem. Of all War Ministers of the period he was the most favourably disposed towards the Jews, yet did nothing practical to ease their position: 'I believe that it has been and still is the case that in the army a young man of the Israelite faith does not become a reserve officer for the simple reason that he is a Jew.'[3] Einem at least showed some sympathy; his successor, von Heeringen, showed none.

In spite of the wealth of evidence produced by Jewish societies, in spite of the defence of religious liberty by certain members of the Reichstag such as Eugen Richter, Barth, Schrader, Eichhoff, and Müller-Meiningen, and in spite of the far-reaching emancipation of German Jewry, the position of the Jew in the German army worsened during this period. How was it possible for the army to stand out against such a strong opposition, and to emerge from every skirmish unscratched?

The army excluded Jews from the ranks of the Officer Corps by two simple methods. The first was simply not to elect them to the mess, for a commission in the army was dependent on being elected by the assembled officers of the regiment in which one wished to serve. The other method was to refuse promotion on the grounds of 'weakness of character'. Criticism of these devices was easily countered by reference to the fundamental right of the Officer Corps to recruit members without intervention from civilians who were not qualified to judge the

---

[1] BA Koblenz, HO2-1/21, 183.
[2] Kopsch, *Die Juden im deutschen Heer*.
[3] Ibid.   [4] Ibid., RT, 19-3-04.

military qualities of the aspirant, and by stressing the danger of disrupting the carefully poised harmony of the Officer Corps. Moreover since there were no objective standards for judging character how could the army's decisions be questioned? Thus, although no Jew had become a reserve officer in Prussia since the early 1880s the War Minister von Heeringen blandly claimed in a letter dated 12 April 1910 that no Jew had been refused a commission on religious or racial grounds.[1] Heeringen was not allowed to get off so lightly, and at times admitted that all was not well. In an article in the *Vossische Zeitung* he wrote, 'it has been rumoured that one-year volunteer N.C.O.s were not appointed, at the end of their year of service, as potential officers on the grounds that in spite of the zeal they had shown and their good knowledge of military affairs they were not suitable to be superiors through lack of character. If this was the case then they should never have been made N.C.O.s.'[2] In other words even a man well known for his antipathy towards the Jews, such as the War Minister, had to admit in the light of overwhelming evidence, that all was not well in the army. But those who hoped for reform had little to hope for from Heeringen. It is noticeable that his objection was not that Jews were being refused reserve commissions, but that they had been made N.C.O.s during their one year of service. Heeringen claimed that the 'lower orders' did not like serving under 'our Israelite fellow-citizens', adding that although this attitude might be reprehensible, it had to be taken into account.[3]

The simplest method to ensure that the 'lower orders' did not have to suffer any such embarrassment was to ensure that no Jew should be allowed on to the first step of the ladder towards a commission. In many regiments men who were considered suitable for a commission, mainly as reserve officers, were given special training as potential officers (*Offiziersunterricht*). By closing the door at this stage there was little hope of a Jew ever becoming an officer. Similarly many one-year volunteers who were considered suitable material for reserve officers were made N.C.O.s, and although this by no means guaranteed a later

[1] Loewenthal, *Das jüdische Bekenntnis als Hinderungsgrund*, p. 11.
[2] *Vossische Zeitung*, 25-2-1911; Loewenthal, *Jüdische Reserveoffiziere* (Berlin, 1914).
[3] Loewenthal, *Das jüdische Bekenntnis als Hinderungsgrund*, p. 11.

commission, it was an important step forward. Few Jews got even as far as this.[1]

In the surviving archives there are examples of Jewish potential officers who managed to get beyond these first stages, but were turned down later for unconvincing reasons. These cases were uncomfortable for the army administration, for the further the candidate climbed up the ladder of advancement, the less easy it was for them to explain refusals on grounds of lack of character or of military qualities. Thus in 1895 the one-year volunteer Wolff was refused a commission in the reserve, although his military record was excellent, on the grounds that his mother's family had a bad reputation in Hamburg (although no reason was given why), and because his father owned a cigar factory.[2] In 1897 one Guggenheim complained of discrimination, having been refused a commission. Again his military record was good, and the selection officer had spoken in his favour. Although this case aroused the interest of the War Minister von Einem, the decision was not revised, on the grounds that after all his military record was not as good as it had at first seemed, his father was a shop-keeper, and some of the officers in the regiment to which he had applied did not approve of his character.[3] In another case a Jewish candidate was turned down because 'after the customary enquiries it appears that he does not enjoy that degree of esteem and trust which is an essential precondition for promotion to the rank of reserve officer'.[4] In 1910 the *Frankfurter Zeitung* took up the case of the 18th Infantry Regiment, 'Prinz Ludwig Ferdinand', where Jewish candidates had been refused commissions on thin excuses. Two years previously an established lawyer had been refused a commission, in spite of brilliant military testimonials, with the remark that 'he was unable to provide sufficient evidence that he had that feeling for social tact which must be asked of a reserve officer'. Now another case had arisen. The one-year volunteer Gross again had excellent reports, 'a thoroughly decent young man . . . highly capable . . . has done really good work in all fields'. But the same adjutant had turned him down with the same arguments, 'as a comrade . . . he did

[1] Loewenthal *Das jüdische Bekenntnis als Hinderungsgrund*, p. 28.
[2] Bayr.HSA, Abt. IV, KA, M.KR.2072.
[3] Ibid.   [4] Ibid., 2073.

not win any sympathy', and he did not have the 'necessary tact'.[1] The Bavarian War Minister when taxed with this case simply remarked that religion was all too often used as an excuse by people who simply were not good enough to be given commissions.[2] The *Berliner Tageblatt* was harsher in its assessment of the Gross affair, and described it as 'this striking abuse of the nationally accepted principle of the equality of all citizens'.[3]

One of the easiest ways for a Jewish potential officer to show 'character', and therefore to stand a good chance of selection was to get baptized. One candidate passed all his exams as the best in his group, only to be told that he could not become an officer because he was a Jew; the selection officer suggested to him that he should get over this little difficulty by being baptized.[4] There were a number of Christian sons of Jewish parents who became officers.[5]

This veto on Jewish officers was not confined to the sons of cigar manufacturers or shop-keepers, but included the highest in the land. Albert Goldschmidt-Rothschild with a fortune of 80 million marks, who had given enormous sums to charity, who regularly went to court, could not become a reserve officer in spite of the personal intervention of the Chancellor Bülow, who wished to reward him for his excellent work at the Foreign Office.[6] Zedlitz-Trützschler remarked on this occasion, 'if it is suggested to our military chauvinists that a Jew may be an officer of the reserve, they see red, and yet there have been many Jewish officers who fought the enemy with distinction in time of war'.[7] Walter Rathenau wrote to Frau General von Hindenburg in December 1917,[8] 'even though my ancestors and I served this country as best we could, I am, as you should well know, as a Jew a second-class citizen. I could not become a political civil servant, and in peace-time not even a lieutenant. I could have escaped this discrimination by changing my faith,

[1] *Frankfurter Zeitung*, 25-5-1910.
[2] Bayr.HSA, Abt. IV, KA, M.Kr.2073.
[3] *Berliner Tageblatt*, 26-5-1910.
[4] Loewenthal, *Das jüdische Bekenntnis als Hinderungsgrund*, p. 31.
[5] Ibid., p. 37.
[6] Spitzemberg, *Tagebuch*, 2-4-1905.
[7] Zedlitz, *Twelve years*, p. 217.
[8] The good lady was not the wife of a more famous Hindenburg.

but this would only have given encouragement to the illegal actions of the ruling class.'[1]

Jews were not only discriminated against in the army in that it was virtually impossible for them to become officers, but also in that the military authorities made it extremely difficult for them to practise their religion. An order from the War Ministry in Berlin dated 3 October 1913 read: 'the War Ministry cannot regard it as desirable to allow soldiers of the Jewish faith to have ritually prepared food sent to them in the barracks when they desire.' The War Ministry claimed that the provision of kosher food was militarily impossible and that the Rabbis made no allowance for this. Clearly the order was designed to wean Jewish soldiers away from what seemed to the military authorities to be merely a bad habit. Jewish soldiers could, however, be excused from eating in the canteens, and could go to Jewish restaurants outside the barracks, but it was not possible to claim the cost of the canteen food as was sometimes allowed when soldiers had to eat away from their barracks.[2] In Württemberg this order was modified in that Commanding Officers could allow Jewish soldiers to receive ritual food from outside, provided that 'it did not cause inconvenience'.[3] Since in most garrison towns there were no Jewish restaurants, even this amounted in effect to a virtual prohibition of ritual food in the army.

Jewish authorities were less worried about the problems of ritual food than that Jewish soldiers should be allowed to attend Synagogues, partly because they had a perfect right to do so, but also out of fear that soldiers unable to attend religious services with reasonable frequency might be lost to the faith. Thus they demanded the right for soldiers to attend Synagogues without the express permission of their officers to do so. In 1897 the Commanding General of the XIIIth Army Corps reluctantly agreed to this request, but added testily that he could see no reason why they should not go to the Synagogue on Friday evenings, for this would interfere less with their military duties. In the area of the XIIIth Corps, Württemberg, the Minister for Churches and Schools backed up these demands, agreeing that

---

[1] Walter Rathenau, *Briefe* (Dresden, 1926), i. 243.
[2] Bayr.HSA, Abt. IV, KA, M.Kr.2357.
[3] Heeresarchiv Stuttgart: WKM, AApA (A): Band 932.

the general's offer was not sufficient. In the following year the Commanding General wrote to the Württemberg War Minister saying that he agreed with the Jewish point of view, and had ordered that Jews should be instructed as to the religious significance of the Oath to the Flag (*Fahneneid*) in the Synagogues. In 1902 the Jewish authorities again complained that not enough Jews were being allowed to attend Synagogues. The Commanding General of the XIIIth Corps replied that he would try, where possible, to allow time once a month for Jews to attend the Synagogue, but at the same time refused to force Jews to attend religious services as the governing body of the Israelite church (*Israelitische Oberkirchenbehörde*) had requested. Shortly afterwards the Commanding General reiterated his views, but this time claimed that the Jewish authorities wanted Jewish soldiers to be marched to the Synagogues simply to give them a bit of cheap propaganda, and that he could not be expected to agree to this. In the face of such opposition the Jewish authorities reduced their demands, but repeatedly asked that Jewish soldiers should be commanded to attend religious services on the occasion of the Kaiser's birthday. The Jewish authorities had some reason to push their claims at this time, for the Prussian War Minister von Einem had shown a reasonable interest in their demands and had repeatedly ordered that Jews should be allowed time off for religious services and festivals, and that they should be allowed ritual food 'so long as it does not conflict with their duties'.[1]

Von Einem was certainly no liberal in these matters, but at least, he did show some interest in the crasser cases of abuse. His successors did not. Falkenhayn, the author of the 1913 order, was impeccably anti-Semitic.[2] In this order of 3 October 1913 it was stated that Jewish soldiers could be allowed time off on Saturdays, provided that the commanding officers so wished. The order hastily added that the commanding officers were under no obligation to grant this right. Similarly, it was stated that free time should be given for Jewish festivals, with the proviso that this would very seldom be possible as it would almost certainly harm the 'interests of military duty'.

Within the different armies of the Reich there were some

[1] Heeresarchiv Stuttgart: WKM, AApA (A): Band 932.
[2] See. H. von Zwehl, *Erich von Falkenhayn* (Berlin, 1926).

differences as regards the position of Jews. Bavaria enjoyed the reputation of being less antagonistic towards Jews, with the result that many Jews from northern Germany tried to go there for their period of military service. In fact the liberal attitude of the Bavarian authorities was largely a myth. In 1909 there were 46 Jewish reserve officers and 42 Landwehr officers in Bavaria, which amounted to an average intake of 3·3 per annum.[1] This was not a very remarkable achievement considering that there were 56 Bavarian regiments to choose from, but at any rate it was a gleam of hope when one remembers that in Prussia there were no Jewish reserve officers. In May 1909 the journal of the League of German Citizens of the Jewish Faith, *Im deutschen Reich*, published an article warning against anyone having high hopes of becoming an officer in Bavaria. With the Jewish problem as with military policy, the article noted that Bavaria was 'following more and more in Prussia's footsteps'. Nor did the enormous influx of the hopeful from northern Germany help matters. 'The larger garrisons are literally teeming with North-German Jews.' The Bavarian War Minister was delighted with the article, and wrote in the margin 'pretty accurate'.[2] Moreover, the Prussian military authorities were sharply critical of even these feeble concessions which they regarded as a danger to the army.[3] This attitude made it extremely difficult, if not impossible, for any liberal elements within the Bavarian army to advocate reform.

Although Siegfried Westphal claimed that 'the army was not friendly to Jews, but it was also not anti-Semitically inclined', there is evidence enough to the contrary. Anti-Semitism was one of the fundamental creeds of the German Officer Corps. Characteristically Colmar von der Goltz, one of the finest military brains of his time, wrote in 1911 on the question of Jewish demands for justice in the army, 'as if the salvation of the Fatherland depended on our accepting a few dozen useless Isidores, Manasses and Abrahams as confessing

---

[1] Bayr.HSA, Abt. IV, KA, M.Kr.2073. Reservists who had completed their term of service were transferred to the Landwehr 1st levy which was designed to support the reserves on mobilization; they were then transferred to the Landwehr 2nd levy whose war-time role was purely defensive.

[2] Ibid.

[3] Demeter, *Das Deutsche Offizierkorps*, p. 202.

THE ISSUE OF ANTI-SEMITISM 47

Semites in our Officer Corps'.[1] The 'liberal' and cultured
Groener remarked with regret on the cultural life of the 1890s:
'in the cultural sphere there was a tendency, not yet predominant but certainly existing, to spread Jewish points of view'.[2]
An English officer who served with the German army, in an
objective account of his experiences, stressed the anti-Semitism
of the Officer Corps.[3] Even Lt. Bilse, in his sharply critical novel
which caused a scandal by portraying the abuses of the Officer
Corps, agreed with his erstwhile brother officers in their attitude towards Jews.[4]

In one matter the Officer Corps was prepared to make concessions. It was considered 'suitable' (standesgemäss) for an
officer to marry a Jewish girl, but only on condition that she
was rich. This led predictably to a number of jokes in the
satirical papers.[5] This inter-marriage was not without a future
significance, for the very fact that many officers married into
wealthy Jewish families led these officers to underrate the extent of Hitler's anti-Semitic plans, since they felt confident that
their own families would be excepted.

From the outbreak of hostilities in August 1914 Jews were
again able to serve as officers, as they had done in 1866 and
1870–1, and they served with the same distinction. Rabbis
rivalled priests in their patriotic sermons. Here was a just war
against the 'Barbarian Empire in the East', against 'Muscovite
tyranny', for the freedom of the Jews in the East from the yoke
of Tzarist despotism. The war was sent to prove the Jews worthy
in God's eyes to return to a home of their own, and to fight for
their own cause.[6] Other Rabbis praised military virtues in
extravagant terms and called for 'comradeship, equality, to-
getherness', and also for 'obedience, subordination, discipline;
the abstention from any sort of fault-finding, censure and
criticism; silent obedience'.[7] So determined were the Jews to

[1] Generalfeldmarschall Colmar Freiherr von der Goltz, Denkwürdigkeiten
(Berlin, 1929), p. 334.
[2] Wilhelm Groener, Lebenserinnerungen, Jugend, Generalstab, Weltkrieg (Göttingen,
1951).
[3] The German Army from Within, by an Officer who Served with it (London, 1914).
[4] Lt. Bilse, Life in a Garrison Town.
[5] Franz Conring, Das deutsche Militär in der Karikatur (Stuttgart, 1907).
[6] Der Krieg und wir Juden (Berlin, 1915).
[7] S. Carlebach, Das Heereswesen und die jüdische Erziehung (Lübeck, 1915).

prove their worth after years of discrimination that some of these pronouncements seem today somewhat exaggerated even though they were made in the style of the day. But after years of hard and fruitless struggle such enthusiasm is easily understandable, for the way was now open for a Jew to become a first-class human being, a Prussian Lieutenant.

III

THE OFFICERS' CODE OF HONOUR

THE Officer Corps regarded its code of honour, and the right to defend it in a duel, as an essential condition of its continued existence as a special caste. So deeply rooted was this belief that, although throughout the reign of William II the army was continually attacked for preserving what seemed to the opposition to be an antiquated and barbarous practice, they refused to concede to the reformers anything but a few mumbled assurances. It was felt that since the Officer Corps held a pre-eminent position in the life of the nation it had to maintain a particularly rigorous sense of honour, and thus set an example to lesser mortals. One writer expressed this idea thus: 'If duels were to disappear the customs of the lower orders of society would, in many cases, get the upper hand.'[1] The officer's sense of honour, and his readiness to defend it in a duel served to preserve the class-consciousness of the Officer Corps, and this was one reason why the Social Democrats opposed this doctrine.[2] The attitude of the Officer Corps was well expressed in a memorandum dated 3-4-1914 by the War Minister Falkenhayn to the Staatsministerium and the Chancellery. Falkenhayn insisted that, 'the roots of the duel are embedded and grow in our code of honour. This code of honour is a valuable and, for the Officer Corps, an irreplaceable treasure. It is the aim of the Reichstag to change or even destroy it. I cannot agree that this aim is justified . . . one would not be very far from the mark in claiming that the Reichstag, at least the democratic part of it, is less interested in fighting against the duels, than in attacking the code of honour of the officers and those circles near to them . . . I consider it to be my duty to

---

[1] A. von Boguslawski, *Die Ehre und das Duell* (Berlin, 1896), p. 89.
[2] Ibid., p. 5.

stand up to all attempts by Parliament directly or indirectly to exert pressure on the ideas and the spirit of the Officer Corps.'[1]

A memorandum by the Catholic General and writer on military affairs, von Loë, underlines the importance which officers attached to the preservation of their notions of honour. 'The strength of the Officer Corps lies in its homogeneous composition and in its exclusiveness. Neither a title nor riches give one the right to hope to become an officer, but an innate feeling for duty, education and the aristocracy of character. The more exclusively we concentrate on that section of the community from which we wish to draw our recruits, the more certain we are to be able to protect our profession from alien elements, in spite of the general mania for equality . . . the duel must not be thought of as an act of revenge, but as a confession of faith . . . an act that shows fidelity to one's beliefs and also an act of justice, the necessity and moral justification of which lies deep in noble human feelings.'[2]

The rigorous code of honour, and the duels formed part of an attempt by the army to preserve its exclusive position in the state by underlining the differences between the military and the civilian population, by claiming for itself a higher sense of honour and human values, and by binding the members of the Officer Corps closer together in a corporate attitude to life that remained distinct from, and in many ways opposed to, the generally accepted ideas of the day.

The problems of the Courts of Honour and of duels were made particularly obscure by the fact that the actual legal and constitutional position of the army and in particular the Officer Corps could not be exactly defined. There were frequent cases during the second Reich when the civil and military authorities clashed over points of law and no adequate decision could be made. A work published in 1939 made a manful attempt to unravel the confusion, but in spite of thorough research the problem could not be solved.[3] How far did measures of military discipline, military punishments and the courts of honour contradict the spirit of the constitutional

---

[1] BA Koblenz: P135-8037.

[2] Heeresarchiv Stuttgart: Denkschriften Sammlung, Band 82.

[3] E. Sossidi, *Die staatsrechtliche Stellung des Offiziers im absoluten Staat und ihre Abwandlung im 19 Jahrhundert* (Berlin, 1939).

state? Did officers serve the state, or did they owe direct allegiance to the Kaiser? Where were the limits of the Kaiser's power of command (*Kommandogewalt*) and his disciplinary power (*Diziplinargewalt*)? The answers to these problems eluded contemporaries just as they have subsequently troubled constitutional historians. In practice decisions as to the limits of the army's power were not made by constitutional lawyers but by the conflicts of practical politics, from which the army usually emerged victorious. As far as the army was concerned the legal position was quite clear. A memorandum of the War Ministry dated 16-5-1913 reads, 'the regulations governing the officer's courts of honour in the Prussian army emanate from His Majesty's power of command and as such are outside the competence of the Reichstag'.[1] This remained the opinion of the War Ministry, and indeed of the majority within the government throughout the period; and a united front was established against the claim of the Reichstag that the courts of honour sprang from the disciplinary authority of the Kaiser and therefore came under the control of the Reichstag.

These considerations played an important part in ministerial discussions of the Army and Navy estimates in December 1912. Valentini, the chief of the Civil Cabinet, telegraphed to Bethmann on 5-12-1912: 'I recommend that the War Minister should show the greatest caution in his remarks on the resolution (on the prohibition of duels) and in any case uphold the principle that the Reichstag has no right to interfere in questions of the power of command.' The War Minister agreed and wrote on 21-12-1912 that any investigation into the problems of duelling would weaken the position of the army, the main pillar of the state, and at the same time undermine the Kaiser's authority. Tirpitz however was more concerned with the estimates than with the army's activities in duelling, and wrote to Bethmann on Christmas day that if the government was not prepared to give way to the Centre Party on the question of duels it might very well refuse to vote for the estimates. The War Minister agreed that the Centre could cause trouble, but insisted that the army had to stick to first principles.

The Minister was able to convince his colleagues, including Tirpitz, that any attack on the army would be a disaster, and

[1] BA Koblenz: P135-8037.

Tirpitz's fears about the Centre turned out to have been unjustified. Voting against the estimates was too high a price to pay for moral scruples about duelling.[1] Once again the army had won the day, and although the question was brought up once more in March 1918, it was again left unsettled.

Although duelling was forbidden by civil law and officially discouraged by the AKO of 1-1-1897 many potential officers were asked about their attitude to duels and were refused commissions if they did not accept them. In an army order of 28-1-1901 it was forbidden 'during the election of officers to question candidates on their attitude towards duels'.[2] In spite of this the abuse continued with the army authorities turning a blind eye. Indeed among the papers of the Bavarian War Ministry there is a cutting from the *Beilage zur Post* dated 12-1-1901 which reads

in the Prussian Officer Corps there should be no room for people who do not accept the duel, otherwise it will no longer remain what it is. Anyone can be against duels as much as he likes, but then he should not try to enter the Officer Corps in which he must be fully aware that an unconditional obligation to duel exists.

With this cutting is a note from the War Minister approving the sentiments expressed.[3] Whether the Minister changed his opinion after publication of the army order a few days later is at least open to doubt. Certainly the practice continued, and the Prussian War Minister von Einem was obliged to repeat the order on 10-12-1906.[4] He laid down that a potential officer was not to be questioned as to his attitude to duelling; furthermore a corps student should not be asked whether or not his corps practised duelling. Owing to the virtual impossibility of any form of control it is doubtful whether this put an end to the matter, the more so since Einem's successors were known to favour duels as a means of preserving the homogeneity of the Officer Corps.

Previous to the AKO of 1-1-1897 an officer could be dismissed from the army for refusing to duel. Thus the *Vossische*

---

[1] DZA, Potsdam: Reichskanzlei, 754.

[2] Heeresarchiv Stuttgart. Persönliche Angelegenheiten des Württ. KM, Bd. 34, p. 42.

[3] Bayr.HSA, Abt. IV, KA, M.Kr.2072.

[4] Ibid., 2073.

Zeitung reported on 24-4-1896 a particularly crass case where the accused in court challenged the *Gerichtsassessor* to a duel. Both were reserve officers, and therefore brought the matter before a court of honour. The court was unable to reach a decision and suggested that they should fight a duel. The *Gerichtsassessor* refused and was then dismissed from the army.[1] Those who had hoped that the AKO would change matters were soon disappointed, and the army remained in direct conflict with the law. Thus 'whoever fought a duel was locked away by the State, but whoever did not duel was chased away by his fellow officers by summary dismissal'.[2] The official attitude of the army, although not explicitly stated, was that duelling was all right as long as no one died as a result of it.[3] This was in fact a wilful misinterpretation of the law. Officers continued to be dismissed for refusing to duel, for duelling was felt to be the basis of the officers' code of honour, and therefore of the Officer Corps itself. In von Blomberg's papers there is a typical example of this. Blomberg's brother had a great friend; in 1913 at a mess party, one knocked the hat off the other's head. The incident was observed by a civilian who reported the matter to a superior officer. They were brought before a court of honour which decided that they should fight a duel. The duel took place and the two friends shot in the air. As a result both were dismissed from the army.[4] One Captain Hoenig criticized the historical writings of the General Staff on the Franco-Prussian war. He was then challenged to a duel by Bernhardi who was then head of the historical section of the General Staff. He refused on the grounds that he was half blind, and was promptly deprived of his uniform by a court of honour.[5]

This lack of respect for civilian law was a result of the belief that the courts of honour were more efficacious than civilian courts when a man's honour was at stake, and therefore the punishment was bound, by its very nature, to be more severe. In a decision of 1-1-1897 the following remark occurs:

The notion that the punishment of the offender by a court of honour

[1] *Vossische Zeitung*, 24-4-1896.
[2] F. C. Endres, *Archiv für Sozialwissenschaften*, p. 306.
[3] DZA, Potsdam: Reichskanzlei, 754.
[4] BA Koblenz: 1108—52/1, Depot von Blomberg, 8.
[5] Alfred Vagts, *A History of Militarism* (London, 1959), p. 26.

does not provide satisfaction for the injured party may be justified in serious cases, but as a general rule it cannot be accepted. In all cases conviction of the offender by a court of honour, confirmed by His Majesty, is a far more effective form of satisfaction than even the most severe civilian court can give.[1]

How this worked in practice can be seen in the case of a lawyer named Feldhaus who was insulted by a young man. Since he was an officer of the Landwehr he reported the case to the court of honour. He then sued the young man and the case came before a civil court. Feldhaus was promptly dismissed from the army for trying to seek satisfaction outside the court of honour, and for refusing to fight a duel.[2]

The attitude of the army towards duelling was underlined by the fact that regular officers who were wounded in duels were given pensions. This was clearly absurd in that duelling was forbidden by law. In 1906 the Centre tried to stop this abuse but failed to do so. The military writer Gädke pointed out quite correctly that this was a useless way of trying to stop duels as reserve officers were not given pensions and it was precisely the reserve officers who duelled most. In addition it was only fair that those officers who were forced into duelling by their superiors were compensated should they be wounded.[3]

The basis of the officers' code of honour and of the duel lay in the idea of the ability to give satisfaction (*Satisfactionsfähigkeit*). This notion served to cement the sense of caste that existed in the Officer Corps. If on the one hand a man of honour had to defend that honour, conversely a man without honour had no honour to defend. This meant that an officer could insult a workman, for example, as much as he liked, for the workman had no honour to defend. Heinrich Mann satirized this unattractive attitude in his novel *Der Untertan* by showing the delight with which the hero insulted those who were unable to demand satisfaction, and the sense of superiority which this gave to him. The notion of the specific sense of honour of the upper classes found its passionate defenders.

[1] Heeresarchiv Stuttgart. Persönliche Angelegenheiten des WKM, Bd 34, p. 42.
[2] Heeresarchiv Stuttgart: Persönliche Angelegenheiten des WKM, Band 25, p. 50.
[3] Ibid.

Not everyone can damage our honour. He who does not live up to the demands of honour cannot harm us, for he either does not know them, or if he does he does not regard them as binding. Turning to the relationship between officers and *bourgeois* circles this means that only he can give satisfaction who, like the officer, submits himself to the same code of honour, which is accepted by the educated classes and is practised by them.[1]

The officer's sense of honour thus bound him to the upper classes and cut him off from the lower orders.

It would be a mistake to think that the army did nothing to reduce the number of duels, or that the order of January 1897 was entirely without effect. Time was running against the army, and the code of honour of the Officer Corps looked increasingly antiquated in the eyes of a growing proportion of the population. Nor could the vigorous attacks of the Social Democrats and the Centre in the Reichstag be ignored. More and more cases were settled in the courts of honour, and did not therefore lead to duels. The idea became widespread that those officers who had acted in a dishonourable way could not be considered *satisfactionsfähig*, and were therefore dismissed from the army, unable to defend themselves in a duel. Adulterers, or officers who had made wounding remarks under the influence of drink, were often treated in this manner.[2] It is impossible to obtain accurate statistics for the number of duels, for so many were fought in secrecy, or were not reported by commanding officers; but the number of cases settled by the courts of honour certainly increased, and other evidence does suggest a considerable drop in the number of duels after 1897.

The decrease in the number of duels was due not so much to the active intervention of the army authorities, but rather to a changing atmosphere in society as a whole. The notions of honour upheld in the Officer Corps became increasingly difficult to justify to the world outside, and the officers cannot have failed to notice, however reluctantly, that these notions no longer commanded automatic admiration in the circles in which they moved. Contrary to this change in society's attitude to honour and duels the military authorities continued to insist on the right of an officer to defend his honour in a duel, indeed on

---

[1] von Schaible, *Standes und Berufspflichten des deutschen Offiziers* (Berlin, 1891), p. 17.
[2] Demeter, *Das Deutsche Offizierkorps*, p. 134.

the necessity of doing so. Thus a decision of 31-10-99 reads: 'An officer who, before completion of the proceedings of a court of honour, resorts to a duel, is not directly acting against an interdiction of the AKO of 1-1-97.'[1] That the courts of honour could turn a blind eye was shown in the decision of 12-11-1901: 'The council of honour (*Ehrenrath*) should not recommend a duel if a reconciliation of the parties proves impossible, but the AKO of 1-1-97 does not exclude the possibility of a duel under all circumstances.'[2] This was again repeated on 14-1-1906 with the remark that an officer had to be 'the defender of his own honour', and therefore did not need the recommendations of a court of honour before fighting a duel, should the court fail to bring the affair to a satisfactory conclusion.[3] Moreover, the attitude of the court of honour could be influenced by an officer's behaviour in a duel. Thus the court had to wait for the decision of the court martial trying the officer for duelling before coming to a decision of its own. For 'it is extremely important for the court of honour to know how an officer is able to defend his wounded honour'.[4] In spite of these many loopholes the courts of honour tried to make the two parties reach a satisfactory agreement without resorting to force. An order dated 21-8-02 said that the 'Council of honour must recommend reconciliation according to its own discretion, officers are duty bound to offer their hands in friendly reconciliation, and a reconciliation is to be worked for'.[5]

The army was therefore in an awkward situation. Although duelling was forbidden, many leading military authorities, from the War Minister downwards, believed that it was essential for the preservation of the Officer Corps, and at the same time this attitude was increasingly difficult to justify in a world which had less and less patience with romantic notions of chivalry. In the regular Officer Corps this led to a reduction in the number of duels; the reserve officers, on the contrary, tended to duel as much as before if not more. Anxious to ape their idols in the regular army, they were all too ready to seek an excuse for a duel, which certainly earned them the admiration of their colleagues in the regular army. Apologists claimed

---

[1] Heeresarchiv Stuttgart; Persönliches Angelegenheiten des Württ. KM, Bd. 34. p. 42.
[2] Ibid.   [3] Ibid.   [4] Ibid.   [5] Ibid.

that the reserve officer tended to duel more because he came into more frequent contact with civilians who lacked the fine sense of honour of the professional soldier. This argument is not entirely convincing, but it may be that the reserve officer was anxious to prove his warlike skill and his unimpeachable valour to those who, even on Sundays, did not wear the 'King's jacket'.

In Bavaria there were fewer duels than in Prussia, perhaps because military courts were more often open to the public, a supposition suggested by the fact that in the 1850s there had been considerably more duels in Bavaria than in Prussia.[1]

The protests against duels increased. In the Reichstag questions were frequently asked by members who resented the way in which the army did so little in theory to discourage, and so much in practice to encourage, behaviour that was expressly forbidden by the law. Their protest was echoed by the novelists. Theodor Fontane in *Effi Briest* and Jacob Wassermann in *Christian Wahnschaffe* attacked the folly and cruelty of duels in works of the highest literary merit. The popular novelists did not lag far behind; Franz Adam Beyerlein in *Jena oder Sedan* and Bilse in *Aus einer Kleinen Garnison* showed how men were forced to fight duels for bagatelles, and how often the duels themselves bordered on pure farce. A society against duels, the *Anti-Duell-Liga (ADL)*, was formed with its own newspaper and a number of prominent members, by no means all of whom were liberals or on the left.[2]

In spite of all this activity duelling continued in the favoured circles of Junker and officer, civil servant and student. To duel was the mark of a real man, a sign that one belonged to the privileged class. It was for this reason that the students of the Technical Hochschule of Aachen clamoured for the right to duel.[3] But times were changing. Even the passionate defender of the duel, von Boguslawski, had to admit that the courts of honour were sometimes in conflict with the laws of the land.[4] Duels were on the wane, certainly those which resulted in death,

---

[1] Demeter, *Das Deutsche Offizierkorps*, p. 137.
[2] BA Koblenz: P135–8037.
[3] Ibid.
[4] Boguslawski, *Die Ehre und das Duell*, p. 95.

and the opponents of the duel were increasingly better organized, within the Reichstag and without. But the wistful remark of *Vorwärts*, that if the laws of libel were considered adequate why was there a need for duels at all, remained unanswered.

The army not only regarded the courts of honour as a means of binding the Officer Corps more closely together, but also as a useful weapon to control former officers. It thus tried to exercise direct control over officers who were no longer on the active list, particularly those whose ideas it found dangerous or whose political views differed from its orthodoxy. In matters of honour, used in its widest, and usually in its political sense, it considered that ex-officers came under exactly the same military control as regular officers. This attitude led quite naturally to a number of struggles with the Ministry of Justice which regarded ex-officers as civilians, and therefore as coming under the jurisdiction of civil law.[1] This problem was particularly acute in the case of officers writing for the press. The most spectacular example of this indirect form of censorship was the case of Oberst a.D. Gädke.

William II had a strong dislike of officers writing for the daily press. He had an aversion to officers writing in journals whose general political ideas he found bordering on the treasonable, and furthermore he did not wish to see military affairs discussed too openly in public. The mystique of the army had to be preserved. In 1892 he tried to stop all officers from writing in the daily press, but this was clearly a violation of the press law of 7 May 1874 and of article 27 of the constitution. He was therefore obliged to settle for a compromise measure. In the AKO of 13-6-1894 he threatened to bring officers before a court martial or a court of honour if he did not approve of their articles. This had the quite natural result of causing a sharp decrease in the number of articles published by officers, even in purely technical journals, with the result that fruitful debate on military matters was severely restricted. In the AKO of 31-1-1897 officers were encouraged to write for the military journals, such as the *Militär-Wochenblatt*. Effective control was exercised in that the majority of the articles were first presented to the General Staff for approval. After the publication of the first

[1] BA Koblenz: P135–7870.

volume of Hohenlohe's memoirs, which caused a considerable scandal, Moltke wished to extend this censorship to officers' memoirs. Although many submitted drafts to the General Staff a direct control was not brought into effect.[1] The problem of controlling former officers writing for the daily press was much more difficult, as can be seen from the Gädke case.

Gädke, a retired colonel, had been the commanding officer of the 2 Niederschlesische Feldartillerie Regiment number 41. On leaving the army he became the military correspondent of the *Berliner Tageblatt*. He was without a doubt one of the finest military commentators of his time, and the papers of the Württemberg War Ministry show that his articles were taken seriously by high military officials.[2] But Gädke was sharply critical of certain aspects of military life, and therefore became increasingly obnoxious to the military authorities. An article on the murder of King Alexander I of Serbia by a group of officers in June 1903 gave them a chance to take action. Gädke had argued that this showed that there could be a conflict between an officer's duty to the monarch and his duty to his country. The War Ministry decided to bring him before a court of honour and strip him of the title of Colonel and the right to wear uniform.

This procedure was not without precedent. The author of the critical book *Sine ira et studio*, Oberstleutnant a.D. von Wartenburg, had been brought before a court of honour and deprived of his title shortly before the Gädke case began.[3] The Wartenburg case had caused a considerable amount of criticism of the army, particularly in the liberal and left-wing press, and many felt that another such scandal would be certain to harm the army. The Minister of Justice wrote a carefully worded note to the War Minister on 10-7-1905 suggesting that the army did not in fact have the right to use the court of honour against retired officers, and thus recommended that the case against Gädke be dropped.[4] The War Minister was, however, out for Gädke's blood, and wrote to the Ministry of Justice on 11-9-1905 that, since the title of officer was granted by the Kaiser, and the

[1] Demeter, *Das Deutsche Offizierkorps*, p. 154.
[2] Heeresarchiv Stuttgart: Denkschriften Sammlung, Band 405.
[3] *Berliner Tageblatt*, 2-5-1905.
[4] BA Koblenz: P135–8588. JM to KM, 10-7-05.

Kaiser alone, then clearly the Kaiser had the right to withdraw the title.[1] A court of honour decided in February 1904 that Gädke had lost the right to wear uniform and to call himself Colonel; but Gädke refused to accept the decision, claiming that the courts of honour had no jurisdiction over retired officers, since retired officers no longer came under military law. The War Minister therefore claimed that Gädke was using a title to which he was not entitled, thus committing a legal offence. Under pressure from the War Ministry the Minister of Justice wrote on 27-9-1905 that he could not guarantee the success of a trial against Gädke, but added that there was a faint possibility of finding him guilty.[2] At this stage the War Minister began to have second thoughts as to the wisdom of prosecuting Gädke; he did not wish to risk the humiliation of an acquittal, and after the Minister of Justice's note this seemed highly probable. On 25-10-1905 the War Minister wrote to the Chancellor: 'Under these circumstances it would be much better to give up the idea of starting criminal proceedings against Gädke, even taking into account the danger that he might continue his attacks. In my humble opinion the advantages that a criminal prosecution might have bear no relationship to the consequences that an unfavourable decision, which is quite probable, certainly would have.' The Minister added that in future retired officers should only be allowed to use their titles under certain specific conditions, so that a repetition of the Gädke case could be avoided.[3] This proposal was clearly unacceptable.

In spite of the War Minister's desire to drop the case, the affair continued to take its course. On 29-11-1905 the War Minister repeated to the Minister of Justice the claim that retired officers came under the jurisdiction of the courts of honour.[4] Meanwhile a jury-court (*Schöffengericht*) had returned a verdict of 'not guilty' on Gädke on the charge that he had been using a title without authority to do so. This decision was fiercely debated. The First State Prosecutor (*Oberstaatsanwalt*) of the Supreme Royal Court of Justice stated on 16-2-1906 that

---

[1] BA Koblenz: P135–8588. KM to JM, 11-9-05.
[2] DZA, Potsdam: Reichskanzlei, 1305; JM to KM, 27-9-05.
[3] Ibid.
[4] BA Koblenz: P135–8588; KM to JM, 29-11-05.

courts of honour had no jurisdiction over retired officers, and that the title of Colonel could not be taken away from Gädke, even by the application of the Kaiser's power of command over the army, for he was no longer in the army in the constitutional sense.[1] However another state prosecutor claimed that the sentence of the jury-court was wrong and appealed against the decision. The First State Prosecutor repeated his point of view on 19-5-1906: 'The fact that the accused accepted the right to wear uniform and the honours that go with this on leaving the army can under no circumstances be regarded as a voluntary submission by him to the new regulations governing courts of honour.' The War Minister for his part argued that retired officers had to be regarded as members of the Estate (*Standesgenossen*) and therefore as part of the army, this being clearly shown by the fact that they were saluted by regular soldiers, and therefore they had to accept the officer's code of honour and the decision of a court of honour.[2] On 5-10-1906 a compromise solution was reached. The appeal by the state prosecutor was turned down on the grounds that Gädke had not had his exact legal position with regard to the courts of honour explained to him when he left the army. The law demanded such an explanation. On the other hand the principle that courts of honour had legal powers over retired officers was upheld.[3] Gädke then claimed that according to an order of the War Ministry of 21 April 1849 the courts of honour had no right to try a man for his political views.[4] The decision of 5-10-1906 did not satisfy the War Ministry, the more so since Gädke had sharpened his attacks on the army in the pages of the *Berliner Tageblatt*, but the Minister of Justice sought to defend it in a memorandum dated 17-12-1906 'the great significance of the judgement lies in the fact that the Supreme Court accepts the legal validity of all the clauses of His Majesty's regulations of 2-5-1874 governing courts of honour, so that even retired officers who retain the right to wear uniform are subject to the jurisdiction of the courts of honour'. The Ministry found further justification for the decision of the court by adding: 'there

[1] BA Koblenz: P135–8588; KM to JM, 29-11-05.
[2] Ibid., KM, 22-6-06.
[3] Ibid., 5-10-06.
[4] *Berliner Tageblatt*, 10-10-06.

is however no really convincing evidence that before the criminal proceedings began he (Gädke) knew of the decision which denied him the right to use his rank as an officer'. This memorandum also mentioned that Gädke had refused to go to the court of honour in person, and therefore his conviction was *in absentia* and could not therefore be considered binding. The Minister of Justice suggested that Gädke be brought before a second court of honour so as to obviate this confusion, and 'to protect the prestige of the Crown'.[1]

The army was not satisfied with the outcome of the case, and sought to fill in the gap through which Gädke had managed to escape. By the AKO of 27-12-1906 it was established that decisions of courts of honour did not have to be given in person, but that a signed copy of the sentence sufficed.[2] Gädke was at once up in arms, and wrote in the *Berliner Tageblatt* on 12-2-1907 that 'the Cabinet order of 27-12-1906 is suspect in that it uses an army order to instruct the State Prosecutor, and this seems to me to be contrary to the constitution'.[3]

Unconstitutional or not, the attack on Gädke continued. On 22-4-1907 he was tried again before the jury-court in Berlin, and once again was found not guilty, the court having decided that: 'A retired officer is not a person subject to the power of command, nor is he a soldier.'[4]

Although Gädke had been by now acquitted several times on 9-9-1907 he was tried again and fined 150 marks with the alternative of 15 days imprisonment. Meanwhile the second court of honour had reached a decision and the sentence was read to Gädke through the use of AKO 27-12-1906. His appeal against the decision was turned down on 25-2-1908. Gädke, who for nearly four years had stood up against the army, had at last lost. From now on his articles in the *Berliner Tageblatt* could no longer be signed '*Oberst a.D.*'.[5]

The Gädke case was certainly not an isolated one, for exactly the same methods were used in 1907 and 1908 against a member of the Reichstag, Paasche, who had criticized the life in the officers' messes in Berlin. Paasche was a major in the

---

[1] BA Koblenz: P135–8588; JM, 17-12-06.
[2] Ibid.
[3] *Berliner Tageblatt*, 12-2-07.
[4] BA Koblenz: P135–8588.
[5] Ibid.

Landwehr, and like Gädke was submitted to the full pressure of the courts of honour to make him retract these remarks.[1]

The cases of Gädke, Wartenburg, and Paasche were examples of the way in which the army used all the power at its command to force officers, even when they had left the regular army, to keep to the path of political orthodoxy, resorting, where necessary, to methods which were constitutionally highly dubious. Gädke himself underlined the dangers of this abuse in the *Berliner Tageblatt*: 'What is the implication of the use by the military authorities of the courts of honour against reserve officers who, apart from the time they spend on manoeuvres, are legally entitled to use their full political rights? It amounts to an act of force, a strong moral pressure, which is used to bind the individual officer to a particular political line and to make him submit to an utterly one-sided view of the state. Like the demonstrative behaviour of the Crown Prince in Parliament, like the agitation of the Admirals and the Colonial Generals, like the favouritism shown to the aristocracy, the misuse of the courts of honour amounts to an interference by the army with ordinary politics, it means a suppression of civil freedom and honour by the power of command.'[2]

---

[1] Heeresarchiv Stuttgart: Denkschriften Sammlung, Band 82.
[2] *Berliner Tageblatt*, 13-11-11.

IV

ALFRED GRAF VON WALDERSEE
AS A POLITICAL GENERAL

WALDERSEE was born in Potsdam in 1832. His father was Commanding General of the Vth army corps, and later the military governor of Berlin. His mother, who had been a lady-in-waiting to the Duchess of Cumberland, also came from a military family. Her father, Generalleutnant Freiherr von Hünerbein, had been a friend of Queen Louise. Waldersee's early career was that of a well-placed young aristocrat from a military family who was set on following in his father's footsteps. Having first been a page at court, he was commissioned in an artillery regiment of the guards. In 1865 he became adjutant to Prince Karl, the commander of the artillery. After the war of 1866, in which he had served with the Prince, he became a General Staff officer in Hanover. In 1870 he was appointed military attaché in Paris; there he looked forward to the war which he was convinced would come, and wrote in his reports that the time was ripe to strike. In his diary he noted: 'Since 1866 every one of us who was at all perspicacious had the feeling that the unity of Germany could not be achieved without a war with France. Our preparations for war are being made largely in this direction.'[1] As a sign of particular favour in May 1870 Waldersee was appointed A.D.C. to the King of Prussia.

Waldersee played no conspicuous part in the Franco-Prussian war, but merely accompanied the General Staff doing nothing in particular, for which he was awarded the Iron Cross 1st Class. After a short period as chargé d'affaires in Paris he became commanding officer of the 13th regiment of Uhlans. By 1873 he was chief of the General Staff in the Xth corps and in 1882 was appointed Quartermaster General at the General

[1] Waldersee, *Denkwürdigkeiten*, Vol. I, 30-4-70.

Staff. In this office he became the confidant of the ageing
Moltke, and soon his most likely successor. In 1888, on Moltke's
retirement he was appointed Chief of the General Staff. In 1873
he became engaged to an American, Marie Esther Lee, the
widow of Prince Friedrich zu Schleswig-Holstein-Sonderburg-
Augustenburg. This marriage brought him not only wealth but
also greater influence in court circles.

By the time Waldersee was appointed Chief of the General
Staff, one of the most influential positions in the Reich, his
political views were already firmly established. Having been
unable to play a particularly dramatic role in the wars of 1866
and 1870–1 Waldersee looked forward to the next war, in
which he hoped to be able to show his sterling military qualities.
His choice of an enemy was soon made. Germany had defeated
both Austria and France, therefore the next on the list was
Russia. Thus the mainspring of his political aims was his desire
for war with Russia.

In 1873 Waldersee considered the problem of Russia in his
diary, and noted that recent reforms in the Russian army would
cause a strengthening of her military position. He believed that
the construction of an effective railway system would make a
second Crimean war impossible, and also that the introduction
of universal military service for a two-year term would give
the Russians an enormous advantage in numbers. At the same
time Waldersee thought that Russia had gone too far in its
liberalization since the Crimean war, and that it was only the
power of the Orthodox Church that was keeping the Empire
together.[1]

After his appointment to the General Staff the problem of
Russia became something of an obsession for Waldersee. In the
Spring of 1882 he discussed the danger of Russia almost daily
with Moltke, and the subject of war with Russia became the
most popular topic in military circles.[2] The General Staff's
reports to Bismarck painted a gloomy picture of the danger of
invasion from Russia, so much so that Bismarck even discussed
with Waldersee the possibility of restoring Poland as a buffer
state against the likelihood of Russian attack.[3] Waldersee's

[1] Waldersee, *Denkwürdigkeiten*, Vol. 1, 13-5-73.
[2] Wolfgang Fornaschon, *Die politischen Anschauungen des Grafen Alfred von Waldersee
und seine Stellungnahme zur deutschen Politik* (Berlin, 1935), p. 97.
[3] Waldersee, *Denkwürdigkeiten*, Vol. I, 27-10-83.

ardent desire for war was frustrated however, and by 1885 he was beginning to despair: 'I see that the only way out for us is a large-scale war in which we permanently cripple one of our foes, France or Russia—but how can one ask that of an 88-year-old Kaiser and a 70-year-old Chancellor?'[1] As the Kaiser and Chancellor remained in command and no war came, Waldersee began to think that it might soon be too late for Germany to fight a successful war: 'I am absolutely convinced that this war, which simply must come soon, offers us better chances the sooner it comes.'[2] Waldersee was also anxious to stir up the offensive spirit of the Austrian allies. In discussions with the Austrian military attaché Steininger in December 1886 Waldersee remarked that he did not believe that the Russians would attack just yet, but that when war broke out the Germans were counting on the Austrians undertaking a 'powerful offensive'.[3]

The spread of Boulangism in France turned his thoughts momentarily away from Russia to the glamorous prospect of a new war with France. In December 1886 he wrote: 'After mature consideration of the possibilities I believe that it would be the best for us to provoke war with France; to wait until our enemies think that the moment is ripe is certainly unwise.'[4] Although Waldersee held that war with France was 'inevitable', he was disappointed to find that his enthusiasm for war was not shared by many of his fellow generals.[5] Among the generals, von Loë and von Heuduck welcomed the idea of a war waged with Austria against France and Russia. Waldersee took every opportunity of publicly announcing his belief that war with France was essential for the security of the Reich which gave him the reputation of being, in his own words, 'a very bad man'; but he comforted himself with the thought that at least the War Minister, Bronsart von Schellendorf, agreed with him.[6]

In February 1887 the new mobilization plans were finished, which transferred a number of troops from the Eastern to the Western front, thus showing the greater emphasis Waldersee had begun to place on war with France. Waldersee believed

---

[1] Waldersee, *Denkwürdigkeiten*, Vol. 1, 15-10-85.
[2] Ibid., 1-5-86.   [3] Ibid., 13-12-86.
[4] Ibid., 28-12-86.   [5] Ibid., 9-1-87.   [6] Ibid., 27-1-87.

that the new seven-year estimates (*Septennat*) which foresaw
sizeable increases in the army would force the French to take
similar steps, and that this would eventually lead to war.
Bismarck, however, was quite convinced that this would not
be the case.[1] By October 1887 Waldersee seemed to be losing
interest in French affairs and noted in his diary that no-one had
the courage to start a new war; he also declared that opinion
in Russia was becoming increasingly anti-German.[2] In
November he discussed the movement of Russian troops towards the West with the Crown Prince (later William II), to
whom he expressed the conviction that the Russians would
attack in the New Year.[3] On the following day he expounded
his views to Moltke, suggesting that the German army should
be mobilized at once, so as to force the Tsar to withdraw his
troops from the western frontier; if the Tsar refused to comply
war should be declared at once. Waldersee claimed that
although a winter offensive was hard, at least it would mean
that the bridge-heads on the rivers could be secured, whereas
a spring offensive would be even more difficult. Although he
claimed in his diary that Moltke was impressed by his arguments he did not think he would get his war. The War Minister
promised, somewhat half-heartedly, to co-operate by encouraging railway building in the East. This was clearly a delaying
tactic, for he probably knew that neither the Kaiser nor the
Chancellor were likely to be convinced of the need for war.[4]
The fact that the Tsar arrived the next day in Berlin for a visit
did not help Waldersee's plans. Indeed the result of the talks
was that the Kaiser believed that, although war was likely
between Russia and Austria, Germany might be able to remain
neutral. However, Moltke told the Kaiser in a loud voice (*mit
gehobener Stimme*) that 'we can never leave Austria in the
lurch'.[5]

Waldersee's endeavours to convince the Austrians of the
necessity of a preventive war against Russia did not escape the
notice of Bismarck.[6] On 7 December 1887 the Chancellor sent
a sharp note to Waldersee asking him to refrain from meddling

[1] Waldersee, *Denkwürdigkeiten*, Vol. I, 5-2-87.
[2] Ibid., 21-10-87.   [3] Ibid., 16-11-87.
[4] Ibid., 17-11-87   [5] Ibid., 26-11-87
[6] See M. E. Howard in *Cambridge Modern History*, xi. 223.

in politics.[1] In an interview with the Kaiser on 17 December Waldersee was appalled to hear that he had no desire to go to war, but he agreed that military talks with Austria should continue.[2] Bismarck was not enthusiastic for these talks, fearing that Austria was trying to force Germany into a war which could only be for Austria's interests. Bismarck stressed that the alliance of 1879 was purely defensive, and that he could not tolerate any interference with his foreign policy which was based on the preservation of peace in Europe.[3]

On New Year's day 1888 Waldersee reviewed his position in the quarrel with Bismarck:

> The Chancellor, in spite of all his skill, has not been able to keep Russia friendly with us, thus the world war, in which we shall fight for our existence, is in sight. The big question is this: should we start the war, which seems inevitable, when the chances favour us, as they do at the moment, or should we wait until our opponents feel ready, in the hope that something can happen that will save us from war? I am convinced that the first is correct, but am also certain that we have chosen the second. The Kaiser certainly does not want war with Russia, and does not trust Austria much. At his age it is, of course, natural that he wants to end his days in peace. The chancellor had even less desire for war, partly for other motives; and thus we are wasting a good opportunity and are, I am convinced, doing our best to make Austria suspicious again, which seems to me highly reprehensible.[4]

Waldersee prided himself that it was only the General Staff which was preserving the Austrian alliance, and he was comforted to hear from the military attaché in Vienna that Franz Joseph thought the same.[5] Bismarck, who feared that the close co-operation between the two General Staffs might encourage Austria to run the risk of war with Russia, told the Austrian Foreign Minister, Kalnoky, that the Austrian army should remain behind the Carpathians in the event of war. Waldersee who thought that this idea was 'hair-raising rubbish' and further evidence of the Chancellor's vanity in that he regarded himself as a military expert, comforted himself with the thought that at least Beck, the Austrian Chief of the General Staff, was

---

[1] Waldersee, *Denkwürdigkeiten*, i. 340.
[2] Ibid., 17-12-87.   [3] Ibid. 30-12-87.
[4] Ibid., 1-1-1888.   [5] Ibid., 25-1-88.

not a coward in this respect and believed in the offensive spirit. In fact the German Ambassador in Vienna was ordered to take back the Chancellor's remarks, but Waldersee saw it as further evidence of a sorry lack of offensive spirit.[1]

Shortly before his appointment as Chief of the General Staff Waldersee repeated his belief in the need for a preventive war: 'I remain convinced that we have the best chance if we, in alliance with Austria and Italy, declare war on Russia and France.'[2]

It became increasingly clear to the army and the government that Moltke was not immortal, and indeed that he was rapidly sinking into senile decay. Moltke enjoyed, even in his old age, the reputation of being a supreme and infallible military genius, but the personality cult of 'Saint Moltke' became increasingly remote from the real facts. Bald, he took to wearing a wig which was styled to make him look like Julius Caesar, but unfortunately this ornament was somewhat too big for him and had the distressing habit of falling off at awkward moments. He was almost stone-deaf, which did not make work with him easier. His capacity for dropping unfortunate bricks was proverbial in Berlin, but amused respect was paid to his advanced age. On one occasion, while still head of the General Staff he paid his humble respects to a Lady-in-waiting, under the impression that she was the Empress, an episode which caused the Empress herself no little amusement.[3] Although Moltke had virtually ceased to do any work at the General Staff, leaving everything to his subordinates, his reputation in the army bordered on idolatry. Von Einem, the later War Minister, describes the army's attitude to Moltke in his memoirs in extravagant but typical terms.

Moltke's genius was supreme, no-one criticized him. We only argued then as to which aspect of his character was more splendid, the military or the human. Marcus Aurelius and Plato were not wiser than he. No General was his superior; he stands in the ranks of the really great: Alexander, Hannibal, Frederick, and Napoleon.[4]

It was unthinkable that Moltke should resign as long as the old Kaiser William lived, for their names were inextricably

[1] Waldersee, *Denkwürdigkeiten*, Vol. I, 31-1-88.   [2] Ibid., 8-4-88.
[3] Helmuth von Moltke, *Erinnerungen-Briefe-Dokumente 1877–1916.*
[4] Generaloberst von Einem, *Erinnerungen eines Soldaten*, p. 30.

coupled with the glorious campaigns of 1866 and 1870, but with the young and active William II his position was less secure. William was determined to free himself from the giants of a previous generation and to go his own way. Quite apart from this Moltke's health made it unlikely that he could remain much longer in office. Even in the General Staff it had become a standing joke that he only recognized one man on his staff, one Claer, whom he called Wright, for that had been his predecessor's name.[1] In August 1888 he resigned, and the Kaiser appointed Waldersee in his place.

Waldersee's appointment caused little surprise. For several years he had virtually acted as Chief of the General Staff, for Moltke's advanced age gave him every opportunity to strengthen his position. Equally important was the fact that he had ingratiated himself with William II. Waldersee heartily endorsed William's dislike of his father's politics, a fact which helped to strengthen the bonds of friendship between the two. His friendship with Prince William was no secret at the court, and he was soon accused of trying to turn him against his father.[2] In a conversation with William, shortly after the death of his grandfather, Waldersee quite openly mentioned his dislike of the new Kaiser, without the Crown Prince raising the slightest objection.

I spoke very openly and said something like this: we all feel that the idea that it would be a misfortune if Kaiser William I died before the Crown Prince has been quite wrong; the new imperial couple would do so many preposterous things that they would prepare the way for the next Crown Prince (William II) in the best possible fashion, it all depended on keeping calm; after a short while the Kaiser (Frederick III) would have to ask him to take on the Regency. The less noticeable it had been until then, the less he had asked for, the stronger would be his position. He agreed thoroughly and left in a friendly manner, expressing the hope that we would have a lot to do with one another.[3]

Waldersee did everything to fan William's resentment against his father, and even more so against his mother who was considered the real instigator of his dangerously liberal

[1] Eberhard Kessel, *Die Welt als Geschichte* (1954) Jahrgang 14.
[2] Waldersee, *Denkwürdigkeiten*, Vol. I, 2-4-1886.
[3] Ibid., 11-3-1888.

tendencies, and constantly flattered him by claiming that William was the only man fit to rule and should replace his sick father. William's vanity and prejudices thrived on such fare, and in return he regarded Waldersee as his right-hand man—a man of impeccably reactionary sentiments and intense martial ardour. Small wonder that Waldersee thought that his appointment as Chief of the General Staff was merely the first step to higher office.

As Chief of the General Staff Waldersee's first objective was to strengthen its independence from the War Ministry, Foreign Office, and Chancellor. While he was still Quarter-master General he had skilfully used the enormous reputation of Moltke to increase the power of the General Staff. The reform of April 1883, which gave the Chief of the General Staff the right of direct access to the Kaiser, without the War Minister having to be present, was largely his work.[1] In the military field he set about removing some of the abuses which had arisen under the lax leadership of Moltke's later years. Manoeuvres became somewhat more realistic and were no longer the 'tourist trips' that they had tended to become. Similarly reconnaissance expeditions ceased to be mere excuses for luxurious tours of Europe; officers were given a proper theme to examine and were expected to give a lengthy report on their return. Waldersee also did something to stop the nepotism and favouritism which tended to determine appointments to the General Staff.[2] Moltke had laid more and more stress in his old age on the study of military history, and much time and energy was expended in the careful analysis of the great campaigns of classical and mediaeval times. Waldersee removed these sub-jects from the curriculum of the War Academy, claiming that Staff Officers had more vital topics to study, although the study of the recent campaigns continued, particularly in the historical section of the General Staff.[3]

Waldersee had insufficient time as Chief of the General Staff to inaugurate any far-reaching changes in strategy and tactics. However, as a former gunnery officer he demanded eighty-four

[1] Generalleutnant von Cochenhausen, *Von Scharnhorst zu Schlieffen 1806–1906* (Berlin, 1933), p. 217; and Hans Mohs, *Generalfeldmarschall Alfred Graf von Waldersee in seinem militärischen Wirken* (Berlin, 1929), p. 35.

[2] Mohs, *Waldersee*, pp. 28–30.

[3] Eberhard Kessel, *Die Welt als Geschichte* (1954) Jahrgang 14.

new batteries and this request led to a fierce struggle with the
War Minister, Bronsart, who after lengthy argument agreed to
grant Waldersee an increase in the strength of the artillery, but
reduced his original demands by two thirds.[1] Waldersee was
convinced that the cavalry had outlived its military usefulness,
having played an insignificant role in the wars of 1866 and
1870-1. The cavalry was still held in high esteem, the result, he
felt, of a fallacious reading of military history, but his efforts to
augment the fire-power of the infantry and increase the artillery
at the expense of the cavalry were flatly turned down by the
Kaiser, who was ever impressed by the sound of thundering
hooves on the manoeuvre ground.[2] Strategically he wanted a
more mobile and offensive plan for mobilization in the West, a
direct result of his desire for a two-front war.[3]

Waldersee's main field of political activity during his time as
Chief of the General Staff was foreign policy. His views were
delightfully simple. Germany would have to fight a preventive
war with France and Russia before she was attacked, therefore
conventional diplomacy should be abandoned to the army. He
had a large number of correspondents, most of whom fancied
themselves experts on foreign policy, with whom he conducted
a voluminous correspondence. Principal among them were the
military attachés, Engelbrecht in Rome, Graf Schmettau in
Brussels, von Deines in Vienna, Huene in Paris, Graf Yorck von
Wartenburg in Petersburg, Goltz the German military expert
in Turkey, and Freiherr von Rechenberg the German consul in
Warsaw. All these men were devoted to Waldersee, and their
reports helped to strengthen him in his fondest prejudices.
These activities were supported by William II, who resented
the fact that the military attachés had been placed under the
Reichskanzler in 1867, and who wished to have their reports
sent directly to him.[4] The military attachés followed the wishes
of the Kaiser, without informing the Foreign Office, and also
kept Waldersee well informed in their private correspondence.
Thus both the Kaiser and the Chief of the General Staff encouraged the military attachés to ignore the instructions which

[1] Cochenhausen, *Von Scharnhorst zu Schlieffen*, p. 248.
[2] Waldersee, *Denkwürdigkeiten*, ii. 2.
[3] Eberhard Kessel, *Die Welt als Geschichte* (1954) Jahrgang 14.
[4] Waldersee, *Denkwürdigkeiten*, ii. 30.

required them to submit their reports to their heads of mission. Even under the old Kaiser William, Waldersee had exploited the fact that he was too old to read the reports of the military attachés himself, and had seen to it that he alone read them to him.[1]

Waldersee's confidant in Paris, the military attaché Huene, filled his reports with hair-raising accounts of the imminence of a French attack. The whole Boulanger movement he saw as evidence that the French would seek the first possible opportunity for revanche, and even after Boulanger's ignominious departure from the French political scene he remained convinced that his spirit had not been exorcised. One of Huene's favourite theories was that the Boulangists were determined to restore the temporal power of the Church, which would lead to war between France and Italy, and Germany would then have the chance to intervene. After Boulanger's departure, and a consequent easing of the tension between France and Germany, Huene warned against over-optimism: 'The present peaceful exterior is only a thin covering over France, a slight puff of wind and the bayonets are through.'[2] Huene's activities had given headaches to both Bismarck and Caprivi. In May 1890 Caprivi saw an opportunity of getting rid of him. Huene had fallen for a lady of somewhat dubious reputation who had been married twice, had an English mother, and had lived for a considerable time in England—a fact which did not recommend her as the wife of a military attaché. Caprivi insisted that if he wished to marry the woman he would have to leave the Paris embassy. Huene, however, was not a man of particularly romantic disposition, and dropped her in favour of his career. But, although the Kaiser insisted that he was irreplaceable, he was soon to fall in Caprivi's onslaught on the attachés.[3]

In Vienna the attaché, von Deines, was a faithful servant of Waldersee, who did all he could to keep alive the offensive spirit in Austria, urging the need for an offensive against Russia through Galicia. Just as Waldersee had received a rap on the knuckles for his activities in preaching preventive war in 1887-8, so his man in Vienna came up against the resolute

[1] Mohs, *Waldersee*, p. 30.
[2] H. O. Meisner, *Berliner Monatshefte* Jg. 15 (1937), pp. 958 ff.
[3] DZA, Potsdam: Reichsjustizamt, 3613. AA 50265.

opposition of the embassy and the Foreign Office. The ambassador, Reuss, was furious that Deines was advocating a policy diametrically opposed to that of Bismarck in Austria.[1] Bismarck severely reprimanded Deines with the remark that 'the foreign policy of His Majesty is conducted not by the General Staff but by me alone'. Even Moltke allowed himself a joke at Deines' expense: 'there is bad news from Austria again, they are peaceful once more!' But in spite of these warnings he continued to whisper into Franz Joseph's ear that preventive war was the only hope for the salvation of the Empire. Like Huene in Paris he enjoyed the unlimited confidence of William II, and therefore thought he could ignore the complaints of the Foreign Office.[2] In his letters to his father he spoke of his colleague Monts at the Vienna embassy as 'that awful Monts' and as a 'repulsive creature'. Indeed his attitude to the diplomats was typical of the military attachés, thinking of them as incompetent, weak-kneed, and unable to accept the obvious reality that preventive war was the only hope of avoiding an eventual catastrophe.[3]

The military attaché in St Petersburg, unlike the other military attachés, held the office of military plenipotentiary (*Militärbevollmächtigten*) and was therefore not under the direct control of the embassy, but was a member of the Tsar's retinue and served as a direct link between Kaiser and Tsar.[4] Yorck von Wartenburg, who held this office whilst Waldersee was at the General Staff, shared his Chief's belief in the necessity for preventive war against Russia and was therefore, in view of his unique position at the Russian court, a particular nuisance to the Foreign Office. Schweinitz, the German Ambassador in Russia, tried to remove him, on the pretext that he had become engaged to a divorced Russian. William II took no notice of his ambassador's complaint, and told Waldersee: 'My military attachés Villaume [Huene's predecessor in Paris and later attaché in Petersburg], Yorck, Deines, and Huene are excellent officers who, when things get serious, will have to do the real

[1] Anton Graf Monts, *Erinnerungen und Gedanken* (Berlin, 1933), p. 173.
[2] Witzleben, *Adolf von Deines*, p. 183.
[3] BA, Koblenz: Nachlass von Deines HO8-32/11, Brief 8-10-1890.
[4] Gustav Graf von Lambsdorff, *Die Militärbevollmächtigten Kaiser Wilhelms II am Zarenhofe 1904–1914* (Berlin, 1931), p. 95.

work.'[1] Waldersee thought that he might have added the name
of Engelbrecht to this list. Engelbrecht was attaché in Rome,
and the sworn enemy of Crispi.

Clearly the activities of the military attachés caused endless
difficulties to the Foreign Office and the Chancellor. The principal attachés were the confidants and admirers of Waldersee,
and Waldersee was the most outspoken advocate of preventive
war. The reports of the attachés were therefore carefully
designed to advocate the need for war. Every troop movement,
every increase in armaments, every remark that could possibly
be construed as anti-German, was at once taken up by the military attachés as incontrovertible evidence that the Reich was
about to be overrun. The Kaiser, who suffered from delusions
of grandeur as far as his military capacities were concerned,
thrived on these reports, and looked forward to the day when he
would lead his army to greater victories than those of his grandfather. Furthermore, the confidence that the Kaiser had in the
attachés brought him closer to Waldersee, and made him take
greater notice of his bellicose conception of foreign policy.
William II firmly believed that the reports of the military
attachés were reliable and objective, whereas those of the professional diplomats were hopelessly optimistic and far removed
from the harsh realities of international politics. One of William
II's remarks characterizes this position: 'the hiatus in reporting
between the civilians and the military is historical. . . . The
civilians never wish to admit or to understand . . . a danger
when the military warn them against it. As soon as the relations
between two countries reach a point where they must be judged
also from the standpoint of military possibilities, the military
point of view is always underrated and ridiculed by the
aggrieved diplomats.'[2]

Bismarck had tried to keep the attachés under close control,
but had not been entirely successful. Virtually all of them had
received sharp raps on the knuckles for meddling with politics,
but, certain of William II's support, they had taken little
notice of these warnings, and had seen it as further evidence of
the perfidious machinations of the Foreign Office. Bismarck
could also use his irony as a weapon against the attachés. In a

[1] Waldersee, *Denkwürdigkeiten*, II, 21-1-1889.
[2] Gordon Craig, *Political Science Quarterly 64* (1949), pp. 65–94.

report to William in March 1890, he ridiculed his fears that war with Russia was imminent, a view which he had gained from the reports of the military plenipotentiary in Petersburg and from Waldersee.

With reference to His Majesty's remark allow me humbly to show your Majesty the enclosed memorandum of Field Marshal Moltke of 30 November 1887 which even then spoke of his conviction that the Russians had begun to deploy troops since the beginning of 1887. However not only has peace been kept for 3 years, but relations with Russia have become much better.[1]

Bismarck found the attachés aggravating, and was prepared to hit back when they got out of hand, but never took the trouble to get them completely under his control. Furthermore, the time when the attachés were at their most active, after 1887, was also one in which the Chancellor's own position was far from secure, and when William II was still under the sway of Waldersee's views on foreign affairs. It was left to Caprivi to grasp the nettle of the military attachés.

Caprivi acted with speed and determination. He was resolved to put an end to this system of double diplomacy and place the military attachés under the control of their heads of mission. He began his offensive shortly after taking office, by writing on 24 April 1890 to Waldersee and to the War Minister, to whom the military attachés were responsible, complaining that the attachés had a distressing tendency to indulge in spying. Waldersee was not perturbed, for the attachés' work by its very nature tended to involve them in a little espionage; he replied that he thought that it would be quite sufficient to give them a warning from time to time to be careful not to compromise themselves with too many dubious activities. This answer did not satisfy the Chancellor, who came out into the open two months later and demanded that the heads of mission should have direct formal control over the military attachés. Caprivi was entirely justified in doing this, for the 1867 regulation made the position of the military attachés in regard to their heads of mission perfectly clear, but William II and Waldersee had chosen to ignore it.

A fierce contest ensued between Waldersee and Caprivi. The

---

[1] GPEK, vi. 364, Nr. 1362.

ร

Chancellor insisted that: 'the military and naval attachés are organs of the heads of mission'. Waldersee noted in the margin that this notion was 'absolutely false'. Caprivi insisted that, to avoid any possible attempt by the attachés to escape his control, their reports be given to the heads of mission who would then stamp them 'read' and forward them to the Chancellor's office.

Waldersee was no longer able to shrug off Caprivi's attacks on the military attachés, and therefore warned them to avoid sending in official reports and to concentrate more on private letters directly to him. On 6 July 1890 he wrote to Engelbrecht in Rome:

I can claim with certainty that S(olms) [German Ambassador in Rome] worked against you during his recent visit to Berlin, although I have no official indication as yet; I have the impression that a campaign has been launched against the position of the military attachés, and S(olms) would certainly joyfully support it. H(olstein) would also join in, for he is a fanatical admirer of Crispi.

It is essential to keep cool in such affairs, all the more so now when H.M. is away, the War Minister and I on holiday, and the Chancellor is alone in Berlin.

I suggest that you do not send any reports and agree fully with your suggestion that it is better to report as little as possible, or not at all, officially, but to keep in contact with me privately. . . . I spoke to Deines and Huene yesterday, both have to put up with attacks, and reached the same agreement that they should be in direct contact with me.[1]

In August he noted in his diary:

To my regret a conflict with Caprivi draws near . . . I have tried for a long time to improve the position of the military attachés. The Kaiser agreed with me entirely, that they should be removed from the control of the heads of mission. Caprivi has now ordered the opposite. They must be completely under the control of the heads of mission, and in their reports must never touch on politics. This order is quite ridiculous and bad for the service. The military attachés are far more intelligent than most diplomats, and that is their crime. The Kaiser likes them, backs them, and values their political reports highly, naturally to the chagrin of the professionals.[2]

Waldersee replied to Caprivi's demands with the comment

[1] Waldersee, *Briefwechsel*, Ed. H. O. Meisner (Berlin, 1928), p. 388.
[2] Waldersee, *Denkwürdigkeiten*, Vol. II, 10-8-1890.

that the Chancellor had insulted the military attachés by suggesting that they were trying to compete with the Foreign
Office, adding that in any case the attachés had nothing whatsoever to do with the missions, but were merely attached to
them so as to be given adequate diplomatic protection. On the
same day, 2 December 1890, Waldersee complained to the War
Minister that the Chancellor was trying to undermine the
Kaiser's power and authority by attempting to cut off this
valuable source of information. In a memorandum which he
wrote on the subject a few days later he spoke of Caprivi's
activities as a dangerous attack on the autonomy of the Officer
Corps. He chose as an example a somewhat curious supposition:
if a military attaché, by some sorry misfortune, lost some of his
horses, he might quite easily be financially embarrassed, and
therefore be obliged to ask the General Staff for financial support. To fill Caprivi's requirements this letter would have to be
read by the Head of Mission. Waldersee bitterly complained
that it would be: 'An interference by the diplomats with the
most intimate matters of the Officer Corps'.

Caprivi took little notice of Waldersee's arguments, and
Waldersee was outraged at his behaviour, which he considered
to be unworthy of an officer.

I cannot regard Caprivi's action as loyal, and find it quite un-
heard of that he, as a General, expects officers to have an unworthy
position. I am determined not to let the matter stand there, and I
am therefore certainly faced with a struggle, but I know that I am
fighting for the interests of the army. I am quite in agreement with
the War Minister over most military questions as many discussions
have shown. He also was annoyed by the treatment of the military
attachés, but at the moment he thinks that as the Kaiser has made
up his mind he can do nothing about it. I do not agree.[1]

On 22 December Waldersee complained to Caprivi that the
attacks on the military attachés were basically an attack on his
own person. Caprivi, of course, denied these charges. Waldersee
still hoped that the Kaiser would back him in his struggle with
the Chancellor, for he had assured Waldersee that he would
still be able to receive his reports from those attachés who were
A.D.C.s, and this was the case in St Petersburg, Vienna, Rome,
and Paris.[2]

---

[1] Waldersee, *Denkwürdigkeiten*, Vol. II, 13-12-1890.   [2] Ibid., 17-12-1890.

It seems likely that the Kaiser was trying to reassure Waldersee and was merely playing for time. With Waldersee's dismissal from the General Staff in January 1891 the lynch-pin of
the whole system was removed and the bitter rivalry between
Foreign Office and General Staff abated.[1] There were however
occasions when the Kaiser lent an uncritical and willing ear to
reports from the attachés. One such case occurred shortly after
Waldersee's dismissal. Huene, whom Caprivi had at last been
able to remove from Paris, was convinced that France was
preparing for war, and told the Kaiser so in a private conversation. In a letter to Waldersee on 11 March 1891 he described
this interview:

> The Kaiser often spoke about my analysis of the situation and
> said that I was quite right, and not the Ambassadors or the Wilhelm-
> strasse. After dinner His Majesty spoke in true German terms about
> these functionaries, but added that he would leave the Ambassador
> in Paris for a while so that the French would not notice that they
> had been found out.[2]

William then wrote to the Foreign Office saying that Huene
was far better informed about French affairs than was the
Ambassador; and Huene himself sent in a report to the effect
that the French would attack in the autumn. When the ambassador in Paris, Münster, heard of Huene's report and the success that it had had with the Kaiser, he was naturally enough
outraged and regarded it as a flagrant insult to his capabilities
that such nonsense was taken seriously. In a letter to Caprivi he
wrote: 'If Major von Huene really believed his alarming reports
he would have written in a quite different style, for he can
write very well, than that of this miserable report which is well
below his usual standards'. The storm, however, soon blew
over, and Münster was relieved that Huene's successor in Paris
—Ritmeister von Funcke—was an altogether cooler head.[3] A
further incident occurred in 1895 when Hohenlohe clashed with
the Kaiser over Engelbrecht, a Waldersee man who had
remained as military attaché in Rome. Engelbrecht's activities
were making the work of the Ambassador, Bülow, increasingly

---

[1] Gerhard Ritter, *Sitzungsberichte der Heidelberger Akademie der Wissenschaften,*
Jahrgang 1959 (for documents on Caprivi-Waldersee dispute).
[2] Meisner, *Berliner Monatshefte* (1937), p. 958.
[3] *GPEK*, vii. 295.

difficult, and there seemed to be every indication that he was aiming to replace Bülow. This prospect was certainly not to the taste of the Foreign Office, and Engelbrecht was reprimanded.[1] But after Waldersee had departed such incidents became increasingly rare, and the role of the military attachés as rivals of the Foreign Office was to be taken over by the naval attachés, particularly in London.

Waldersee's political activities were by no means limited to foreign policy. He had equally definite and radical views on home affairs. In this field his two closest allies were Stoecker and the *Kreuzzeitung*. As a radical conservative, anti-Semite, and intolerant Protestant Waldersee was impressed by Stoecker's ideas. His wife shared these views and was actively involved with Stoecker's '*Stadtmission*', an attempt to lead the working class away from the Social Democrats with a bowl of soup and a bible. Stoecker also had the advantage of being a particular favourite of William's, and it seemed likely that the movement would gain in influence when William became Kaiser. In 1888 Kaiser William I complained that Waldersee's wife, whose religious ideas bordered on the fanatical, had far too great an influence on William, and he clearly wished her to withdraw her support from Stoecker. But neither William nor Waldersee were perturbed by these warnings, and Stoecker's star continued to rise.[2]

At first it seemed that Waldersee's calculations had been correct. In his diary he noted with satisfaction: 'I believe the dislike of the Kaiser for the Jews, on account of their arrogance and unjustifiably large influence, to be so fundamental, that even Bismarck can do nothing about it.'[3] It soon became apparent, however, that William II was not prepared to join forces with Stoecker in an anti-Semitic crusade. Indeed Stoecker was becoming an embarrassment to the court. His name became involved in too many scandals political and otherwise (there were even hints that he kept a Jewish mistress), and it became increasingly clear that his days as Court Preacher were numbered. Waldersee, realizing that Stoecker was unlikely to

[1] Bogdan Graf von Hutten-Czapski, *Sechzig Jahre Politik und Gesellschaft* (Berlin, 1936), p. 289.
[2] Waldersee, *Denkwürdigkeiten*, Vol. I, 17-1-1888.
[3] Ibid., Vol. II, 11-10-1888.

survive the attacks of his enemies, tried to dissociate himself from
him, but he also endeavoured to persuade the Kaiser that
Stoecker's fall would be a triumph for 'Jewish and Progressive
circles' and also for Bismarck's machinations.[1] Stoecker, without the support of the official church, and without powerful
allies in the government, was obliged to hand in his resignation
in November 1890.

Stoecker's fall was a severe blow for Waldersee, for the man
who had seemed a valuable political ally and confidant of the
Kaiser turned out to be a dangerous liability. Stoecker's failure
could only serve to make it clear to Waldersee that this particular brand of extremist reactionary politics could not hope to
command an influential following in government circles. The
hopes that Bismarck's fall from power would mean a collapse
of the Kartell, and therefore give an opening to the extremists,
was shown to be illusory, and the attempts by Waldersee to woo
the Kartell were no longer particularly convincing.[2]

Waldersee's relations with Hammerstein's *Kreuzzeitung*, the
organ of the extreme right, took a similar course. Waldersee not
only shared the political views of the paper, but also had a certain influence on it through his friend Major Scheibert, who
contributed articles on military affairs to it. But Hammerstein
was every bit as uncomfortable an ally as Stoecker. Waldersee
had been attracted to him as the right-wing critic of Bismarck
and the Kartell, and hoped that the supporters of the extreme
right, the so-called *Kreuzzeitungspartei* would gain a powerful
political position after the fall of Bismarck. William II, however, realized that there was no valid alternative to the Kartell
for his political purposes, and regarded Hammerstein's criticisms as outrageous, for they came from a conservative, and
conservatives were expected to be loyal to the government.
Even Waldersee became increasingly impatient with Hammerstein: 'Hammerstein acts fanatically without even stopping to
think'.[3]

[1] Waldersee, *Denkwürdigkeiten*, Vol. I, 25-2-1889.
[2] The Kartell was formed in 1887 and was a Parliamentary alliance of the
German Conservatives, the free Conservatives and the National Liberals, which
gave Bismarck a comfortable majority. Although defeated in the elections of 1890
the Kartell remained the basis of further governments.
[3] Waldersee, *Denkwürdigkeiten*, Vol. II, 6-10-1889.

At first the *Kreuzzeitungspartei* exercised considerable influence on Prince William as it was against Bismarck, and Waldersee's friendship with the Prince seemed to bode well for the future. Some even looked to Waldersee as a possible successor to Bismarck, an idea which was highly flattering to him, but which had little chance of realization.[1] Meanwhile Scheibert expounded Waldersee's views on foreign policy in the pages of the *Kreuzzeitung*, preaching a close offensive alliance with Austria-Hungary and war against Russia and France.[2] By 1889, when it was clear to Waldersee that the *Kreuzzeitung* was unlikely to give him the effective political support which he needed, he moved away from it. Although he tried to reassure the Kaiser that he did not approve of Hammerstein's radicalism, his conversion did not seem particularly convincing, the more so since he still remained in close contact with the group. Certainly Waldersee wanted Hammerstein to be removed, for then there might be a chance to moderate the tone of the paper and win back the ground that had been lost through its ill-considered tactics. This was in fact the view of many right-wing conservatives who were worried by the fact that their connexions with the paper had caused many voters to leave them in favour of the Kartell.[3]

After his fall from favour in 1891 Waldersee returned to his support of the *Kreuzzeitung*, but still had his reservations about Hammerstein. Any remaining doubts were abruptly cast aside in 1895 when it was revealed that Hammerstein had been swindling the paper and had fled rather than face charges ranging from forgery to theft. In 1899 the *Kreuzzeitung* invited Waldersee to address a meeting on the relationship of the paper to the conservative party. Waldersee refused, on the grounds that as 'a regular officer and general adjutant of His Majesty I must avoid becoming politically prominent'.[4] A delightful

---

[1] There were influential supporters for Waldersee's candidature in the army, and even Holstein and Miquel were prepared to use him in their schemes to oust Bismarck, although they had no desire to see him as Chancellor. It would have been impossible to find adequate support in the Reichstag for Waldersee's extremist views. He had alienated the Foreign Office with his use of the military attachés. As the most prominent exponent of preventive war he would have strained relations with France and Russia to a point to which William was unwilling to go.

[2] Fornaschon, *Die politische Anschauungen Waldersees*, p 49.

[3] Waldersee, *Briefwechsel*, p. 216.

[4] DZA, Merseburg: Rep. 92 Waldersee: B II-14.

remark from the most politically active of all William II's officers, but it does suggest that, at least as far as the *Kreuzzeitung* was concerned, he had learned his lesson.

Waldersee's views on domestic politics were of a similar simplicity to those on foreign affairs. Right-wing conservatism was the only possible answer to the complex political and social problems of the day, any other solution was dangerous, suspect and bordering on treason. As a stern protestant he loathed the Centre party and what he described as political Catholicism. He thought of the Centre as being servants of the Pope, and therefore no true German patriot could possibly support them, for they were, in his eyes, separatist and ultramontane to a man. The *Freisinnige* he labelled a 'progressive Jewish clique'. His big guns he reserved for frequent broadsides against the Social Democrats. He believed in a firm stand against any demands from the workers: 'My opinion is that in view of the fact that our working class has been largely undermined any fresh compromise or conciliation will lead to disaster ... up to now it has been our experience that all generous laws, all concessions and wage increases have only increased their greed.'[1] After the failure of Stoecker's Christian Social movement, which he had hoped might win the workers to Conservatism by religion and small material concessions, he came to believe that the only possible answer to Socialism was either a return to Bismarck's anti-Socialist laws, or, better still, a *coup d'état*.

On 9 November 1890, by which time it must have been clear to him that he was unlikely to survive as Chief of the General Staff, Waldersee summarized his political views in his diary. This political testament shows how little he had advanced from Stoecker's ideas. The fundamental weakness of society he saw in the unequal distribution of wealth: the widening gap between rich and poor would lead in the end to catastrophe. This did not mean that Waldersee was an egalitarian. He believed that material concessions to the proletariat would only make them greedy for more and more benefits and would lead to an increasing radicalization of the working class. The weakness he saw more in the greed and materialism of the *bourgeoisie*:

the possibility of earning vast sums by speculation has developed an inclination towards luxury and pleasure in a wide section of the

---

[1] Waldersee, *Denkwürdigkeiten*, Vol. II, 3-2-1890.

community. German family life is visibly going to the dogs. Unhappy marriages, adultery, the early degeneration of youth, the desire for luxury and the wish to seem richer than one is, all gain ground shockingly.

Religion he saw as the only answer to this problem, for religion was 'soothing and equalizing', it would help people to be content with their lot, and would restrain the flamboyant extravagance of the wealthy.

By religion Waldersee meant Protestantism; he regarded Catholicism as simply one further menace to the unity of the Reich. The Catholics he equated with the Ultramontanes, the separatist movements in Bavaria and the Rhineland, and the 'fanatical men from the Centre'. He regretted that the Evangelical Church had been unable to present a united front against this menace, for the Catholic Church was determined to bring back the Jesuits and take over control of the schools. The Kaiser should stand solidly behind the Evangelical Church, take 'the Evangelical flag energetically in his hands and work for the unity of all Evangelicals in Germany'. Although Waldersee had admired Bismarck's *Kulturkampf*, he no longer thought that it would be possible to revive it. The country had become so irreligious that any religion should be supported, but care should be taken that the Catholics did not challenge the dominant position of the Evangelical Church.

One religion he found particularly difficult to fit into his scheme—the Jewish religion. Although he wanted to avoid a crusade of Christians against Jews, he thought that the Jews were given far too much protection by the state, and this should stop. Although never an advocate of a pogrom, his anti-Semitism remained inflexible:

The most efficient way of fighting Jewry would be to try to persuade Christians not to worship the golden calf and to become more modest in their way of life and in their desires. One must not forget that many Christians equal the Jews in avarice and equally ruthlessly exploit anyone who falls into their hands.

Waldersee ended these remarks with an attack on the government, which he accused of being weak, and, with the exception of Miquel, comprised of second-rate men.[1]

---

[1] Waldersee, *Denkwürdigkeiten*, Vol. II, 9-11-1890.

A favourite theme not mentioned in this summary was the reform of the voting system. He did not believe that the voting for the Prussian diet should be as democratic as that for the Reichstag, which was what the Social Democrats demanded, but rather that through some form of electoral geometry all left-wing and democratic parties should be excluded from the Reichstag. In March 1889, when elections for the Reichstag were about to take place, Waldersee feared that the waning of Bismarck's popularity might lead to further gains for the Democratic parties, and he wrote: 'Universal suffrage proves more and more to be a danger since we now have a reasonable Reichstag we must try to bring in a new electoral law.'[1] After the election Waldersee saw his worst fears confirmed, particularly as regards the increased number of Social Democrats in the Reichstag. Fearing that the new Reichstag would refuse to vote the military estimates, and that a new election would only make matters worse he wrote: 'The only thing left to us is to abolish universal suffrage. I want very much to help in this.'[2]

After Caprivi's appointment as Chancellor the relations between Waldersee and William II became increasingly strained. The first sign of trouble was in March 1890 when Waldersee criticized the Kaiser's solution to a tactical exercise. William was furious and started to criticize the problem which had been set in terms which only served to convince those present that his military knowledge, to say nothing of his tact, was minimal. Although William later apologized it is clear that the incident continued to rankle.[3] From this moment on Waldersee's diaries are full of criticism of the Kaiser. He was annoyed that the Kaiser had published an order trying to stop excessive luxury in the officer's messes: 'The army is a body, like a family, whose intimate questions do not belong in public.' Such criticism could only help to provide ammunition for the enemies of the army.[4] The Kaiser, he claimed, had lost the confidence of the army. He was far too interested in the navy and as far as the army was concerned he only had time for the Guards. He failed to treat higher officers with due respect and had the distressing habit of talking badly of senior officers to

[1] Waldersee, *Denkwürdigkeiten*, Vol. II, 26-3-1889.
[2] Ibid., 24-2-1890.
[3] Ibid., 21-3-1890.   [4] Ibid., 18-4-1890.

younger ones. In all he seemed to regard the army as a toy with which he liked to play.[1] In another entry in his diary he criticized the Kaiser more expansively.

The Kaiser does not really have his own ideas in any field and does not know his own mind, he is easily influenced by dangerously skilful men and makes the most extraordinary leaps in all directions. One thought determines all his actions, interest in his own personal position, the desire to be popular! In addition there are his worries about his own safety and his rapidly increasing vanity. I looked upon Kaiser Frederick as an outstandingly vain gentleman, who loved to dress up and pose. The present monarch exceeds him in this by far. He literally pants for applause and likes nothing better than crowds yelling 'hurrah'. Since he has a very high opinion of his own capacities (which is alas a dreadful deception) he finds flattery greatly to his taste. He loves to play the patron, and throws away money without stopping to think. All this has developed so quickly that I am continually amazed.[2]

Although there is much truth in what Waldersee wrote about the Kaiser it stands in marked contrast to the obsequiousness with which he courted him before Caprivi was appointed Chancellor. Clearly Waldersee was unable to forgive William for dashing his political ambitions, which had once seemed to have such outstanding chances of success. It was a characteristic of William that he was apt to turn against his erstwhile friends, but also tended to follow his attacks with touching scenes of repentance and contrition. William's relations with Waldersee swung between these two extremes. Bülow speaks in his memoirs of some marginal comments the Kaiser made on Waldersee which Holstein showed him: 'the epithet "traitor" was the one that recurred most frequently, but there was no lack of still coarser expressions'.[3] Yet William was also to give further evidence of his favour.

Waldersee's position in the General Staff became increasingly insecure, and the incident which spurred on his dismissal happened during the manoeuvres in September 1890. The Kaiser insisted on taking over the command of the VIth corps, having failed to realize that the manoeuvres were so arranged that the corps stood a very good chance of being defeated, and

---

[1] Waldersee, *Denkwürdigkeiten*, Vol. II, 6-5-1890.
[2] Ibid., 11-8-1890.
[3] Prince von Bülow, *Memoirs* (London, 1931), ii. 360.

William was a very bad loser. The Kaiser made a number of disastrous mistakes, the worst of which was that he somehow managed to get the river Neisse between two of his divisions, and his corps was roundly defeated. Even Waldersee's severest critics agreed that his criticism of the manoeuvres was a model of its kind, but the Kaiser, angry at being criticized in front of an imposing assembly of officers and civilians, as well as a number of foreign observers, fought back.[1] These attempts to justify his actions made it increasingly evident that his military knowledge and experience left much to be desired, a fact which further humiliated him. This incident was the culmination of the growing strife between the two men. In the manuscript of his diary Waldersee is unsparing in his vocabulary when describing the complete and utter stupidity of the Kaiser during the manoeuvres.[2] The Kaiser for his part tried to blame the whole incident on Waldersee's inefficient planning of the manoeuvres, and harboured dark thoughts that his Chief of the General Staff had deliberately tried to humiliate him in public.

Moves were already on foot to replace Waldersee, but it was not easy to find a position for him which would not be humiliating. From being Chief of the General Staff to Commanding General of a corps was a considerable step down. Philip Eulenburg, fearing trouble, advised the Kaiser to go slowly.[3] Caprivi suggested, the day after the manoeuvres, that he should be given the post of Commanding General in Stuttgart, with the Order of the Black Eagle as a suitable compensation. Waldersee tried to play for time by suggesting other officers who could take over the command at Stuttgart, but realized that his days at the General Staff were numbered.[4]

The Kaiser bided his time, but Waldersee noted sorrowfully: 'I have realized that I am no longer invited to dinners which are given for the Kaiser, as I used to be.'[5] On 27 January 1891 William told Waldersee that he intended to appoint him Commanding General. Waldersee, having discussed the matter with Schlieffen and Gossler, decided to hand in his resignation. On the following day he told the Kaiser that he was determined to

[1] Wedel, *Zwischen Kaiser und Kanzler*, p. 125.
[2] DZA, Merseburg: Rep 92 Waldersee: A I-15.
[3] Haller, *Eulenburg*, p. 197.
[4] Waldersee, *Denkwürdigkeiten*, Vol. II, 21-9-1890.
[5] Ibid., 15-1-1891.

resign, but the Kaiser would hear nothing of it, saying that he
had decided to send him to Hamburg. William tried to flatter
Waldersee by saying that he needed a particularly good man
in Hamburg to look after Bismarck, for the Kaiser thought that
he was plotting against him, and also because Hamburg was a
dangerous centre of Social Democracy. He continued that he
wished to reduce the importance of the Chief of the General
Staff, and increase the power of the Commanding Generals.
'The Chief of the General Staff must be a sort of amanuensis to
me, and thus I need a younger one.' To which Waldersee
noted: 'He wants to be his own General Staff chief! God preserve the Fatherland!'[1] After repeated threats to hand in his
resignation he eventually accepted the post in Hamburg-Altona,
and left the General Staff blaming the whole affair on Caprivi's
machinations and the Kaiser's maniac desire to emulate
Frederick the Great.

In government circles there was general relief that Waldersee had left the General Staff. Portales wrote to Schweinitz
from Berlin in February: 'Here one is naturally preoccupied
with Waldersee's departure. In confidence I can assure your
Excellency that the speedy end to this situation (Chancellor
versus Chief of General Staff) was highly desirable. Waldersee
simply could not keep his hands off politics.'[2]

Once in Hamburg Waldersee was not slow to get in touch
with the other prominent exile in Friedrichsruh, Bismarck. The
two of them were able to commiserate with each other on the
sorry way in which William had treated them, and soon Waldersee was to become an admirer of his old rival, and would contrast his resolute diplomacy with the flounderings of his successor. 'Our reputation in the world would be really far better
if he was still adviser, and many mistakes at home would have
been avoided.'[3] His friendship with Bismarck led to rumours in
the press that he was plotting to oust Caprivi and bring back
Bismarck. The label of a political general firmly stuck to him,
and he did nothing to remove it.

Waldersee remained sharply critical of the government, and
particularly of Caprivi whom he described as having the

[1] Waldersee, *Denkwürdigkeiten*, Vol. II, 28-1-1891.
[2] General von Schweinitz, *Briefwechsel* (Berlin, 1928), p. 275.
[3] Waldersee, *Denkwürdigkeiten*, Vol. II, 7-4-95.

mentality of an N.C.O. The danger from France and Russia remained uppermost in his mind, and his motto remained the same: 'My favourite theme: armaments and more armaments!'[1] Although he still thought that Poland might be built up as a buffer against Russia he considered that the mild concessions made by Caprivi went too far. His view of the Slavs remained the same: 'Slavs like to be kicked about, they even kiss the boot that has kicked them.'[2] Dreams of *Grossdeutschland* began to fill his head: 'It is still my firm conviction that Germany has not yet reached its zenith, and that I shall live to see a *Grossdeutschland* that will stretch to the Adriatic.'[3] Austria, he feared, might well be falling to pieces under the strain of the different nationalities, and an expansionist German Reich would be the only solution, if the Austrians were unable to force the nationalities to obedience.[4]

Waldersee's fall was in a certain sense a triumph for the constitutional principle, the defeat of an attempt by a section of the army, and to some extent the Kaiser, to win an excessive influence on policy-making, and to reduce the power of the civil authorities. However, the Kaiser never completely rejected the plan, ever popular with his military entourage, of a military *coup d'état* against Social Democrats and Liberals. Waldersee's political ambitions were now centred on returning to the political scene as leader of this putsch. The extremists, in the army and in the conservative party, gave him every possible encouragement. 'I was in Berlin yesterday where I was able to speak to some Conservative deputies and afterwards to Verdy (War Minister 1889–90). All were of one mind that Hohenlohe is incapable of getting us out of our hopeless position, and that drastic measures are needed. They think in terms of a sort of putsch with me as the ideal man to lead it.'[5] Waldersee was, however, dubious as to the determination of the Kaiser to exterminate the Social Democrats. He criticized the Kaiser's 'thoughtless remarks' and 'love of pomp' and said that he was a 'merciless autocrat' and 'unpredictable'; this he thought turned men away from the monarchy and made them into Social Democrats: 'the present Kaiser literally breeds Social Democrats'.[6]

[1] Waldersee, *Denkwürdigkeiten*, Vol. II, 17-9-1891.   [2] Ibid., 17-3-1890.
[3] Ibid., 30-8-97.   [4] Ibid., 12-12-97.   [5] Ibid., 7-2-95.   [6] Ibid., 22-6-93.

In 1896 he thought that his hour had come. A strike broke out in the harbour of Hamburg, and 16,690 men came out on strike. Waldersee hoped that the strikers would give him the excuse to use force to put down the strike and that this might be the beginning of the armed suppression of Social Democracy for which he longed. In his first report to the Kaiser on the strike he said that the strikers were behaving well, and that the police was as yet able to deal with the situation. He added: 'I have taken measures to ensure that serious trouble, which would necessitate the use of the army, will be speedily and energetically put down.' Clearly hoping that the strikers would give him the chance to move in with the army, he suggested moving a battleship into the Elbe as well as some armoured boats belonging to the engineers. He had in fact already contacted the navy and asked that a battleship be kept at the ready. However, the strikers resolutely refused to comply with Waldersee's wishes. In further telegrams he had to report that all was quiet and that meetings had passed without any incidents. The strikers were well financed, some 500,000 marks had been sent to them from various trade unions and socialist clubs both at home and abroad, and Waldersee feared that the strike might be able to continue for some time.[1]

Faced with the prospect of a long trial of strength and unable to use military force, he became increasingly impatient:

People in Berlin must be quite clear that we stand before the precipice, and drastic measures must be taken if we are not to collapse one day. They like to comfort themselves with the army, which in the last resort must shoot down the revolutionaries. It would certainly do that today, but will it be the same in ten years time?[2]

He still had to report that the strikers behaved peacefully and that there had been no attempts to incite the workers against the government. He was relieved that the City Senate had refused to set up an arbitration committee as the ship-builders had suggested, for he feared that this would only encourage the strikers to increase their demands.

Although his reports continued to show that all was peaceful, he increased his military precautions, and now foresaw sending

[1] BA Koblenz: HO2-1/20.
[2] Waldersee, *Denkwürdigkeiten*, Vol. II, 30-12-1896.

two battleships, an icebreaker and sundry other vessels into the harbour. Convinced that the whole strike was a trial of strength, he encouraged the ship-builders to make a resolute stand against the strikers' demands, and assured them of his support. By 23 December the Social Democrats decided to call off the strike, but their resolution was turned down by a two-thirds majority. Money continued to pour in for the strikers and the strike in fact continued until February.

On 22 January Waldersee sent a memorandum to the Kaiser in which he expounded his views on the working class question. He advised William to raise the standard of living of at least a part of the working class, so as to convince them that there was no need to join the Social Democrats. At the same time he insisted that a clash between workers and employers was inevitable, and therefore the state was in duty bound to settle the question once and for all. The longer the Kaiser waited before taking harsh measures against the revolutionary party the larger and more radical it would get. Even the army was becoming increasingly infiltrated by socialist ideas: 'The second generation of a Social Democratic family brings the idea of revolution with it to the colours.' Youth was being poisoned by socialist and materialist ideas: 'The youth of both sexes which is now growing up, shows a moral degeneration and a degree of blasphemy which makes us look with alarm into the future.' Waldersee demanded immediate action. Social Democrats should no longer be protected by the law, but should be wiped out, if need be by a *coup d'état*: 'The state is still strong enough to smash any revolution.'[1]

William, who liked to toy with the idea of a *coup d'état*, was impressed by Waldersee's arguments, and even thought of making Waldersee into his Putsch Chancellor (*Staatsstreich-kanzler*).[2] But common sense prevailed, and Waldersee was never given the role for which he longed. The strike passed off peacefully, and the troops which marched through the streets of Hamburg were never given the opportunity to resort to force. Nevertheless William liked to murmur. 'Yes, if the old chap in Altona had not been there!'[3]

[1] BA Koblenz: HO2-1/20.
[2] Fornaschon, *Die Politische Anschauungen Waldersees*, p. 40.
[3] Mohs, *Waldersee*, p. 355.

Waldersee's position suffered a further set-back during the strike as the result of a different affair. This was set off by the faulty reporting of a speech by the Tsar, carefully calculated to spur anti-Russian feeling in Germany; but the subsequent trial, which took place in December 1896 revealed some of Waldersee's dealings with the press, and helped to damage any prestige he might have won in Hamburg.[1]

The Hamburg strike was Waldersee's last bid for the Chancellorship. He kept up his correspondence with his radical friends, and was untiring in the reiteration of his well-worn themes—preventive war, the slow decline of German prestige, the need for a *coup d'état* against the socialists, and testy references to the shortcomings of all the prominent men in the Reich from the Kaiser downwards. But it became increasingly clear that he was unlikely to play an important political role and he preferred to retire more and more from the political arena.

In August 1900 he once again became the centre of attention. *Faute de mieux* Germany was chosen to appoint a commander-in-chief for the international force to put down the Boxer rebellion in China. William, who regarded the whole affair as a major diplomatic triumph for the Reich, selected Waldersee. To suit William's histrionic sense and his assessment of the importance of the occasion Waldersee was appointed Field Marshal. Paul Metternich describes the scene: 'His Majesty handed him the Field Marshal's baton, making a very fine little speech. Waldersee at once put it at the corner of his thigh in the regular pose of the old copper engravings, as though he had always carried the baton.' He departed for China with such pomp and circumstance that Eugen Richter remarked that he was being given laurels on account.[2] Baroness Spitzemberg, who was certainly no friend of Waldersee, was moved by the splendour of the occasion to write: 'The choice of Waldersee is a further instinctive bull's eye by the Kaiser ... it is a proud feeling that a German General has the complete confidence of all countries as has Waldersee.'[3] Others in government circles were less enthusiastic and feared that Waldersee would be far too independent in China, a fear that was partly justified.

[1] Dieter Fricke, *ZfGW*, Heft 7 (1960) 1597–1603.
[2] Bülow, *Memoirs*, ii. 365.
[3] Spitzemberg, *Tagebuch*, 11-8-1900.

The China expedition was for Waldersee more of a diplomatic than a military trial. On arrival he was furious to learn that General von Lessel, contrary to his express orders, had attacked the Peitang forts and had thus successfully concluded military operations, apart from one or two minor mopping-up operations.[1] He sent his reports directly to the Kaiser, without informing either the Chancellor or the Foreign Office. William found this flattering, and it was only after considerable persuasion from Eulenburg and his A.D.C. Mackensen that he agreed to forward the reports to the Foreign Office.[2] Relations between the various contingents in China soon became strained, and Waldersee, whose strength did not lie in either diplomacy or tact, did little to ease the situation. Particularly difficult were the relations between the Germans and the English, whom Waldersee heartily disliked on account of their liberal political system. He ordered that German officers were not to salute English officers, for he considered that the English were militarily far too sloppy.[3] Waldersee also demanded reinforcements from Germany, which both Schlieffen and the Foreign Office thought would only further antagonize the English, scruples which William and his closest military advisers did not share.[4]

Waldersee returned shortly afterwards to Germany with a victor's laurels and dysentery. Twenty thousand people waited to greet him late at night on the station at Frankfurt, and in other towns the reception was equally impressive. Yet deep in his heart Waldersee was understandably disappointed by the whole affair. An officer who served with him in China wrote of him: 'He often told us officers that it was just as hard for him as Commander-in-Chief to return home without drawing his sword.'[5] Nor can the irony of his new nickname have escaped him—'der Weltmarschall'.

After his return from China Waldersee played no further active part in politics. He bemoaned what he considered to be the Kaiser's growing liberalism, and feared that the conservatives

[1] General Erich von Gründell, *Aus seinen Tagebüchern*, Ed. Walter Oberkircher (Hamburg, 1938), p. 23.
[2] Haller, *Eulenburg*, p. 69.
[3] Kurt von Bülow, *Preussischer Militarismus zur Zeit Wilhelms II* (Schweidnitz, 1930), p. 83.
[4] *GPEK*, xvi. 209.
[5] Kurt von Bülow, *Preussischer Militarismus.*

had less and less influence on politics. The man who had said, 'Germany's future is hopeless unless we spread death to right and left' became increasingly dubious as to Germany's chances in the next war and thought that the army had lost its offensive spirit.[1] Covered with the highest honours, civilian and military, he confined his jeremiads to the pages of his diary. On 5 March 1904 he died, murmuring: 'I beseech God that I do not have to witness what I see coming.'[2]

Waldersee's activities had made him many enemies, and few, even those who had used him in the crisis over Bismarck's dismissal, were prepared to support his political ambitions. Wedel, who was later Governor of Alsace-Lorraine where he was to suffer under the political ambitions of the army, wrote of him: 'Waldersee, in spite of his considerable gifts, was a disturbing element. He interfered in everything, had limitless ambitions and did not desist, I think, from using all kinds of intrigue to achieve his aims.'[3] Bismarck said: 'Count Waldersee was driven by an unhealthy ambition, because he did not wish to confine himself to his military career. Nor can I defend him against the charge of being a pusher.'[4] Von Einem, the later War Minister, said that he was an intriguer,[5] and Philip Eulenburg described him as the classic example of an ambitious wire-pulling general.[6]

Waldersee had little chance of becoming a German Boulanger. He had no popular support. The divisions in German politics were not deep enough for a political adventurer to play one party off against the other. William II was popular enough in the early years of his reign not to need to run the risks of making Waldersee his 'Putsch Chancellor', nor was he a danger —his removal from the General Staff was an inconvenience, but it did not cause any major political upset. He was, as Baroness Spitzemberg suggested, a strong man who was too easy to bully. The political circumstances at the end of the Bismarck era spurred his ambition, but the openings he saw were largely

[1] Karl Friedrich Nowak, *Kaiser and Chancellor* (London, 1930), p. 49.
[2] Waldersee, *Denkwürdigkeiten*, ii. 232.
[3] Wedel, *Zwischen Kaiser und Kanzler*. p. 140.
[4] Fornaschon, *Die politischen Anschauungen Waldersees*, p. 45.
[5] Von Einem, *Erinnerungen eines Soldaten*, p. 41.
[6] Haller, *Eulenburg*, p. 43.

illusory. The man who had played an important part in Bismarck's downfall, who was widely known to be one of the leading figures in the opposition to the old Chancellor, and who many hoped would be his successor, wrote shortly before his death: 'The zenith of the German Reich was during the last years of the reign of Kaiser William I, internally and externally. We have since declined slowly but surely.'[1]

[1] Waldersee, *Denkwürdigkeiten*, Vol. III, 13-2-1904.

V

THE ARMY AND THE IDEA OF
PREVENTIVE WAR

ALTHOUGH to many contemporaries the victory of the Prussian army in the war of 1870 seemed to be the culminating point of a long historical process leading to the reunification of the Reich and the opening of a new era of peace, prosperity, and happiness, many of the leading generals thought otherwise. Moltke had wanted to exterminate France in 1870, to wipe Germany's Western rival off the map of Europe, but had been frustrated by Bismarck. After 1871 he became obsessed with the idea of a further war with France, which he thought was bound to come owing to Bismarck's short-sighted policy and inability to realize the danger that a re-established France would offer to German security. The remarkable recovery of France after the war, in spite of the severe peace terms, further exacerbated Moltke. War with France, he thought, was inevitable, therefore Germany should strike first, so as to have the advantage of surprise and a more carefully planned mobilization.[1] The field-marshal, who was wont to philosophize, also had moral objections to long periods of peace:

Everlasting peace is a dream, and not even a nice one, and war a part of God's order in the world. In war the finest of man's virtues develop: valour and restraint, devotion to duty, self-sacrifice at the risk of one's own life. Without war the world would sink into materialism.[2]

Although Bismarck dismissed Moltke as *cette tête de bois*, his views were regarded by many, particularly in the General Staff, as something approaching revealed truth, and his belief that the

[1] Stadelmann, *Moltke und der Staat*, p. 280.
[2] Helmuth von Moltke, *Gesammelte Schriften und Denkwürdigkeiten* (Berlin, 1892), p. 194.

territories won by Germany in the Franco-Prussian war should have to be guaranteed by a further preventive war, was an article of faith among many influential officers, and an integral part of an officer's political *Weltanschauung*. Soldiers often dream of wars, the senior officers so that they can prove their strategic and tactical genius to all the world, the junior officers in the hope of adventure and promotion; but for many members of the German Officer Corps preventive war was a political necessity if the Reich was to achieve the position in the world which seemed to them its due historical legacy.

Prominent among the propagandists for a preventive war was General Friedrich von Bernhardi, whose theoretical writings achieved a wide popularity, not merely in military circles. The most influential of Bernhardi's writings was the book *Germany and the Next War*, which was published in 1911, soon ran into several editions and was translated into numerous foreign languages. He took Moltke's arguments in favour of a further war to their extreme conclusions and went one step further than Moltke in demanding war as a means of expanding the territory of the Reich.

Bernhardi claimed that war 'gives a biologically just decision, since its decisions rest on the very nature of things'.[1] This being so 'the end-all and be-all of a state is power'.[2] He demanded that this power should be used for an expansionist war which would secure for Germany the mouth of the Rhine as well as conquests in the East. 'The Germany of today, considered geographically, is a mutilated torso of the old dominions of the Emperors; it comprises only a fraction of the German peoples. . . . She has been robbed of her natural frontiers.'[3] He preached a policy of 'Germany for the Germans' and demanded the expulsion of all other races, particularly the Slavs. 'Many Poles are firmly established in the heart of Westphalia. Only fainthearted measures are taken to stem this Slavonic horde.'[4] For Bernhardi, as for many other high-placed officers including Waldersee and the younger Moltke, Germany would have to settle once and for all the question of 'Germanic or Slavonic Supremacy'. He defined this racialist and expansionist policy in the following terms: 'the importance of Germany will depend

---

[1] Friedrich von Bernhardi, *Germany and the Next War* (London, 1914), p. 23.
[2] Ibid., p. 45.   [3] Ibid., p. 76.   [4] Ibid., p. 78.

on two points: first, how many millions of men in the world speak German? Secondly, how many of them are politically members of the German Empire?'[1] Defeat of France was an integral part of his programme: 'France must be so completely crushed that she can never again come across our path.'[2] Bernhardi did not confine himself to foreign policy, but had equally definite views on internal policy. In accordance with the conventional opinions of the Officer Corps he regarded democracy and liberalism as fates from which the Reich was to be preserved at all costs: 'No people is so little qualified as the German to direct its own destinies, whether under a parliamentarian or republican constitution; to no people is the customary liberal pattern so inappropriate as to us.'[3] He also felt, along with a number of other right-wing extremists, that the middle-class should be strengthened and their tax burden be lightened, at the expense of the wealthy capitalists and the stockbrokers whom he regarded with particular disfavour. But the main weight of his argument lay in the notion of preventive war: 'Safety lies only in offensive warfare.'[4] 'In a state which is so wholly based on war as the German Empire, the old manly principle of keeping all our forces on the stretch must never be abandoned out of deference to the effeminate philosophy of the day.'[5]

Frustration that the government of the Reich refused to see the necessity of fighting a preventive war was one of the principle themes of Bernhardi's collected papers.[6] A close friend of Waldersee, he supported his bellicose policy, and condemned Caprivi for his 'N.C.O. attitude'. As military attaché in Berne he wrote to a friend in 1891: 'Every thinking man knows that we should have gone to war years ago. It is terrible that it has not yet happened.'[7]

Bernhardi's promotion was speedy. In 1897 he became a regimental commander in Karlsruhe, and in the same year was appointed Chief of Staff to the XVIth Army Corps in Metz. The following year he was given the influential position of

[1] Friedrich von Bernhardi, *Germany and the Next War* (London, 1924), p. 83.
[2] Ibid., p. 106.
[3] Ibid., p. 108.
[4] Ibid., p. 109.   [5] Ibid., p. 110.
[6] Friedrich von Bernhardi, *Denkwürdigkeiten aus meinem Leben* (Berlin, 1927).
[7] Ibid., p. 134.

chief of the historical section of the General Staff in Berlin. Bernhardi was by this time one of the most influential and respected military theorists of his day, well connected with the leading figures of the military establishment.

Among Bernhardi's friends was the War Minister, von Einem, whom he tried to persuade that Germany's political problems could only be solved by war. In 1904 Einem, along with many other leading officers, was thinking in terms of war with France. Bernhardi was elated, but once again his hopes were dashed.[1] In 1908 Einem again agreed with Bernhardi that Germany should go to war, but the 'illusion of everlasting peace' was still too strong.

In 1907 Bernhardi became Commanding General of the VIIth Army Corps, where he continued his propaganda campaign for war. In the same year he dined with the Kaiser, and did not let the occasion slip for propounding his ideas to his Supreme Warlord. He tried to convince William that Germany should attack France, to which the Kaiser replied: 'Who knows what I am doing?' Bernhardi at once said that the army would be delighted at the idea of war.[2]

Europe remained at peace, and Bernhardi became more and more frustrated, lashing out against the Kaiser and his love of peace and his Christian scruples against war, against the illusions of the Reichstag that peace could be preserved, and against the feeble policy of Bethmann Hollweg. How could Germany possibly try to be a *Weltmacht* without fighting a war, he asked?

Bernhardi was closely connected with the *Alldeutsche Verband* and other chauvinist organizations, and was also much in demand as a lecturer. A French journalist who attended one such lecture given to the Military Society in Berlin, an assembly of high-ranking officers, mostly from the General Staff, along with some university professors and civil servants, reports Bernhardi as saying:

we realize that Prussia's historic mission is not yet completed for that mission is to form the core around which all the dispersed elements of the German race will group themselves; she will extend her sphere of influence so as to put herself in harmony with her

[1] Friedrich von Bernhardi, *Denkwürdigkeiten aus meinem Leben* (Berlin, 1927), p. 308.
[2] Ibid., p. 293.

political limits, she will give and guarantee to Germanism the place it deserves in the world.[1]

Many of Bernhardi's ideas were also found in the works of von der Goltz. Goltz was more concerned than Bernhardi with purely military problems, and his more practical turn of mind did not lead him to think in terms of Prussia's historic mission or of a racial crusade against the Slavs, but he also was an outspoken advocate of preventive war. Coming from a family of impoverished Junkers, he had taken to writing newspaper articles and historical novels when he was a young lieutenant in order to pay his mess bills. Having failed at first to get into the General Staff, he thought of leaving the army to become a writer; but the success of his second attempt made him change his mind, although he continued to write novels under an assumed name, and even achieved a certain success with them. His first important military work was *Leon Gambetta und seine Armee* which was published in 1877. Although the work was largely concerned with a military analysis of the Franco-Prussian war, Goltz used the opportunity to propound his views on Germany's encirclement by France and Russia and the need for a two-front war. Curiously enough the book gave Goltz the reputation of being a liberal. He spoke out in favour of a two-year period of service as a better means of training a larger army which would be needed in the war he advocated, rather than the three-year service which was still in effect. Such ideas were anathema to William I, and although Moltke's support kept him on the staff for a while, he was soon posted as a company commander.

In his book *Volk in Waffen* he developed his ideas further, advocating a large mass army and an offensive war to be fought outside Germany's frontiers.

It is necessary to make it clear to ourselves and to the children growing up around us, whom we have to train, that a time of rest has not yet come, that the prediction of a final struggle for the existence and greatness of Germany is not a mere fancy of ambitious fools, but that it will come one day, inevitably, with full fury.[2]

[1] André Chéradame, *L'Allemagne, la France et la Question d'Autriche* (Paris, 1902).
[2] Generalfeldmarschall Colmar von der Goltz, *The Nation in Arms* (London, 1906) p. 475.

Volk in Waffen was soon to prove a best seller running rapidly into several editions, and was translated into several languages. In spite of the upset over his first book Goltz was soon recognized as one of the leading brains in the younger generation of German officers. In 1883 he was posted to Turkey and set about reforming the Turkish army. Although these reforms had little success when put to the test in 1912 and 1913,[1] Goltz's mission was not without profit for Germany as he was able to secure important orders for Krupp, Mauser, Löwe, and the Schichau shipyard. Although the younger Moltke referred to Goltz as the 'man who ruined the Turkish army', the industrialists had every reason to be pleased with his activities in Turkey.

While in Turkey Goltz sent frequent reports to Waldersee, and like the despatches of the military attachés these reports had a distinctly political flavour. Preventive war was a favourite theme. In August 1890 he wrote:

The 'preservation of world peace' is not the sort of aim that will give to the thoughts and power of a nation a unified goal and the necessary vitality. The discovery of an external aim which we should pursue, and the awakening of general understanding for this, would be the best service one could give to the German people. One only needs to look at the great effect which a much milder and paler idea of revanche has even today in France, to be convinced of this.[2]

War was for Goltz a means of creating national unity, and above all a way of turning men's minds away from the social problems of the day:

I hold it as a most questionable prospect if in the near future, by that I mean for some decades to come, we have no war. For we are nearing great social changes and that which your excellency tells me of ideas on this topic in influential circles gives me less hope for a satisfactory treatment of them than I have in the outcome of a possible war.[3]

The army increases of 1892 he thought might lead to war: 'Our neighbours in East and West must really raise their hackles at the discussions and perhaps that will bring the decision earlier

[1] The Turkish army had however defeated the Greeks in 1897. Goltz immediately wrote a book in praise of the Turkish campaign: Colmar von der Goltz, *Der Thessalische Krieg* (Berlin, 1898).
[2] DZA, Merseburg: Rep 92 Waldersee, BI-21, Von der Goltz.
[3] Ibid.

than we think.'[1] But Goltz was beginning to doubt whether the government could be convinced of the need for a preventive war. War with Russia was essential, for the Russians were waiting for the best opportunity to attack Austria: 'Thus it would be best if we chose the most suitable moment for us to attack! But we have grown old and frightened and are therefore unlikely to make such an important decision.'[2]

In 1898 Goltz returned to Germany for a while as inspector of fortresses. His old notions of an offensive war now took second place to his desire to increase his own importance in the army, and he demanded a chain of fortifications around the Reich; this notion predictably horrified Schlieffen who saw it as a negation of his own strategic ideas, as well as the War Minister Gossler who probably did not like the idea of footing the bill. Although Goltz had by no means abandoned the idea of an offensive war, such was the obsession in the army with attack at all costs that the mere suspicion of defence-mindedness was enough to make it virtually impossible for him to continue to work with Schlieffen and the General Staff, and in 1901 he resigned from the position of inspector of fortresses.

Inspired, as were many Germans, by the example of the Boers, who were fighting for 'Faith, Freedom, and Fatherland', Goltz began to concoct grandiose schemes for war against England. Germany should ally with Holland and invade England whilst Turkish troops should take Egypt and then march to the Indian border.[3] But he was realistic enough to accept the fact that for the moment such notions were pipe dreams: 'A Chief of the General Staff who, for example, made all necessary preparations for the opening of hostilities with England, as he should, would not keep his job long.'[4]

The failure of Germany to go to war over Morocco in 1911 was another disappointment for him. 'That the Wilhelmstrasse in dealing with this question of prestige was largely carried away by economic interests, and preferred to submit to a severe diplomatic defeat, rather than to demand a warlike decision, depressed him deeply', wrote his biographers.[5]

[1] DZA, Mersebnrg: Rep 92, Waldersee, BI-21, Von der Goltz.
[2] Goltz, *Denkwürdigkeiten*, p. 149.   [3] Ibid., p. 220.   [4] Ibid., p. 259.
[5] Goltz, *Denkwürdigkeiten*, p. 326. The memoirs are adorned by a breathless and uncritical biographical commentary by Friedrich von der Goltz and Wolfgang Foerster.

The years passed and no war came. Goltz began to despair. Prosperity had made the Germans soft and effeminate, the Germany of East Prussia, poor, hardworking, tough, and war-like, was losing ground to the feeble and undisciplined prin-ciples of the industrial and commercial west. The virtues which he admired in the Japanese and the Boers, patriotism, self-sacrifice, and martial ardour, he felt were lacking in a Germany which seemed no longer interested in war and neglected the army at the expense of Germany's security.

Like Bernhardi, Goltz also played an important role in the para-military and extremist organizations of the time. As chairman of the Young German League (*Jungdeutschlandbund*), with 750,000 members by 1914, his influence was considerable, and his activities were supported by the government. Into such organizations Goltz tried to inject those values which he felt to be lacking in the Reich, to inspire Germany's youth eagerly to await the next war.

Bernhardi and Goltz were not isolated prophets in the wilderness, but the leading military theorists of Germany, respected, influential, and admired; their books had con-siderable success and not only in military circles. Their views were symptomatic of an army which thought that peace had lasted too long, who distrusted the official foreign policy of the Reich, and who felt that Germany did not have that place in the society of nations which she deserved. These views were also shared by some pan-Germanic professors, the most notable of whom was Theodor Schiemann. Schiemann's book *Videant Consules* was inspired by the 'war in sight' crisis of 1887 and sought to justify Waldersee's aggressive policies. Schiemann argued in favour of a two-front war, and demanded that France should be attacked first as France represented in the long run the greater danger, quite apart from the fact that the Russians would most probably retire into the steppes and refuse to fight a decisive battle. The book was full of warnings that Germany's position was unstable owing to the question of Alsace-Lorraine and the ideas of revanche in France, the menace of pan-Slavism in the East and the nationalities' problem in Austria-Hungary which weakened Germany's principal ally. Only preventive war could solve these problems and give Germany the security she needed for further development.[1] There is indeed some truth in the remark made by a French journalist in 1913: 'l'armée est moins impatiente d'aller aux champs de bataille que ne le sont les professeurs de l'y envoyer.'[2]

The more bellicose among the generals became increasingly frustrated as Germany became diplomatically isolated and the government resolutely refused to see the need for a further war. The Kaiser was at times convinced by the reports from the military attachés that war was imminent, and would rattle his sabre in the secure confines of the imperial palace in front of an enthusiastic audience of officers, but such episodes only served to increase the suspicion that the Kaiser was at heart a peace-loving man influenced by the starry-eyed idealists in the Foreign Office.[3]

The Morocco crisis of 1905 had seemed to give the war party the chance for which they were longing. Holstein was determined to put pressure on France in the hope of straining the Anglo-French Entente to breaking point, and also of putting pressure on the links between Paris and St Petersburg. Holstein who was very friendly with Schlieffen knew that he could count on the Chief of the General Staff to back what was probably, for Holstein, a bluff and not a serious attempt to bring about a preventive war. The two used to meet almost weekly in a *chambre séparée* in the Berlin restaurant Borchert, and Holstein was well acquainted with the details of Schlieffen's plan. Indeed the Schlieffen plan itself was a reflection of Holstein's idea of bullying France away from her allies.[4]

Schlieffen, who had not in fact seen Holstein for some time before the crisis broke out, realized—and it certainly did not need a military genius to see it—that the chances of fighting a successful war were excellent, with Russia losing a war against Japan and the British not yet recovered from the Boer war. The General Staff were convinced that their planning was an infallible recipe for success; even Schlieffen believed that he was 'safely in possession of the secrets of victory'.[5] The army was ready to go.

[1] Theodor Schiemann, *Videant Consules* (Paris, 1890).
[2] Paul Pilant, *Le Péril allemand* (Paris, 1913), p. 18.
[3] Schweinitz, *Briefwechsel*, p. 280.
[4] Boetticher, *Schlieffen*.
[5] Generalfeldmarschall Graf Alfred von Schlieffen. *Gesammelte Schriften* (Berlin, 1913), p. 456.

Holstein probably never seriously considered forcing France into war over Morocco; indeed, by April 1905 he knew from the German ambassador in Paris that Rouvier was prepared to drop Delcassé and to co-operate more closely with Germany. Schlieffen, however, was unaware of these diplomatic exchanges, and therefore did not bother to press for war himself, preferring to wait until France and Germany fell upon each other. Groener, who during the crisis was head of the railway section of the General Staff, describes the atmosphere: 'it was not known that Schlieffen had spoken out in favour of war, but we all more or less had the same views as Count Schlieffen.'[1]

On New Year's Day 1906 William II told his Commanding Generals that Schlieffen had resigned and that he had no intention of going to war over Morocco. The War Minister, von Einem, who would have welcomed the idea of war, wrote that the generals were 'visibly moved' but realized reluctantly that they would have to follow the orders of their Supreme Warlord.[2] The War Party now had nothing to do but to follow in anger the proceedings of the conference at Algeciras.

Shortly after the first Morocco crisis the German military attaché in London, Graf Schulenburg-Tressow, visited Schlieffen.

He talked about the military and political situation very openly and said that England in future would be on the side of our enemies, therefore it was a necessity of state in 1905 either to exploit the favourable military situation, or to come to a real agreement with France over Alsace-Lorraine. . . . He did not understand the ideas and ways of German politics, but thought that the time was very suitable for the inevitable war, since Russia was out, and he stressed that it was not the English fleet, but the battles in France that would decide the war.[3]

The Morocco crisis was a turning point for the army. War had seemed very near in 1905, and henceforth thoughts of the next war were uppermost in the minds of many leading officers.[4] Some feared that the opportunity of 1905 to fight a successful war would not recur; as one officer put it: 'We missed the boat in 1905. Then the old Hohenzollern principle of

[1] Groener, *Lebenserinnerungen*, p. 83.
[2] Von Einem, *Erinnerungen*, p. 114.
[3] BA Koblenz: HO8-58/1, Nachlass Graf von der Schulenburg-Tressow.
[4] Groener, *Lebenserinnerungen*, p. 135.

putting our enemy in the wrong and showing our superior strength was still a possibility.'[1]

Moltke, who succeeded Schlieffen at the General Staff, in contrast to Schlieffen had certain reservations about his own qualities and showed growing nervousness at the possibility of an anti-German entente. He was therefore determined to establish better relations with the Austrian General Staff, which Schlieffen in his imperious manner had tended to ignore. 1906 also saw changes in the Austrian General Staff, Beck being replaced by Conrad von Hötzendorf, an outspoken advocate of a preventive war and of an expansionist policy in the Balkans. Conrad needed German backing for his schemes just as much as Moltke needed Austria's closest co-operation in the event of a two-front war. In 1909 when agitation broke out in Serbia the two Chiefs of General Staff discussed their problems in an exchange of letters.

On 1 January 1909 Conrad wrote to Moltke saying that Serbia and Montenegro were backed in their anti-Austrian activities by the support of Turkey, England, and Italy, but most of all by Russia, and that in the event of war between Austria and Russia over the Balkans Germany would have to join in on the side of the Monarchy 'in the spirit of the alliance of 1879'. Conrad presumed that this would lead to war between France and Germany, and asked Moltke how he proposed to deploy his forces in the event of a European war.[2] Conrad's purpose in this letter was quite clear. He wished to get unconditional support from Germany for a punitive war against Serbia and Montenegro, even if this led to a general European war. Such activities were certainly not in the spirit of the 1879 alliance, which was designed by Bismarck as purely and solely a defensive treaty. Bismarck had had no desire to encourage Austrian expansion in the Balkans, but wanted to guarantee the territorial status quo of the Monarchy. Bismarck however had seen the danger that the treaty of 1879, and the Roumanian treaty of 1883, might encourage provocation of Russia.[3]

Moltke replied on 21 January. Although he insisted at the

---

[1] Heeresarchiv Stuttgart: Nachlass General von Schnürlen. Briefwechsel mit Generaloberst Freiherr von Falkenhausen 1909–1917, Falkenhausen 12-1-1909.

[2] Feldmarschall Conrad, *Aus meiner Dienstzeit* (Vienna, 1921) i. 631–4.

[3] *GPEK*, iii. 273. Bismarck to Reuss, 28-9-1883.

beginning of his letter that the treaty of 1879 was designed as a
defensive guarantee in the event of a Russian attack on Austria,
he later made it quite clear that he also thought that the treaty
could be used as a pledge to Austria of German support, if
Austrian activities in the Balkans led to war with Russia: 'I
believe that only Austria marching into Serbia could cause a
Russian intervention. This would constitute for Germany the
"casus foederis".' He also felt that it was unlikely that France
would stand by in the event of war between Russia and Austria
and Germany. France would almost certainly mobilize when
the Germans mobilized; 'Two mobile armies like those of Germany and France could not stand face to face without fighting.'
Moltke then outlined the German war plans for a massive
attack on France which would lead to a speedy victory. Moltke
argued that: 'There is no doubt that the French army will move
to the frontier if it does not go on the offensive. Thus a decision
will be made soon after the end of the deployment.' He further
assured Conrad that the chances for a two-front war were not
bad for the allies: 'I believe, even if France joins in, that the
situation of the allied empires would be serious, but would not
have to be described as menacing.'[1]

Conrad had every reason to be pleased with Moltke's reply.
Moltke had accepted the somewhat dubious reading of the 1879
treaty which Conrad had suggested, had assured the Austrians
of Germany's unconditional support, and had given Conrad
every encouragement that the Central Powers had little to fear
from a war on two fronts. Furthermore, the letter had been
sanctioned by the Kaiser and by the Chancellor. Moltke's letter
of 29 January 1909 can be seen as the first blank cheque issued
by the German government, on the sole initiative of the General
Staff, to support Austrian ambitions in the Balkans.

It is clear that both Moltke and Conrad wanted war in 1909
over Serbia, and were exceedingly angry that the diplomats
thought otherwise. On 14 September, after the crisis had blown
over, Moltke wrote to Conrad:

> In this private letter may I say that I regret most profoundly, like
> Your Excellency, that the chance has passed and has not been taken
> when for some time such advantageous conditions are unlikely to

---

[1] Conrad, *Aus meiner Dienstzeit*, i. 379–84.

recur. I am absolutely convinced that it would have been possible to localize the war between Austria-Hungary and Serbia and that the Monarchy, having fought a successful war, would have been more secure internally, externally strengthened, and would have won a preponderance in the Balkans which could not have been easily challenged. Even if Russia had been active and a European war had developed, the situation for Austria and Germany would have been better than it is likely to be in a few years. All the same, Your Excellency, let us look confidently to the future. As long as Austria and Germany stand side by side, both ready to recognize the 'Tua res agitur' of the other, we will be strong enough to break an encirclement. Many will break their teeth on this central European block.[1]

Conrad soothed his disappointment with such unequivocal support from Berlin. In his annual report for 1909 he wrote: 'Germany works with rich resources, constant determination and resolution to develop the army and navy, especially to organize the army for a war on two fronts and is always prepared not only to make an instrument of war, but also to use it when needed.'[2] Discussions between Berlin and Vienna continued, with Moltke insisting that 'the destiny of Austria will be finally decided not on the Bug but on the Seine', and Conrad anxious that he should have some support from Germany in the initial stages of the war against Russia. Moltke got quite carried away with the idea of the next war, and spoke in terms of 'a struggle between German and Slav culture . . . to prepare for this is the duty of all states who are the standard bearers of Germanic culture.'[3] Conrad, well aware of the fact that 47 per cent. of the subjects of the Monarchy were Slavs, was not so enthusiastic about the idea of a racial crusade, but hoped that war would come before the Slavs in the Monarchy were drawn into the Pan-Slav camp.

Russia's mobilization in 1912 increased Moltke's nervousness, and he was determined that this should not be allowed to happen again. On 18-2-1913 he sent a memorandum to the General Staffs in Bavaria, Württemberg, and Saxony which read: 'As has been already mentioned the Russian army has been told (by the Russian government) that the declaration of mobilization must be regarded as the opening of hostilities'.[4]

[1] Conrad, *Aus meiner Dienstzeit*, i. 165.
[2] Ibid., i. 269.   [3] Ibid., iii. 145.
[4] Bayr.HSA, Abt. IV, KA, M.Kr.1711.

This was repeated two months later by the War Minister at a meeting with a group of Reichstag members. The Minister insisted that Germany could not allow Russia to mobilize again, and should this in fact happen he would call up the reserve. He pointed out that this had not happened in 1912 because France would have followed suit and Europe would have plunged into war.[1] Thus the Chief of the General Staff and the War Minister accepted the principle that Russian mobilization would in future lead to a European war. Another important step had been taken towards the disaster of August 1914.

At the same meeting the question of Belgian neutrality was raised. At first the War Minister tried to avoid answering the question by saying: 'Whether Belgium is considered as a possible theatre of war cannot be said, since the attitude of France is decisive. All statements depend on assessments, calculations and observations by our General Staff.' Asked on the following day to give a unequivocal guarantee of Belgian neutrality the War Minister replied that it was a matter for the Foreign Office. Some days later Jagow, speaking for the Foreign Office, assured Noske that Germany intended to respect Belgian neutrality. The War Minister however insisted that war had little to do with politics: 'War breaks out when the vital interests of a people are endangered; then no treaties help.' Jagow then answered further questions with the statement: 'I can only *confidentially* say, we will not give the French a hint as to where to await us.'[2] The diplomat's hands were firmly tied by the General Staff.

The war party was encouraged by the vast increases in the army in 1913, which, although they by no means met the original requirements of the General Staff, dispersed any possible doubts that Germany was the strongest military power in Europe. The General Staff knew, however, that these increases stretched the financial resources of the Reich to a point where further increases could only be made at the expense of the naval programme, and doubted whether the government would tolerate any economies in that sector. Furthermore Germany's actions were bound to be answered by similar increases in France and Russia. War fever spread throughout the army. In

[1] Heeresarchiv Stuttgart: Württ. Militärbevollmächtigter Berlin, Band 41.
[2] Ibid.

his traditional address to the Commanding Generals at New Year 1914 the Kaiser voiced his opinion that war would come that year. This was promptly repeated by General Deimling in Strasburg, and General Tülff von Tschepe und Weidenbach told his officers in Koblenz: 'Gentlemen, I have to tell you that this year we'll get cracking!'[1]

Too much emphasis should perhaps not be placed on these remarks which were typical of William when in a sabre-rattling mood, but they were symptomatic of the atmosphere of the time. In January 1914 the German military attaché in Vienna, Graf Kageneck, told Conrad that Moltke was in favour of war, but that 'the authorities' were for peace.[2] In a further exchange of letters both Moltke and Conrad agreed that they were militarily in a particularly strong position, with the Russians frantically trying to reform their army and the French army in some confusion after the introduction of the three-year service.

On 12 April 1914 Conrad travelled to Karlsbad, where Moltke was undergoing a cure, to discuss the military situation. In the course of the conversation Moltke insisted that the longer they waited for war the less would be the chances of success, and criticized his government for waiting for England to make up her mind what she would do in the event of war. Moltke also told Conrad that he expected that Germany would be able to defeat France in six weeks, and would then turn her forces to the East.[3]

The murder at Sarajevo was greeted by the General Staff as a golden opportunity for the preventive war for which they had waited so long. The Saxon Military Plenipotentiary in Berlin wrote to his War Minister on 3 July: 'I have the impression that one thinks that it would be a good idea if war came now. Our situation and chances will not get any better.'[4] The Saxon Envoy also had the impression that 'the military are pressing for war now while Russia is not yet ready'.[5] In Vienna Hoyos was under the impression that the military in Berlin would welcome a war.[6]

[1] Fritz Fischer, *HZ*.199 (1964), 337.
[2] Conrad, *Aus meiner Dienstzeit*, iii. 596.   [3] Ibid., iii. 669–73.
[4] Imanuel Geiss, *Julikrise und Kriegsausbruch* (Hanover, 1963), i. 75.
[5] Ibid., i. 72.
[6] *Österreich-Ungarns Aussenpolitik 1908–1914*, viii. 235.

The War Minister, Falkenhayn, however, was not particularly impressed by the warlike utterances from Vienna, and thought that the Austrians would try to use diplomatic pressure rather than war. On 5 July, after a conference with the Kaiser and the Chancellor at Potsdam, he advised Moltke not to interrupt his cure, and assured him that he would tell him of any further developments.[1]

After the initial excitement the General Staff became confident that Austria would do nothing that might lead to a European war. Moltke remained in Karlsbad, and on 8 July the Quartermaster General in the General Staff, Waldersee,[2] also went on leave, followed shortly afterwards by the head of the 2nd department who was also partly responsible for mobilization.

It was not until the evening of 25 July that Moltke returned to Berlin. Falkenhayn, who had taken a short leave, returned on the morning of that day. On the following day the General Staff gave the Foreign Office a note to be handed to the Belgian government claiming that the French were about to attack Germany through Belgium, and that therefore the German army would be obliged to march through Belgian territory.[3] It is therefore clear that the General Staff were almost certain that the breakdown of diplomatic relations between Vienna and Belgrade would lead to a two-front war.

On 29 July the Bavarian Military Plenipotentiary in Berlin reported to the Bavarian War Minister that:

The War Minister supported by the Chief of the General Staff urgently desires military measures which would meet the politically tense situation and the real imminent threat of war. The Chief of the General Staff wants to go even further, he uses all his influence to try to use the unusually favourable situation to bring about a war; he points out that France is at the moment in military difficulties, that Russia does not feel militarily secure at all; also the favourable time of year, the harvest is mostly gathered and the year's training finished.[4]

His Saxon colleagues reported to his War Ministry in much the same terms. 'It is unquestionable that the Chief of the General

[1] *Die Deutschen Dokumente Zum Kriegsausbruch 1914*, i. xii.
[2] Not to be confused with the older Waldersee who died in 1904.
[3] Geiss, *Julikrise*, ii. 12.
[4] Ibid., ii. 297.

Staff is for war, whereas the Chancellor prevaricates.' He was, moreover, convinced that war was inevitable.[1] Varnbüler, the Württemberg envoy in Berlin, also reported that: 'Already the reins are slipping noticeably out of the hands of the diplomats into those of the War Department'; the General Staff was optimistic as to Germany's chances, and was pressing the diplomats to accept German military measures against the partial mobilization in Russia and the troop movements in France.[2]

The War Minister, Falkenhayn, according to his somewhat uncritical biographer was pressing for war on the 29th, whereas Moltke was trying to hold back the order for mobilization.[3] Whatever the truth of the first part of this statement, there can be little doubt that the second part is inaccurate. On the same day Moltke sent a memorandum on the military situation in Europe to the Chancellor, which, although full of peace-loving sentiments, ended with the words: 'The further our neighbours' preparations go, the sooner their mobilization will be finished. The military situation will thus worsen for us from day to day, and may, if our potential opponents continue undisturbed to prepare for war, have disastrous consequences for us.'[4] Moltke also commented on a report from the military attaché in Petersburg, which arrived at the General Staff on the 29th, that if Germany did not hurry up with her mobilization Russia might well defeat Austria before Germany was ready, leaving Germany defenceless on the Eastern front.[5] It is therefore quite clear that Moltke was pressing for German mobilization, and by no means trying to dampen the warlike enthusiasm of the War Minister.

On the following day Moltke conferred with Falkenhayn and Bethmann, and this time there was no possible doubt that he was in favour of speeding up German mobilization, and therefore of bringing on war. Moltke was, however, anxious that Germany should not seem to be the aggressor. He told Captain Fleischmann, an Austrian officer attached to the General Staff in Berlin, that Germany would not mobilize until war had

[1] Geiss, *Julikrise*, ii. 299.
[2] Ibid., ii. 300.
[3] Zwehl, *Falkenhayn*, p. 56.
[4] *Die Deutschen Dokumente Zum Kriegsausbruch 1914*, ii. 62–66.
[5] Geiss, *Julikrise*, ii. 118.
[6] Zwehl, *Falkenhayn*, p. 57.

actually broken out between Russia and the Monarchy, since Germany's mobilization would automatically lead to war. Fleischmann at once telegraphed this to Conrad in Vienna.[1] But at a meeting of the Prussian State Ministry on 30 July Falkenhayn pressed for further steps towards mobilization in Germany.[2] Moltke received the Austrian military attaché and told him that Austria should mobilize against Russia, and that Germany too would mobilize. Moltke had decided on war.

The military attaché promptly telegraphed details of this conversation to Vienna, and the telegram landed on Conrad's desk on the 31st. Having read the telegram aloud to Berchtold the latter exclaimed: 'Who rules: Moltke or Bethmann?'[3] Berchtold was perfectly correct in his suspicion that the military had gained the upper hand. Bethmann agreed with Moltke's proposal that a final decision on German mobilization should be made at midday on the 31st. Moltke who only received the news of the mobilization of the Russian army at 7 a.m. on the 31st, was so certain of his position that he had already telegraphed to Conrad the previous evening that Germany would mobilize. From now on the diplomatists were trapped by the military time-tables and the strategic planning of a dead man, Count Schlieffen.

Confirmation of Russian mobilization came from the German embassy in St Petersburg towards midday on the 31st. From then on the army leaders urged Bethmann to give his sanction for the mobilization of the German army as soon as possible.[4] Rumours that England and France might remain neutral, which were discussed in Berlin on 1 August, occasioned an outburst from Moltke that the mobilization plans, which foresaw a swift attack on France, could not possibly be changed.[5] Moltke and Falkenhayn were determined not to give way in the face of the Kaiser's sudden change of mind. Moltke was getting increasingly angry with Bethmann's prevarications, and told Tirpitz on 2 August that it was about time that the General Staff should take over the political control of the Reich.[6] He

[1] Conrad, *Aus meiner Dienstzeit*, iv. 130 ff.
[2] *Die Deutsche Dokumente Zum Kriegsausbruch 1914*, ii. 162–6.
[3] Conrad, *Aus meiner Dienstzeit*, iv. 152.
[4] Geiss, *Julikrise*, ii. 386.
[5] Moltke, *Erinnerungen*, p. 19.
[6] Alfred von Tirpitz, *Politische Dokumente* (Berlin, 1924), p. 20.

did not have to wait long. The following day Bethmann declared war on France.

It would be a distortion of the facts to suppose that the German military leaders were solely responsible for the outbreak of the war, but it is equally untenable to claim that they did not play a decisive part in bringing it about. Military leaders had pressed for preventive war in the past, and frustration that many promising chances of fighting a successful war had been neglected was an important factor determining the attitude of the General Staff throughout the July crisis. The activities of the General Staff helped to make war more probable. In 1909 Moltke had encouraged the Austrians to be firmer in the Balkans and had assured them of German support. The telegram to Conrad on the 30th was one of the decisive events which led to war. The doctrine that Russian mobilization would automatically lead to a European war was in no way in accordance with reality. Moreover, even if it was true that for Germany mobilization meant war this did not necessarily apply to other states. Their inability to work out an alternative to the Schlieffen plan robbed the German government of any freedom of action during the final days of the crisis. Lastly, the army's dislike of the diplomatists, and the lack of any close co-operation between the General Staff and the Foreign Office not only had a disastrous effect at the time, but was a portent for the future.

VI

THE ARMY AND THE CIVILIANS

THE re-unification of the Reich by blood and iron gave the
army an immense popularity; amongst patriotic Germans,
who regarded the foundation of the second Reich as something approaching a miracle, admiration for the army was
unbounded. At the same time the army, flattered by this praise,
was only too willing to return some of the attention lavished
upon it. An American friend of the Kaiser, who knew Germany well, wrote, 'in the halcyon days which succeeded 1870
there was the most cordial fellowship between soldiers and
civilians. Officers in uniform were a familiar sight at the hotel
tables of small garrison towns'.[1] These halcyon days were however numbered. As memories of Königgrätz and Sedan faded,
and the Reich seemed to be less of a miracle and more of a
commonplace, the army lost its popularity and retired from the
hotel tables to the exclusiveness of the mess. Within a few years
the cordial relations between the army and civilians became
increasingly strained until they virtually ceased to exist.

Whilst serving in Thuringia Goltz wrote that officers
'naturally' had nothing to do with the civilians.[2] Life was indeed depressing for Goltz in his small garrison, 'in one of the
15 officers' families the stork was always on the way, or there
was scarlet fever or mourning; we had isolated ourselves completely from the civilians'.[3] Bilse in his popular novel on the
scandals of the army in a small garrison town laid great stress
on the hostile attitude of the army towards the civilians. One of
the characters in his book said, 'self-conceit is the curse of our
profession and likely to alienate more and more the army
officers from the civilians, although the contrary is earnestly to

---

[1] Poulteney Bigelow, *Prussian Memories 1864–1914* (New York, 1916), p. 58.
[2] Goltz, *Denkwürdigkeiten*, p. 90.
[3] Hermann Teske, *Von der Goltz* (Göttingen, 1957), p. 31.

be desired'.[1] Seeckt's biographer, von Rabenau, also stressed the growing split between civil and military in this period.[2] The army's attitude was expressed succinctly by a major in the *Kreuzzeitung* in 1895, 'one can ask oneself why on earth officers and the people should sympathize with one another!'[3] It is hardly surprising, therefore, that the official commission established to examine the army after the first World War pointed out that much of what had happened in the years before the war had contributed to a weakening of the officer's authority when it came to war. Dr Herz spoke to a sub-committee set up to examine this question in 1926, of 'the great gulf between the Officer Corps and the *bourgeoisie* which was one reason why antipathy towards the officers was so widespread among the people'.[4]

There were exceptions to this self-enforced segregation. Groener writes in his memoirs that in Swabia and in Southern Germany officers used to mix freely in the cafés with all sections of the community, even with workmen, and claims that this liberal attitude was the foundation of Southern German democracy.[5] Even Goltz prided himself that when he was a commanding general in Königsberg he would sometimes invite civilians to the mess, but only, he added, when they were well educated.[6]

The limits of 'Southern German democracy' were, at least as far as the army was concerned, very carefully drawn. In Bavaria a reserve lieutenant who in civilian life was in the transport business had been observed drinking a glass of beer with 'station masters, engine drivers and conductors, &c.', whereupon he was refused any further promotion and transferred to the second levy of the Landwehr. Using a familiar tone to someone who was his social inferior was the end of a reserve officer's career.[7] What applied to the reserve officer applied equally to a regular officer, and it is doubtful if Groener's

---

[1] Lieutenant Bilse, *Life in a Garrison Town*, (London, 1904), p. 54.

[2] Hans von Seeckt, *Aus meinem Leben 1866–1917* (Leipzig, 1938), p. 28.

[3] Volkmann und Hobohm, *Ursachen des deutschen Zusammenbruchs im Jahre 1918*, 4 Reihe, i. 256.

[4] Ibid., i. 271.

[5] Groener, *Lebenserinnerungen*, p. 35.

[6] Goltz, *Denkwürdigkeiten*, p. 258.

[7] Bayr.HSA, Abt. IV, KA, M.Kr.1863.

fellow officers had any wish to run the risk of a fate similar to that of the unfortunate lieutenant of the reserve.

The army tended to pay very scant regard to the problems of civilian life, and this was particularly true of its attitude to reserve officers. The Ministry of Justice, for example, sent frequent complaints to the War Ministry that lawyers were being called up for service in the reserve too frequently and without sufficient notice, thus often causing considerable difficulties to the Ministry.[1] The army also frequently disregarded the regulations and called up reservists without informing their superiors. This naturally enough led to complaints against such a high-handed attitude.[2] Civil servants also complained that the time they spent on manoeuvres was subtracted from their holidays, and the War Minister was prepared to support their claim that reserve training should not be treated as a holiday.[3] Although many ministries asked their employees to co-operate as far as possible, many still resented the somewhat inconsiderate attitude of the army.[4]

The distinction between the army and civilians was nowhere more striking than in their respective legal positions. Throughout the period there was a strong movement demanding that soldiers be tried for civilian offences in civil courts. This encountered the steadfast opposition of the War Ministry. Military courts almost inevitably gave milder punishments to soldiers who were on trial for civil offences. Thus after one fight in a restaurant between soldiers and civilians the soldiers were all acquitted, but the civilians involved had also to be acquitted because all the witnesses declared that they had been acting in self-defence.[5] In another case a lieutenant general, who was fined twenty marks because his dog had bitten a boy in the face, refused to pay the fine, and demanded the right to be tried by his equals in a military court.[6] Equally picturesque are the 'regulations for officers of the prostitution department' of 1914. In the section dealing with the arrest of prostitutes it was stipulated that 'immediate action should be avoided when a

---

[1] BA Koblenz: Justizministerium, P135-2869; P135-2867.
[2] Ibid., P135-2869.
[3] Bayr.HSA, Abt. IV, KA, M.Kr.2072.
[4] Ibid.
[5] *Vossische Zeitung*, 31-11-1894.
[6] *Volks-Zeitung*, 31-8-1898.

woman is found in the company of an officer in uniform, whether she is being charged for a breach of the laws on prostitution or for any other offence'. The police were ordered to treat officers in this unfortunate position with the respect due to their rank and 'special consideration should be paid to the interests of his profession'.[1] These and other examples of the army enjoying a particularly favoured position in the eyes of the law did not help the establishment of good relations between the army and civilians.

The fact that the army had a privileged position in society was not of its own enough to cause the degree of animosity that existed. Even more important were the encroachments the army made on the basic rights of civilians, usually when the army was called in to act as a police force. One particularly vicious example of this happened in 1894. In a small village the inhabitants had quarrelled with the local squire (*Gutsherr*) over the right to collect firewood. Since the inhabitants refused to concede their rights the army was called in to settle the matter by force. The result of the operation was that two men were killed, one of them aged sixty-eight, the other sixty-nine, four were severely injured, and thirteen wounded. One peasant got seventeen bayonet wounds in his back and one in the backside. None of the soldiers were injured, although the army claimed that resistance had been particularly hard.[2] In 1892 there were a number of cases of sentries firing on civilians. In order to show his active support for the army the Kaiser sent a personal note of congratulation to a soldier involved in one such case, along with a signed photograph. The man was promptly promoted.[3]

The army's activities were not confined to police actions, it also interfered directly in purely civil matters. In 1912 a group of citizens of Rastatt decided to erect a statue to Carl Schurz who had come from their town. Schurz had been a *Freischärler* in 1849 and had shortly afterwards emigrated to America where he became a general and a statesman. The army command in Karlsruhe objected strongly to the plan, saying that the statue would serve as a bad example to the troops, and that the whole

---

[1] *Volks-Zeitung*, 3-1-14.
[2] Dieter Fricke, *ZfGW*, Heft 6 (1958), 1298–1310.
[3] J. Alden Nichols, *Germany after Bismarck*, p. 215.

idea came ominously from a group of 'democrats'. General
Huene, who had heard of the plans to erect the statue, went to
see the Minister for the Interior of Baden, and expressed his
horror at the idea. The Minister agreed with the General that
the statue was a monument to revolution and *Umsturz*, and that
it was clearly an attempt to make the troops break their oath of
allegiance to the Grand Duke of Baden. The Minister's colleagues in the Baden government did not share his anxiety and
were unwilling to undertake anything against the 'Monument
to Revolution'. Enraged at the government's failure to take any
action, Huene wrote a frantic letter to the War Ministry in
Berlin about the dangers of allowing the statue to be erected.[1]
The army was fortunate in that the new mayor of Rastatt,
elected at this time, agreed with its views and was opposed to
the building of the monument. In America the members of the
'Deutsch-Amerika Club' protested to the German Ambassador.
The army remained adamant in its view that the monument
would be 'a serious insult to the Prussian and Baden troops
stationed in Rastatt, and a grave danger to the discipline of the
same'. The War Minister endorsed this attitude in a letter to
the Chancellor of 21-8-1913. The monument was never built.[2]

These incidents, some comic, some tragic, could only occur
in a state where the army had excessive influence, and the
influence of the army could only be maintained with the active
support of a wide section of the *bourgeoisie*. The army was prepared to make some concessions to the *bourgeoisie*, partly out of
the need for a larger army, but more important as a means of
building up a bloc of influential supporters for its reactionary
views. The essential role the army played in the state made the
task easier. The *bourgeois* was only too anxious to share something of the glamour and glory of the army, and a lieutenant's
epaulettes or an invitation to the mess was a low price for the
army to pay for loyal support against liberalism and democracy.
The civilian thus profited in that his social status was enhanced
and he was brought closer to the seats of power; and the army
gained in that military rank and attainments were taken, in
civilian life, as absolute standards for judging a man. Entry to
the officers' mess was essential if a young man wished to have a

[1] BA, Koblenz: HO2-1/22.
[2] Ibid.

successful career in any part of the public service. Baroness
Spitzemberg records in her diary that although the expense was
considerable she decided to allow her son to accept an invitation to dine regularly at the officers' mess as she knew that he
would be bound to meet a number of influential people.[1] What
seemed to the Baroness highly desirable was, to lesser mortals,
a matter of social life or death.

There were other aspects of the army which made it popular
in some sections of the community. It was estimated that an
average infantry regiment brought a garrison town 900,000
marks a year, money which did not all go to those who could
hope to entertain military ambitions.[2] Nor can the glamour of
army uniforms be denied. Bernhardi writes in his memoirs,
'working-class girls were particularly proud of their soldiers.
They willingly paid up to 6 marks, according to the smartness
of the uniform, when they wanted to go out with them on
Sundays. The humble infantry cost about 3 marks.'[3] But it
was not the small shop-keepers nor the amorous young girls who
ultimately determined the relations between soldier and
civilian. The army remained exclusive and found a ready and
obsequious ally in the *bourgeoisie*. Secure in its position, un-
fettered by any form of liberal democracy, it paid little regard
to the rights of civilians who remained outside its orbit. As this
situation increasingly failed to correspond with the fundamental
changes in German society, tension was bound to increase.
Bebel wrote, 'the numerous professional soldiers who, through
lack of any serious work to do, concentrate on the outward
trappings, and in particular the attempt to make an artificial
rift between the army and the people and to create a certain
antagonism between the two, have made the army what it is.'[4]

The system of reserve officers was an effective and popular
way of assimilating the *bourgeoisie* into an aristocratic and
monarchical state.[5] The army was able to thrust its ideology
on to a considerable and influential section of the civilian middle-
classes, in return for the glamour and privilege of wearing the

---

[1] Spitzemberg, *Tagebuch*, 2-11-1890.
[2] Emil Obermann, *Soldaten, Bürger, Militaristen* (Stuttgart, 1958), p. 196.
[3] Bernhardi, *Denkwürdigkeiten*, p. 260.
[4] August Bebel, *Nicht Stehendes Heer!* (Stuttgart, 1898).
[5] Eckart Kehr, *Die Gesellschaft* (1928) ii. 492 ff.

'King's jacket'. Being a reserve officer brought with it social advantages, giving one access to the upper stratum of society and a sense of belonging to an army which had done so much to form the Reich. For the State it had the considerable advantage of ensuring the sound conservative support of an important section of society, and it further enhanced the prestige and influence of the army.

The reserve officer was immensely proud of his rank, and was a passionate defender of the army to which he had the privilege of belonging. This feeling was almost universal, and by no means confined to a small section of social-climbers or ambitious go-getters. An influential majority of the *bourgeoisie* wished to become reserve officers, and those who counted themselves lucky enough to have reached this goal were often more proud of their military rank than they were of their often considerable attainments in civilian life. Thus one of Bülow's finest hours was when he was appointed colonel in a Hussar regiment. Michaelis was a lieutenant-colonel, and the Finance Minister von Scholtz, who had been a sergeant in the reserve, was overcome with joy when he was appointed to the dizzy rank of lieutenant.[1] A delightful example of this attitude is the case of an eminent professor who was asked what title he would like on the occasion of his seventy-fifth birthday. It was suggested that he should become a *wirkliche Geheime Rat*, a high civilian distinction which carried with it the right to be addressed as *Excellenz*. The professor declined this offer saying that he wished to be promoted to the rank of captain in the reserve as he was only a lieutenant.[2] Equally indicative is the attitude of Max Weber. Weber loathed his time as a recruit and had written many letters home damning the army. Once he became a reserve officer his attitude changed radically. On manoeuvres as a reserve officer he wrote. 'Military life was really exhausting in the last few days, but otherwise it is now really very nice and quite interesting. . . . The Captain thinks that I should look on these 8 weeks as a cure, and he is quite right.' His widow wrote of this changed attitude toward the army, 'the final result of his military training was a tremendous respect for the "machine",

[1] F. C. Endres, *Archiv für Sozialwissenschaft 58* (1927), p. 293.
[2] Demeter, *Das Deutsche Offizierkorps*, p. 225.

in addition a warlike and patriotic attitude which made him hope that one day he would be able to go into the field at the head of his company'.[1] Here, as in many other cases, the institution of reserve officer had worked its magic.

The problem of reserve officers is treated in some detail in a work which was sharply critical of the reactionary tendencies of Wilhelmine Germany.

Life in the mess is well designed to remove anything that might harm conservative ideas and prejudices, particularly the liberal press. The *Deutsche Adelsblatt* is an adequate substitute, particularly when the *Kreuzzeitung* is also at hand. This is the atmosphere that greets a reserve officer.

If the young man learned as a one-year volunteer and reserve N.C.O. to look upon the army as the Monarch's bodyguard, and upon himself as a subject and musketeer of His Majesty, the reserve officer during his manoeuvres came into an even more feudal milieu, rooted in even more distant centuries.

In the mess he sees what a vast number of small Prussian aristocratic families exist, and what an important role their titles play, something which no democracy in Prussia as yet has been able to stop.

In the mess the young reserve officer learns of the respect which high military officials pay to the landed aristocracy, that circle of squires who for a long time have acted as a brake on the cultural development of the country.

It is self-evident that these impressions gained in the mess change many of the civilians' ideas about the aristocracy. There he learns that a 'decent fellow' in Prussia is a conservative, for all the gentlemen in the mess are more or less conservative.

Even for a young man who was brought up as a liberal this discovery is not without effect, especially when, as often happens, as a result of life in the mess, frequent contacts between the reserve officer and the regular officers and their habitual guests develop. Regular manoeuvres strengthen the impression. In addition the reserve officer today is almost bound to become a member of the *Kriegerverein*, in which the most conservative elements usually congregate. The *Kriegervereine* are not only organized by the military: the police and the Landrat officially supervise its patriotism and ensure that anyone who has anything to do with the Social Democrats, even economically, is excluded from it. Thus the reserve officer is literally

---

[1] Marianne Weber, *Max Weber, Ein Lebensbild* (Tübingen, 1926), p. 85.

forced to take sides politically, and the side he has to take is the reactionary one.[1]

The reserve officer, acutely conscious of his rank and with an unconditional admiration for the regular army, was anxious to show his devotion to the army, and to prove his sterling military qualities. This attitude often made him appear simply ridiculous as he aped the habits, and more often than not the bad ones, of the active army. Fontane was led to cry in despair, 'these everlasting reserve officers'.[2] But foolish as he must have often appeared to the more enlightened he fulfilled an essential function in German society, serving as the vital link between the army and civilians and as propagandist for the increasing militarization of public life.

A useful way of finding jobs for ex-soldiers, and at the same time of further strengthening the links between the army and the professions, was the system of *Militäranwärter*. Jobs were found for ex-soldiers, usually in the Civil Service, particularly in the prison service and as clerks in the law courts. This idea, which seemed to be a good method of finding suitable employment for former soldiers, in fact led to a great deal of strain within the Civil Service.

The *Militäranwärter* soon began to complain that they were underpaid, and that no proper account was taken of the years they had served in the army as far as seniority in their new jobs was concerned. They argued that it was unjust that civil servants, who had not served in the army, and who were thus much younger than they were, had better and more responsible jobs. In order to force through their demands for better pay and conditions they organized the *Verband deutscher Militäranwärter und Invaliden*.

The civilians were not particularly pleased by such activities. Many employers were not impressed by the performance of the *Militäranwärter* in their civilian jobs, and accused them of 'ignorance, crudity, and stupidity'. Civilian employees founded a counter-organization to that of the *Militäranwärter*, known as the *Kartellverband der Zivilanwärter*'. The fronts had once again

---

[1] *Die Reaktion in der inneren Verwaltung Preussens* (1908), pp. 28–29, quoted in H. Pross, *Die Zerstörung der deutsche Politik, Dokumente 1871–1933* (Frankfurt am Main, 1960), pp. 33–34.
[2] Theodor Fontane, *Briefe an Georg Friedländer* (Heidelberg, 1954), p. 305.

formed between civilian and military within the Civil Service.

The War Ministry had mixed feelings about these developments. On the one hand they were anxious to help ex-soldiers and to secure good positions for them in civilian life, the more so as pensions for soldiers were quite inadequate. On the other hand they did not like the idea of the *Verband*. The army had a strong dislike of any organization over which it did not have complete control, and did not trust a pressure group which demanded better conditions. It seemed altogether too much like a trade union. On 23-4-1900 the War Ministry sent out a memorandum suggesting that since there were a number of jobs open in the Civil Service it might be possible to find better positions for the *Militäranwärter*. At the same time the Minister stressed that he did not regard the *Verband* as the legal and official representative of the interests of the *Militäranwärter*. The War Minister took steps to reduce the influence of the *Verband*. Its official journal *Reveille*, each issue of which sold over 13,000 copies, was banned in the army. Regular soldiers were forbidden to join the organization, and all links between the army and the *Verband* were severed. The Minister of Justice replied shortly afterwards that the *Verband* was well known to be 'thoroughly disruptive' and 'harmful to discipline', and agreed with the War Minister that it should be given no official support. At the same time the Minister said that it would be quite impossible to reserve any positions in the Civil Service for the *Militäranwärter*.

The struggle between the two organizations within the Civil Service led to a number of incidents and particularly libel actions. In 1897 the *Verband* sued the *Hessische Morgenzeitung* for an article on *Militäranwärter* which included the remark, 'lack of education and tact cannot be compensated by 'good will' or by a military bearing and a vast moustache. Ignorant men have a continuously demoralizing effect, at work and socially, and everywhere create an extremely unfavourable impression.'

The *Verband* had few allies. At a meeting of the *Staatsministerium* in 1899 it was agreed that, although the *Verband* was essentially patriotic and 'loyal', it was nonetheless to be condemned as 'demagogic'. The *Kriegerverein* also refused to give the *Verband* any support, and the central committee of the *Kriegervereine* denounced the *Verband* as 'dangerous'.

The system of reserving positions within the Civil Service for ex-service personnel also came under fire. The *Vossische Zeitung* claimed that in 1897 there were 6,670 jobs open in the Justice department alone, of these exactly half were reserved for ex-soldiers. The paper considered that this was too high a percentage, and suggested that needy civilians should be given a much better chance.[1]

In November 1904 the problem of the *Militäranwärter* was discussed in the Prussian diet, but the debate did not reach any useful conclusion.

Meanwhile the attitude of the military authorities towards the *Verband* was changing. This was in line with other similar developments. As hostility between the army and civilians tended to increase, the army was more anxious to support organizations whose general policy it accepted, even if it criticized certain aspects of their activities. Even a difficult ally was better than none. Thus in 1905 the War Ministry published a memorandum saying that the *Verband* was no longer as 'irresponsible' as it had been, and the army was prepared to co-operate with it. Although N.C.O.s of the regular army were still not allowed to join the *Verband* the War Minister decided to allow members of the *Verband* to lecture to active N.C.O.s on some of the problems of finding employment in civilian life. The Minister thought that many of the complaints voiced by the *Verband* were justified, adding that he thought it essential, both for the army and the State, for N.C.O.s to be given good jobs in civilian life. Other ministeries did not share the War Minister's enthusiasm for bettering the lot of the ex-soldiers; the Finance Minister, for example, claimed that any such reform would be far too costly.

The War Minister's efforts to secure better jobs for ex-soldiers caused a number of clashes with career civil servants. In an article in the *Berliner Tageblatt* in 1909 a postal official pointed out that a number of *Militäranwärter* were simply not good enough to take on good jobs in the Civil Service. 'The authorities turn a blind eye when selecting candidates so that the army administration has little trouble finding jobs for N.C.O.s and the incentive of a good civilian job remains to

---

[1] *Vossische-Zeitung*, 7-7-1897.

help recruit new N.C.O.s.'[1] In fact far more jobs were reserved for the *Militäranwärter* than was strictly necessary, which made it extremely difficult for the civil authorities to plan their own recruiting programme. Equally resented was the attitude of the army that the Civil Service should provide good jobs so as to obviate the need to pay adequate pensions.

As an increasing number of women were employed in clerical positions in the Civil Service the *Verband* launched a campaign against the employment of women, claiming that it was a direct cause of unemployment and economic distress. The War Minister backed up these claims and wrote to the Ministry of Justice in 1912 that women were only being employed to save money, and that the Minister was wilfully refusing to see the social necessity of securing adequate civilian employment for ex-soldiers.[2]

The problem was exactly the same in Württemberg. The minutes of a commission established to examine the problems of the *Militäranwärter* in Württemberg show that the commission was sharply divided. The army claimed that Württemberg did far too little for ex-soldiers and complained that the jobs provided for them were worse than in any other part of the Reich. The Württemberg War Minister claimed that if the situation was not improved it would be impossible to get any good men as N.C.O.s in future. The civil authorities pointed out that the men had not been adequately trained before leaving the army, so that they were unable to do their jobs properly, and that if better jobs were provided it would only cause even more bad feeling among those who were already in the Civil Service.[3]

An apologist of the Imperial Army wrote: 'the N.C.O.s who left the army after twelve years faithful service were generally regarded as excellent civil servants. The characteristics of the German civil servants, which were widely admired, were largely due to the fact that they had been N.C.O.s.'[4] In fact the reverse was true. The system of placing ex-soldiers in the Civil Service was the cause of constant strife between civil and mili-

[1] *Berliner Zeitung*, 24-1-1909.
[2] For all the above see BA Koblenz: Justizministerium, P135-2285; P135-2286; P135-2306.
[3] Heeresarchiv Stuttgart: Denkschriften Sammlung, Band 361.
[4] General Ernst von Eisenhart-Rothe, *So war die alte Armee* (Berlin, 1935), p. 194.

tary authorities, and qualities which had proved effective on the barrack square were not always those demanded of a civil servant.

A similar system worked for officers, but as fewer officers sought employment on retirement the problem was not so acute. Between 1894 and 1897 only four officers worked in the Prussian Civil Service, three of whom had only reached the rank of lieutenant.[1] By 1901 the *Offiziersverein* claimed that there were 350 officers seeking employment in the Civil Service. The *Verein* demanded better pay and conditions for such officers. Once again a struggle broke out, as in the case of N.C.O.s, between the army and the Civil Service. The *Kreuzzeitung* published an article in 1912 claiming that, in order to keep the army young to increase combat effectiveness, officers were often forced to leave the army young, and therefore with inadequate pensions. The state had a duty to provide suitable jobs for them so that 'the Officer Corps should not lose its aristocratic character—in the finest sense of the word'. Goltz entered the ring with the remark that 'an Officer Corps which is uncertain of its social position . . . will have few enterprising soldiers'. He bitterly complained that retired officers did not have the same chance for promotion as the 'gentlemen with degrees'. Goltz argued that 'we live at a time when a great mistake is made by over-estimating knowledge which is often moribund, and under-estimating the importance of character, of practical ability, of worldly wisdom and of action'.[2]

In the face of mounting discontent among officers the War Ministry proposed in 1913 to establish an 'Information Bureau for Civil Positions for Officers', to find jobs for retired officers, not only in the Civil Service, but also in trade and industry.

An officer who retired after a relatively long period of service was given a pension equal to about half his previous pay. For those who found employment in the Civil Service the pension was used to bring his salary up to the level of his service pay. Thus one captain with twenty-five years service earned 5,030 marks per annum. His pension was 2,515 marks, exactly half pay. He was given a position in the Civil Service with a salary of 2,940 marks per annum, and thus the pension was reduced to 2,090

[1] BA Koblenz: P135-3860.
[2] *Kreuzzeitung*, 2-5-1912.

marks so that his total income equalled his full army pay. If the salary of his new job was so low that even with the addition of his pension it did not equal his previous pay no increases in the pension were allowed.[1]

For the financially better placed it was an easy step from the army into the Diplomatic Corps. Some officers went to the Foreign Office for a short period of service. In one case a young officer went to the embassy at Stockholm, as he felt it was good for his health, since he was suffering from respiratory troubles. The Foreign Office was keen to recruit smart young officers, usually to help with social functions. The diplomatic service was, however, the preserve of the wealthy. The Foreign Office insisted that a candidate should have a private income of 12,000 to 15,000 marks per annum, and in St Petersburg 18,000. In 1900 the Foreign Office started an intensive campaign to get officers to serve in the Diplomatic Corps, and there seems to have been no great shortage of candidates. On the whole the War Minister favoured the idea, for it tended to strengthen the links between the Diplomatic Corps and the army. The Bavarian War Minister was, however, not keen to allow Bavarian officers to serve at embassies in cities where there was already a Bavarian representative. But in practice it was quite easy for a Bavarian officer to get round this restriction.[2]

Since it was relatively easy to move on from the army to the Diplomatic Corps those who had sufficient financial support would sometimes enter the army merely as an easy way into the Foreign Office. At least in the case of the army and the Foreign Office there were few cases of strife. No one was losing a job or being held up in promotion, nor were financial considerations involved. With a private income of 12,000 marks financial security was not seriously at stake.

The unique position of the army in German society was also upheld by a number of organizations whose express purpose was to increase the power and influence of the army and to strengthen the conservative order. As the Social Democrats gained more and more members for their organizations, increasing emphasis was placed on strengthening the 'patriotic'

[1] BA Koblenz: P135-3860.
[2] Bayr.HSA., Abt. IV, KA, Alt Reg. 18, M.Kr.175.

organizations as a bulwark against revolution and as a fortress of monarchical and conservative sentiment.

The oldest, and in many ways the most important of these organizations was the *Kriegerverein*. The *Verein* was founded in the early 1840s, and on 22 February 1842 was officially recognized by the King of Prussia. In the revolution of 1848 it took a firm stand for the King and for the conservative order, but in the period after 1848 it began to lose members and influence, and no longer seemed to have any significant role to play. The wars of unification gave the *Verein* a new lease of life, and in 1872 it was reorganized and centralized. With the reorganization came a declaration of political intent. Social Democracy became the principal enemy of the organization. The declaration of intent read: 'Love of and fidelity to Kaiser and Reich, Sovereign and Fatherland, will be cherished by its members, put into action and strengthened, national consciousness will be enlivened and strengthened, the ties of comradeship, even in civil life, will be preserved and cherished by its members.' At the same time membership was refused to anyone who was a member of the Social Democratic Party, and even to anyone who was heard to say anything in favour of the Social Democrats.[1]

The *Kriegerverein* was not confined to Prussia, other German states had similar organizations. In 1898 all the *Kriegervereine* throughout the Reich were united in the *Kyffhäuser Ausschuss* formed as a central committee of the various *Kriegervereine* later reorganized into the *Kyffhäuser Bund*. In 1898 the membership of the *Kyffhäuser Ausschuss* was 1,220,615.[2] The *Kyffhäuser Bund* was not formed without difficulty. Baden, for example, resented the political agitation of the Bund, particularly against the Social Democrats. In a memorandum to the secretary of the Württemberg cabinet, which was passed on to the Chancellor, the cabinet of Baden wrote that:

The Prussian state *Kriegerverband* has 'the fight against Social Democracy' as one of the principal aims of the new organization. It needs hardly to be mentioned what an extremely difficult task the organization is taking on, and that it is somewhat dangerous for the Southern German organizations to give power to the Berlin central

[1] Prof. Dr. H. Westphal, *Das deutsche Kriegervereinswesen* (Berlin, 1903).
[2] BA Koblenz: P135-1057.

organization in this, for it has a quite different political situation to consider.[1]

Such reservations were dismissed by the Prussians as an example of Baden particularism, and indeed these protests did little to shake the dominance of Prussia within the *Kyffhäuser Bund*; they did little more than slow down the process of unification.

The Prussian War Ministry was less worried by such outbursts of local patriotism than it was by the formation of rival organizations. One such group was the Veterans' League (*Verband deutscher Veteranen*) which was founded in Leipzig in 1894. The League demanded better pensions for soldiers and an 'honorary payment' for all those who had taken part in the recent wars. It was promptly condemned by the government of the Reich as a group of agitators dominated by Social Democrats.[2] The *Kriegerverein* joined in the struggle against the Veterans' League and condemned it as a socialist organization.[3] The *deutscher Kriegerbund*, a parallel organization to the *Kriegerverein*, and of equally conservative principles, condemned the Veterans' League in its annual report for 1898, at the same time taking the opportunity to underline its own impeccably monarchist beliefs. The recent modest increase in army pensions had sharpened the quarrel between the two latter groups. The *Kriegerbund* countered the claims of the Veterans' League with the following statement: 'It is quite untrue to say that the subsidies of 120 marks which were paid last year to needy veterans are due to the activities of the Veterans' League. Not one single word of that is true. It was His Majesty the Emperor alone whose initiative the veterans have to thank for this help.'[4]

In October 1898 the Prussian State Ministry decided that everything possible should be done to diminish the power of the Veterans' League. All civil servants who were members were ordered to resign, and no member of the regular army was henceforth to have anything to do with the organization.[5]

[1] DZA, Potsdam: Reichskanzlei, 2257. Geheim-Kabinett SKH Grossherzogs von Baden zum Kabinettsekretär des Königs von Württemberg, 1898.

[2] DZA, Potsdam: Reichskanzlei, 2257.

[3] BA Koblenz: P135-1057.

[4] *Deutscher Kriegerbund, Jahresbericht 1898.*

[5] BA Koblenz: P135-1057.

The close co-operation between the state and the *Kriegerverein* had only recently been established. The War Ministry had been worried that the *Verein* might wish to follow an independent policy, and also that socialists and anarchists might work their way into the organization. In 1887 the Prussian War Minister ordered the local army commanders to put trusty men into the *Kriegerverein* to make certain that they toed the line. This appeal did not meet with complete success, for the Minister had to repeat it two years later, urging officers to play a more active part in the *Kriegerverein*. In many places the local area commander (*Bezirkskommandeur*) became the honorary chairman of the local *Kriegerverein*. The question of regular officers being members of the *Kriegerverein* is an interesting example of the 'politics' of the army. Since the *Kriegerverein* was generally considered to be a political organization officers were forbidden to join it, but since the *Kriegerverein* was essential to the army, and since the army wished to keep the closest possible control over its activities, officers could become honorary members.[1] Thus the War Ministry was in the curious position of saying that officers should not be members of the *Kriegerverein*, and at the same time encouraging them to join. The emphasis for and against did, however, change under different War Ministers.[2] General von Heeringen, who was War Minister from 1909 to 1913, was particularly anxious that officers should co-operate with the *Kriegervereine*, and encouraged reserve officers to join.

When the *Kyffhäuser Ausschuss* was formed in 1898 it gave a striking demonstration of its monarchical spirit by erecting an enormous and uniquely hideous monument to Kaiser Wilhelm I on the *Kyffhäuser*, chosen no doubt for its mythical associations with Frederick Barbarossa. The monument cost 1,452,241 marks and 42 pfennigs, a considerable sum for that time, which left the committee 232,132 marks in debt as the local *Vereine* did not prove as generous with funds as had been expected.[3]

As time passed the political activities of the *Kriegerverein* became increasingly pronounced. In 1903, when the member-

---

[1] Heeresarchiv Stuttgart: WKM, AApA (A) 936 (Report of Württ. Militärbevollmächtigte, 11-7-1900).
[2] Ibid., Band 937.
[3] BA Koblenz: P135-1057.

II—G.O.C.

ship had increased to 2,097,527, the *Verein* again expressed its determination to fight the Social Democrats in its official programme.[1] It stressed the necessity of educating members so as to combat the evil forces of socialism, and of turning the organization into an active conservative political force.[2] This development was welcomed by the government. The Ministry of the Interior stressed, in a note to the Ministry of Justice, that the *Kriegerverein* should be given every possible support, for it had proved itself to be a stronghold of 'monarchical and patriotic sentiment'.[3]

By 1909 there were 16,533 *Kriegervereine* in Prussia alone with a membership of 1,439,145. The *deutscher Kriegerbund* had 19,625 *Kriegervereine* with 1,687,990 members. The *Kyffhäuser Bund*, which included all the *Kriegerverbände* of the various states, had increased its membership to 2,528,667. By now the Prussian War Minister had no doubts as to the loyalty of the *Kriegerverein*; he agreed to give the *Verein* the names and addresses of soldiers as they were demobilized, so that the *Verein* might more easily gain new members.[4]

One of the weaknesses of the *Kriegerverein* was that, in spite of the encouragement given to officers to join as honorary members, they were loath to do so. Officers feared that they would lose caste if they joined the *Verein*, for they were called upon to treat ex-soldiers as their equals. The *Militär-Wochenblatt* discussed this problem in an article published in 1895. 'Joy and thankfulness are in every breast when numerous officers join in the celebrations and meetings. Of course the position of officers to other members is by no means easy. The officer must mix in a friendly way with men who were perhaps previously his subordinates, at the same time he must always inspire respect which, as an officer, he is entitled to demand.' The article concluded with the thought that officers should for that very reason work with the *Kriegerverein* so as to show the Social Democrats that the whole notion of class war was nonsensical.[5] Class-consciousness was not so easily forgotten, however, and it remained a problem for the *Kriegerverein* that officers and the more influential mem-

[1] Heeresarchiv Stuttgart: WKM 936.
[2] Westphal, *Das deutsche Kriegervereinswesen.*
[3] BA Koblenz: P135-1057.
[4] Heeresarchiv Stuttgart: WKM, AApA, 936.
[5] *Militärwochenblatt*, Nr. 75, 24-8-1895.

bers of the *bourgeoisie* showed no little reluctance to join the *Verein*.[1] In an attempt to convince the *bourgeoisie* of the importance of joining the *Verein* it appealed to the various ministries to call upon their members to co-operate with the *Kriegerverein*. In 1903 a propaganda offensive was launched to gain the support of this influential section of society. One hundred thousand pamphlets were printed and distributed among officers and civil servants stressing the vital work which the *Kriegerverein* had done to strengthen monarchical and patriotic feeling. The Minister of Justice was particularly forthcoming and sent out a circular calling upon members of his ministry to co-operate with the *Kriegerverein*, adding that trained lawyers could make an important contribution to its work.[2]

Finance also remained a problem. As the debts which were left after the building of the Kaiser William I monument on the *Kyffhäuser* showed, members were not particularly forthcoming with funds. The *Kriegerverein* was anxious to strengthen its financial position, for it was all too well aware of the much greater financial strength of the trade unions which were able to provide superior insurance and benefit schemes for their members. As the *Kriegerverein* stood in many ways in direct competition with the unions this weakness could not be ignored. The *Verein* complained that the unions mulcted their members of 20 pfennigs per week; yet an attempt to get its own members to pay a subscription of 30 pfennigs per annum met with fierce resistance.[3] The *Kriegerverein* was however able to make up for this lack of funds with generous support from the government. The *Verein*'s newspaper, the *Kyffhäuser-Korrespondenz*, a propaganda sheet with little journalistic merit, was financed by the Ministry of the Interior at the express wish of the Chancellor who had been asked for financial support by the *Kyffhäuser Bund*.[4]

In spite of the inadequate financial resources of the *Kriegerverein*, and in spite of the reluctance of officers, civil servants and members of the upper *bourgeoisie* to join it, it played an important part in German society of the time. Particularly in local

[1] Westphal, *Das deutsche Kriegervereinswesen*.
[2] BA Koblenz: P135-1057
[3] Westphal, *Das deutsche Kriegervereinswesen*.
[4] DZA, Potsdam: Reichskanzlei, 2258.

politics it exercised considerable influence, being one of the most important centres of conservative opinion. The hero of Heinrich Mann's novel *Der Untertan* managed to establish his position in the small town where he lived through the influence of the *Kriegerverein*. For such ambitious characters the *Kriegerverein* was a useful vantage point from which important contacts could be made with the more influential circles of the Reich.

On the national level the *Kriegerverein* concentrated on its mission as a stronghold against Social Democracy and the *Umsturz*. Professor Westphal, a prominent apologist for the *Kriegerverein*, expressed the hope that it would become 'the crystallization point for the meeting of all patriots against the revolutionary efforts of the Social Democrats, and for the salvation of our people and our beloved Fatherland'.[1] The *Militär-Wochenblatt* expressed the hope that membership of the *Kriegerverein* would guarantee that no member would vote for the Social Democrats. 'Our members on joining their *Kriegerverein* have sworn love and fidelity to Kaiser and Reich, Sovereign and Fatherland. How can one break this oath more effectively than by voting a man into a legislative assembly who wants to destroy all this?'[2] The *Kriegerverein* also tried to increase its effectiveness by drawing members not only from ex-soldiers who had been through the 'school of the nation' and who were therefore considered on the whole to be more reliable, but also from young men who had not yet served so that they might be brought up as good patriots.[3] It seems however that some of these 'soldiers in civilian clothes', as the members of the *Kriegerverein* were known, were unable to resist the temptation to vote for the Social Democrats, even at the risk of breaking their solemn oath to Kaiser and Fatherland. In 1898 General von Spitz, the chairman of a *Kriegerverein*, spoke at a conference in Weissenfels of such people as 'hypocrites and traitors', and threatened to expel them from the *Kriegerverein*.[4] But in spite of von Spitz's gloomy prognostications it seems unlikely that the Social Democrats ever gained a secure foothold in the

---

[1] Westphal, *Das deutsche Kriegervereinswesen*.
[2] *Militärwochenblatt*, Nr. 21, 8-3-1899. See also BA Koblenz: HO2-1/22.
[3] BA Koblenz: P135-1057.
[4] Jerussalimski, *Die Aussenpolitik und Diplomatie des deutschen Imperialismus*, p. 86.

Kriegerverein; certainly they were unable to do anything to moderate its violent outbursts of jingoistic nationalism and its uncritical admiration of King and Emperor.

If the *Kriegerverein* worked closely with the government, after an initial period of distrust, the government took some time before it finally made up its mind about the activities of the Army League (*Wehrverein*). The *Wehrverein* was founded in 1912 by General Keim[1] and was the army equivalent to the Navy League (*Flottenverein*), which had been founded in 1898 as a propaganda organization to support the construction of the large fleet which was so dear to the Kaiser's heart. With an immense membership and powerful contacts with the navy and with the captains of industry the *Flottenverein* played an important political role which, with the exception of minor ups and downs, was encouraged by the government. Keim himself had served on the General Staff, had been the personal assistant of Caprivi on military affairs, and he was active in organizing official propaganda in favour of the army increases in 1893. After a period as Regimental Commander in Aachen he left the army feeling that his career was prejudiced through his close relations with Caprivi, and with the War Minister Walter Bronsart von Schellendorf, who had fallen from office in 1896. Keim was a good example of the new type of German officer, the 'pure soldiers', highly professional men who were neither landowners nor Prussians, who called for fundamental reforms in the organization and equipment of the army, and who demanded above all a large army; this they regarded as an essential condition of winning the two-front war for which they longed.

Possessing valuable connexions with the General Staff and with conservative politicians, Keim became, on leaving the army, one of Germany's leading military propagandists. He

---

[1] Keim came from an old Hessian military family, and had fought in the Hessian army against Prussia in 1866. He joined the Prussian army after the amalgamation of the Hessian and Prussian armies in 1866. In 1881 Keim joined the General Staff in Berlin. In 1889 he was forced to resign from the General Staff at Bismarck's insistence, having written a strongly worded article against France in the *Hamburger Nachrichten*. Supported by Caprivi and Walter Bronsart von Schellendorf he returned to Berlin in 1892 as official propagandist for the army. In 1896 he was given command of a regiment and two years later, seeing little chance of further promotion, he retired from the army.

was the military expert of the Pan-German League, the fore-most chauvinistic organization of the Second Reich.[1] He soon worked his way up in the *Flottenverein*, becoming the most active spokesman for an increase in the fleet at any cost, regardless of political considerations. In 1908 when ship-building was momentarily reduced, in the hope of establishing better rela-tions with England, Keim launched an all-out attack on the government. The Kaiser was infuriated by Keim's criticism of the government, and forced him to resign from the *Flottenverein*. Keim was by no means put off by this sign of imperial dis-favour, but feared that the Kaiser had become the prisoner of blind and incompetent politicians. He then turned his attention to the schools, and came to the conclusion that education was no longer 'German' enough, but had become 'Roman', 'Greek', and even worse, 'humanistic'. This he put down to the evil influence of Erasmus, whom he described as 'Ungerman', 'poisonous', and 'cowardly'.[2] In order to lead German youth back to the paths of nationalistic righteousness, Keim founded the Youth League (*Jungendverband*). A further enterprise was the formation of the *Vaterländischen Schriften-Verband*, a publishing house for nationalist literature which was later to become the propaganda section of the *Wehrverein*.

Keim founded the *Wehrverein* in 1912 in order to back up the demands for an increased army in the estimates for 1912 and 1913. As a master propagandist Keim soon had a large member-ship. He claimed to have some 100,000 members by 1913. The Social Democrats claimed that the membership was only 78,000, but had to admit that there were over 200,000 associate members.[3] Nearly 300,000 members in little over one year was a remarkable achievement. Keim had prepared the ground carefully, and was certain of the support of the Pan-Germans, and therefore of an important section of the press. The Pan-Germans, who had constantly demanded a preventive war, against France in 1905, against France and England in 1911, and against the Triple Entente in 1912, had also for a long time demanded a larger army, and an all-out attack on pacifists and other unpatriotic elements. Furthermore, the Pan-Germans

[1] Lothar Werner, *Der Alldeutsche-Verband 1890–1914* (Berlin, 1935), p. 154.
[2] Generalleutnant A. Keim, *Erlebtes und Erstrebtes* (Hanover, 1925), p. 154.
[3] Kurt Stenkewitz, *Gegen Bajonett und Dividende* (Leipzig, 1960), p. 74.

believed the next war would be decided on land, and were worried that the navy was getting too large at the expense of the army. They therefore demanded vast increases in the size of the army, urged that all those who were passed as militarily fit should in fact serve in the army, and called for far-reaching organizational reforms. All increases in the army brought in by the government were criticized by the Pan-Germans as being insufficient. General von Liebert, who was chairman of the Imperial League against Social Democracy as well as a prominent member of the Pan-German League, criticized the army increases of 1912 as, 'quite unbelievably inadequate'. Keim spoke for the Pan-Germans when he demanded, 'an army so strong and so well organized that in the event of war we shall be able to attack on two fronts'. No wonder that the Bavarian War Minister spoke in despair of the 'stratagems of the Pan-German military fanatics'.[1]

The outspoken activities of the *Wehrverein* led to a number of discussions in the government as to whether or not the *Verein* should be considered a political organization and therefore active officers barred from joining it. A memorandum from the Minister for the Interior, dated 19-3-1912, denied that the *Wehrverein* was a political institution, but added that Keim was very much of a politician, who was certain to do all he could to influence 'the legislature and the administration', and that the *Wehrverein* was determined to press for increases in the size of the army even if the government was not in favour. The War Minister replied that he did not think it wise for the *Wehrverein* to be branded as a political club, for he was anxious that officers should become members, possibly so that they might exercise a moderating influence on its activities and restrain its attacks on the government. At the same time the War Minister found harsh words for Keim who was leading an otherwise praiseworthy institution astray.[2] The War Minister's hopes that the *Wehrverein* might become more moderate if it was given a small measure of official support proved ill-founded. The criticism of the government became sharper after the army estimates for 1912, which the *Wehrverein* regarded as totally inadequate, a fact which led the War Minister seriously to

[1] Werner, *Der Alldeutsche-Verband 1890–1914*, p. 156.
[2] DZA, Potsdam: Reichskanzlei, 2273.

consider declaring the *Verein* a political organization. In a War Ministry memorandum dated 3-12-1912, this view was expressed in outspoken terms.

> Owing to the criticism of the *Wehrverein*, which is wide of the mark, utterly irresponsible and insulting in character, and which at the moment is aimed at measures which His Majesty has approved for the army, it is highly undesirable that active officers should have anything to do with the League in the interests both of the good name of the army and of its inward coherence.

The memorandum suggested that a declaration to this effect should be included in the Kaiser's speech to the commanding generals at the New Year.[1]

A further memorandum of February 1913 from the General War Department of the War Ministry to the War Minister repeated this theme. It suggested that officers should not be allowed to join the *Wehrverein*, for it could no longer be denied that it was mixing in politics and, even worse, was criticizing the policy of H.M. the Kaiser. In his reply the Minister stated that he was prepared to remain neutral towards the *Wehrverein* provided that it did not continue its agitation among officers, inducing them to criticize the government.[2]

In spite of these misgivings the War Ministry saw the *Wehrverein* as a potentially valuable ally. The introduction of the new army estimates in April 1913 helped to ease the strained relations between army and *Wehrverein*. The considerable increases in the army which resulted from the new estimates took much of the fire from the *Wehrverein*. Indeed it thought that the new estimates were the direct result of its own propagandist activities.[3] It was therefore no longer so critical of the government, and thus certain of governmental support.

The establishment of good relations with the *Wehrverein* made the War Ministry all the more determined to keep a closer watch on its activities. Discussions took place between the *Verein* and the ministry, in which the latter made clear its conditions for continued support. In one such debate between Major Deutelmoser, a press attaché of the War Ministry, and representatives of the *Wehrverein*, the major urged the *Verein* to

---

[1] BA Koblenz: HO2-1/22, 386.
[2] Ibid.
[3] Keim, *Erlebtes*, p. 177.

be more moderate in future, otherwise they would merely provide excellent propaganda material to the Social Democrats, Left-liberals, and Centre.[1] More important than the efforts of the War Ministry was the fact that the army increases of 1913 had taken much of the wind out of the *Wehrverein*'s sails, so that its activities were no longer directly critical of the government. The attitude of the army leaders was one of conditional approval, but among regimental officers the *Wehreverein* found many new members. In some regiments the entire officer corps joined it.[2] The *Wehrverein* remained a radical and outspokenly nationalist organization. Its philosophy was simple, and was summed up neatly by Keim: 'Active politics and offensive war have always been, since history began, the safest foundation, and guarantee of success both in politics and in war.'[3]

The activities of the *Kriegerverein* and the *Wehrverein* were incomplete without a militarist youth movement. The state realized the importance of such an organization, the more so since the Social Democrats had achieved considerable success with their youth organizations, the importance of which was constantly stressed by Karl Liebknecht.

In a memorandum of the War Ministry of April 1910 von Heeringen claimed that the existing youth organization, the *Staatliche Jugendpflege*, had failed to achieve adequate results: it was essential for the army that such organizations should give the youth of Germany a proper military background.[4] In January 1911 reform of the youth organization began in Prussia. Committees were formed throughout the country and given generous financial support by the Ministry of Culture. The links with the army were from the beginning very close, for the new plan was based on the recommendations of General von Bissing, a man who had achieved some notoriety for his belief that the army should be used to put down the Social Democrats by force of arms. In the same year General von der Goltz founded the *Jungdeutschlandbund*, a semi-military and nationalist organization, whose main aim was to keep youth out

[1] Heeresarchiv Stuttgart: Denkschriften Sammlung, Band 527.
[2] Stenkewitz, *Gegen Bajonett und Dividende*, p. 74.
[3] Generalmajor Keim in *Der Tag*, 29-10-1912.
[4] Stenkewitz, *Gegen Bajonett und Dividende*, p. 65.

of the hands of the Social Democrats. Goltz enjoyed the favour of the Kaiser in this enterprise and worked closely with the Ministry of Cults (*Kultusministerium*).[1]

Goltz was held in high esteem by the military authorities, and was therefore able to gain the close support of the army for his youth organization. The local groups of the *Jungdeutschlandbund* were thus able to use many of the facilities of the local barracks, such as swimming baths, gymnasiums, and even the barrack square for drill. Members were also allowed to use military trains at reduced fares. They were also given good places at manoeuvres and parades. Further the War Minister wrote to all General Commands that officers and N.C.O.s should be given every possible encouragement to co-operate as volunteers with the work of the *Jungdeutschlandbund*, particularly with their military exercises and war games.[2]

Every year the members of the *Jungdeutschlandbund* took part in military exercises, the *Jungdeutschland-Übungen*. This pre-military training included, 'war games, camp practice, tests of attentiveness etc. in fresh air, first-aid practice and the like under experienced instructors'.[3] The military emphasis of the *Bund* can clearly be seen in the fact that of the 62 officials (*Vertrauensmänner*) of the *Jungdeutschlandbund* 49 were high ranking officers, and the remaining 13 were reserve officers.[4]

The military training of the *Jungdeutschlandbund* was not confined to giving members a rudimentary military training that would ease the work of the army when they were called to the colours. It was also directed against the 'enemy within'. In Meiningen the *Bund* carried out manoeuvres, the object of which was to train members in putting down a revolt by Social Democrats, which it was felt was bound to break out in the event of a European war.[5]

The official journal of the movement, the *Jungdeutschland Post* devoted much of its space to war propaganda. In an article published in January 1913 on the topic of the next war the youthful members of the *Bund* were given a striking example of such dubious material.

[1] Goltz, *Denkwürdigkeiten*, pp. 336–8.

[2] DZA, Merseburg: Rep 77, Tit. 924; Stenkewitz, *Gegen Bajonett und Dividende*, p. 67.

[3] DZA, Merseburg: Rep 77, Tit. 924.

[4] Stenkewitz, *Gegen Bajonett und Dividende*, p. 67.   [5] BA Koblenz: HO2-1/22.

For us as well the great and glorious hour of battle will one day strike. . . . Yes, that will be a great and happy hour, which we all may secretly look forward to . . . quiet and deep in German hearts the joy of war and a longing for it must live, for we have had enough of the enemy, and victory will only be given to a people who go to war with joy in their hearts as if to a feast . . . let us laugh as loud as we can at the old women in men's trousers who are afraid of war and therefore complain that it is ghastly or ugly. No, war is beautiful. Its greatness lifts a man's heart high above earthly things, above the daily round. Such an hour awaits us. We must wait for it with the manly knowledge that when it has struck it will be more beautiful and wonderful to live for ever among the heroes on a war memorial in a church than to die an empty death in bed, nameless . . . let that be heaven for young Germany. Thus we wish to knock at our God's door.[1]

The army and the Civil Service did everything possible to bring all youth organizations under the aegis of the *Jungdeutschlandbund*. By the outbreak of the first World War this policy had been largely successful. Under the *Jungdeutschlandbund* came the *Pfadfinder*, a kind of boy scout movement with pronounced military emphasis, and the *Jugendwehr*, a pre-military organization. Also included were the *Akademische Sportbund*, the *Deutsche Turnerschaft* and the majority of youth sport clubs, the *Flottenverein* and similar organizations with young people among their members, and other institutions such as the *Alt-Wandervogel*, the *Deutsche Stenographen-Bund 'Gabelsberger'* and the *Katholischen Jünglingsvereinigungen Deutschlands*.[2] Only a few youth organizations refused the embrace of the *Jungdeutschlandbund*, often so as to preserve their autonomy, rather than through differences as to the fundamental aims of the movement. By 1914 the *Jungdeutschlandbund* had 750,000 members.[3]

The *Jungdeutschlandbund* enjoyed the unrestricted support of the army and government as well as of the churches. The Minister of Cults was particularly impressed by the military training of young people and stressed its moral and pedagogic worth; his sentiments were endorsed by the Chancellor and the

[1] *Jungdeutschland Post*, 1913, Nr. 4. Quoted Stenkewitz, *Gegen Bajonett und Dividende*, p. 67.

[2] Georges Bourdon, *The German Enigma;* and Stenkewitz, *Gegen Bajonett und Dividende*, p. 69.

[3] Goltz, *Denkwürdigkeiten*, p. 338.

Prussian Minister of the Interior. In a joint note to the Kaiser they wrote, 'The organization lays stress on the military fitness of youth, furthers its physical and spiritual development, and deepens and strengthens its religious convictions.'[1]

Thus it was that the army exercised close control over a large and influential section of German society virtually from the cradle to the grave. The boy would join an organization which came under the *Jungdeutschlandbund*, he would then serve in the regular army for his period of military service, afterwards he was welcomed in the *Kriegerverein*. Such a man was an ideal subject of the Kaiser and a true patriot. Although it was beyond the capacity of even the German army to achieve by those means a full militarization of public life its achievements in this field were quite remarkable. Nearly five million Germans were either directly or indirectly connected with the army. Nevertheless in its principal aim this enormous apparatus failed. Under the stress of war it was incapable of containing the great upsurge of the Social Democratic movement, and even before the outbreak of war the Social Democrats had emerged as the strongest party in the Reich.

[1] DZA, Merseburg: Rep 77, Tit. 924.; Stenkewitz, *Gegen Bajonett und Dividende*, p. 73.

VII

THE ARMY AND
SOCIAL DEMOCRACY

IN spite of the many divisions within the Social Democratic party there was general agreement that the army needed to be reformed. The army was seen to be one of the main pillars of a form of society which the Social Democrats rejected. As Rosa Luxemburg said, 'giving up the struggle against the military system is virtually the same as giving up the struggle against the present order of society'.[1] Militarism, it was argued, was the inevitable result of a capitalist society. 'Militarism is the most concrete and important expression of the capitalist class-state and if we do not fight militarism then our struggle against the capitalist state is nothing but an empty phrase.'[2] Conversely, as Liebknecht declared at the Mannheim party conference in 1906, the best way to fight militarism was to remove its cause by abolishing the capitalist system. 'We have always realized that militarism is a concomitant of capitalism and that there is no better way of fighting militarism than by attacking capitalism.'[3] On the right wing of the party, among the revisionists, the theory of the intimate relations between capitalism and militarism was not so strongly underlined; yet the right agreed that the army had to be reformed, and that it constituted a formidable barrier against the eventual success of even moderate socialist reforms. If the left attacked men like Noske, Schippel, Heine, or Vollmar, it was not so much that there was a radical difference in views on the army question, but rather that the left accused the right of failing to place due emphasis on the importance of the attack on militarism, and of not criticizing the army frequently enough in the Reichstag. Although these

[1] Rosa Luxemburg, *Ausgewählte Reden und Schriften* (Berlin, 1955) ii. 47.
[2] Ibid., ii. 87.
[3] See Karl Liebknecht, *Gesammelte Reden und Schriften*, i. 201 (Berlin, 1958).

differences proved important in the subsequent development of German Social Democracy, at the time they did not seem so fundamental, and at least in the army it was thought that the Social Democrats were, to a man, the sworn enemies of everything which the army held holy.

The principal demand of the Social Democrats was for the abolition of the standing army and its replacement by a People's Army (*Volksheer*). Bebel, one of the most eloquent defenders of the idea of a People's Army, published his thoughts in a pamphlet in 1898.[1] He argued that the only purpose of an army should be to defend a country in the event of a 'frivolous attack', adding that the army should be organized and armed for this contingency alone. This would mean in fact a larger army, but at the same time a cheaper one, and an army 'which in spirit would be far removed from an aggressive and reactionary militarism'. All that would remain of a standing army would be a small cadre of highly trained instructors. Bebel claimed that the army alone had never been sufficient to deal with real crisis situations, and that 'in all the serious catastrophes of the great civilized countries—England, France, the United States and Prussia—it was the fundamental strength of the people, and not the standing army, which saved the country'. In order to go some of the way to meet the inevitable criticisms of the army, he skilfully used arguments from Goltz's book on Léon Gambetta to back up his theory.

A People's Army, formed of virtually everyone over a certain age, could not be used as a weapon against the 'inner enemy', nor could it support a regime with the point of the bayonet. Above all the army could not be misused as a 'school of the nation', forcing an ideology down the throats of helpless recruits, for it would simply consist of armed citizens (*Staatsbürger in Waffen.*)

Among the Social Democrats there were some pacifists, whose pacifism was a protest against the state itself. They argued that there was no valid reason why the workers should risk their lives fighting the wars of the capitalists for new markets and higher profits. The pacifists, however, were a minority, and the Social Democrats generally supported the idea of a militia.

The Social Democrats' attacks on the army met with the

---

[1] August Bebel, *Nicht stehendes Heer!* (Stuttgart, 1898).

resolute opposition of a majority of the *bourgeoisie*. The effect of three successful campaigns, culminating in the unification of the Reich, had immensely increased the prestige of the army, and many an old liberal had long since lost his objections to it in the face of such achievements. The criticism of the Social Democrats coupled with an ever-increasing membership led many to regard the army as a vital defence against the radical demands of an organized proletariat. Equally important was the fact that to many the army opened the door to a successful career. It had achieved such a dominant social position that members of the *bourgeoisie* were bound to strive for some form of military distinction in order to strengthen their social and often also their financial position. In Bebel's words the army had found 'the ground ... on which the absolutist, military, feudally-organized state power could unite and co-operate with the modern *bourgeoisie*'.[1]

The army for its part was determined to lead a war *à outrance* against the Social Democrats. Not only did these people attack the army at every possible occasion and demand far-reaching reforms that threatened the very existence of the army in its present form; even worse they criticized the basis of a society which it was determined to defend at all costs. The army therefore had a double programme. Firstly, to be ready to deal instantly with any revolt from the Social Democrats which in any way threatened the established order, and secondly to convert men, during their period of compulsory military service, into true subjects of His Majesty. The army was to be a bastion against the creeping evils of democracy, materialism, and socialism.

Although the army was determined to combat the increase in the power and influence of the Social Democrats, it was unable to agree on a common programme of action. Some of this confusion can be seen in the letters written by von Deines, a *Flügeladjutant* and intimate of the Kaiser. Von Deines was a firm believer in Stoecker's Christian Social movement, and he hoped that the Kaiser would implement some of the reforms suggested by Stoecker. In a letter he wrote to his father in 1890 he remarked that he hoped that the Kaiser would be able to win the 'good workers' away from the socialists, thereby stopping 'the common

[1] Reinhard Höhn, *Sozialismus und Heer* (Bad Homburg vor der Höhe, 1959), p. 8.

mistaken belief that all factory workers must automatically be socialists'. A fortnight later he wrote in a different tone: 'Universal suffrage will be put down by powder and lead, the only question is when'. Deines added, in the same letter, that the army was longing for the chance to settle its accounts with the workers. Shortly afterwards he wrote again that he was convinced that the only way of controlling the Social Democrats was by a strict censorship of the press.[1] That Deines could change his mind so rapidly within a short time is characteristic of the army's attitude to Social Democracy. None of the methods suggested were in the last resort likely to be successful. A policy of industrial and social reform seemed too radical, and this policy had few supporters after Stoecker's fall from grace. The blood and iron solution appealed to a number of highly placed officers, but was unlikely to win wide support from any but the extreme right-wing parties. Similarly, many had constitutional scruples against enforcing stringent restrictions on the freedom of the press. Meanwhile the number of Social Democrat voters and members continued to increase.

Some agreed with General Beseler that as long as the army remained strong and the German character remained steadfast all was not lost. But Beseler was full of despair at the successes of the 'disgusting socialists'. In 1893 he wrote: 'Where are we going if the common man has absolutely nothing at all which is holy to him, and if the disgusting greed for pleasure and the good life is the only thing which can satisfy mankind? Where is pride in one's work, where loyalty and patriotism?'[2]

The Social Democrats, spurred on by Karl Liebknecht, were determined to counter the influence of 'patriotic' youth organizations with their own youth movement. The Social Democratic youth clubs concentrated on training young men to be able to counter the anti-socialist propaganda to which they would be subjected in lectures and classes when they went into the army.[3] The success of the movement filled the army with alarm. It was a deliberate and dangerous attempt to undermine the discipline of the army, and to render it useless in the

[1] BA Koblenz: Nachlass von Deines, Briefe an den Vater, 1890–92, HO8–32/II. Letters dated 17-2-1890, 4-3-1890, 19-3-1890.

[2] Werner Conze, *Polnische Nation und deutsche Politik im ersten Weltkrieg* (Cologne, 1958), p. 109. (Beseler 16-5-1893.)

[3] See Karl Liebknecht, *Gesammelte Reden*, Vol. I.

event of a left-wing revolt. A pamphlet published in 1895 discussed this problem at length, and expressed the ominous warning: 'If the Social Democratic movement continues to concentrate as much as it has done on the youth of our working-class, who can guarantee that in ten years' time young soldiers will not fraternize with the revolutionaries and hand over their weapons to them?'[1]

Members of the blood and iron school, such as Massow, were becoming increasingly nervous. They feared that the longer they waited the more chances they would be giving to the Social Democrats to strengthen their position within the army, and thus the army might be unreliable if called upon to put down Social Democracy by force. The General Staff began to wonder whether it would not be better to settle accounts with the socialists before it was too late. In a secret memorandum of the General Staff of 28-1-1897 the problem was considered in some detail, and it was mooted whether,

it is not the duty of the country to see that the situation (i.e. the increasing success of the Social Democrats in the army and outside) is countered by the united efforts of the state. If I raise the question of whether, from a military standpoint it is permissible to let the development of this situation run its course, I can only say, in my view, the answer is 'No'. At the moment there can be no doubt that the army is still loyal, but one cannot deny the view that success in the moral sphere is less marked, the brutishness of youth increases, up to 20 per cent. of the reserves in some corps have been previously convicted.

The memorandum also claimed that there were many Social Democrats among the reservists, and that only drastic measures could help to solve the problem.[2]

Most officers, with their essentially Junker ideology, held 'Saint Manchester' responsible for the growth of Social Democracy. Not without reason they pointed out that German industrial expansion induced an increasing number of countrymen to move to the towns, and it was in the towns that the socialists were naturally strongest. Traditionally the army drew its largest number of recruits from the country, claiming that countrymen were physically fitter than town dwellers; but the

[1] C. von Massow, *Reform oder Revolution?* (see *ZfGW*, Heft 6 (1960), 1378–95.)
[2] DZA, Merseburg: Rep 92 Waldersee, B I-22.

12—G.O.C.

real reason was that agricultural workers and craftsmen were less likely to be supporters of the Social Democrats and were used to the semi-feudal conditions on the land. As more and more went to the towns, and as the army expanded in numbers, the army was forced to draw an ever-increasing number of recruits from the towns. This gave the army an opportunity to combine its traditional antipathy towards anything that smacked of trade with jeremiads on the evil influence of industry on the morale and reliability of the army. In 1911, although only 42.5 per cent. of Germany's population lived on the land, 64.15 per cent. of the army recruits came from rural districts. Only some 6 per cent. came from large towns and 7.37 per cent. from middle-sized towns, whereas 22.34 per cent. came from small towns. If town dwellers were denounced as physical weaklings and drunkards, the real reasons were not very carefully disguised.[1]

By 1903 even Waldersee, a prominent exponent of the blood and iron theory, wrote to a friend that it was no longer possible to wipe out the Social Democrats by force. Waldersee had reached the conclusion that the only hope for Germany and the army was a united front of the Catholic and Protestant churches against the socialist menace.[2]

Waldersee's pessimism was not typical of the army. Perhaps it was because he had several times come near to bringing about the day of reckoning with the Social Democrats, only to be called back to order by everyone from the Kaiser downwards, that he no longer believed that the Kaiser and his government had any intention of staging a *coup d'état*. For most of the army the problem was too serious to be handed over to the Churches. The army was the backbone of the nation; with the army Germany stood or fell. The army alone must solve the problem.

In theory the German officer had to remain aloof from politics. In practice this meant that he had to be a faithful conservative, the struggle against social democracy was never considered to be political, but rather as a matter of self-preservation. Major General Paul von Schmidt wrote in 1904, 'the officer must remain loyal to the Kaiser, even when he no longer wears the glorious uniform of his warlord, for this is the

[1] Bernhardi, *Germany and the Next War*, p. 243.
[2] DZA, Merseburg: Rep 92 Waldersee B II-18, Waldersee 20-7-1903.

politics of the Officer Corps. The struggle against revolution is
not politics, for a struggle for our Kaiser and lord is the life-
work of all loyal subjects.'[1]

Although Bismarck's anti-socialist laws had manifestly failed
to achieve their purpose, many officers thought that the only
hope of preserving the political status quo against the Social
Democrats was to re-introduce the laws. Hans von Seeckt as
Chief of Staff of the IIIrd Corps thought that the only hope for
the future lay in a total ban on the Social Democratic party.[2]
The War Minister, von Einem, considered that, although the
army was not yet 'rotten with Marxism',[3] the danger from the
Social Democrats was still very great. 'Against them only a fight
to the finish can be fought.'[4] Major General Keim thought in
similar terms. In an article published in 1905 in the semi-
official journal *Jahrbücher für die deutsche Armee und Marine* he
suggested that a law should be passed forbidding anyone under
the age of 21 from joining any sort of political party or trade
union. He hoped that in this way recruits would be preserved
from the influence of Social Democratic ideas before joining the
army, and that the army would then be able to make them into
loyal subjects of the Kaiser. Keim also suggested, quite rightly,
that the army was at a considerable disadvantage, in that
officers did not have the slightest knowledge of the basic ideas
of Social Democracy, and were extremely badly informed on
developments within the party. He therefore suggested that the
army should provide officers' messes with copies of the most
important Social Democratic papers and journals. This suggestion was dismissed by an official of the War Ministry as
'rubbish'. Keim also suggested that special laws, other than the
ban on party membership for those under 21, should be passed
to restrict the activities of the Social Democrats. The War
Ministry agreed with these suggestions.[5]

Generalleutnant von Liebert, the president of the league
against Social Democracy, brought most of these arguments

[1] Quoted in Emil Obermann, *Soldaten, Bürger, Militaristen* (Stuttgart, 1958),
p. 104.
[2] Seeckt, *Aus meinem Leben*, p. 57.
[3] Von Einem, *Erinnerungen*, p. 166.
[4] Ibid., p. 67.
[5] *Jahrbücher für die deutsche Armee und Marine*, No. 410, Nov. 1905. For marginal
notes see BA Koblenz: HO2-1/21.

together in a pamphlet published in 1906. Liebert stressed the all-important role of the army as the last line of defence against the encroachments of Social Democracy. 'The army is the most powerful barrier against the secret plans of the party leaders.' The socialist demands to reform the army and convert it into a defensive militia had at all costs to be effectively opposed: 'The threat to her frontiers from all sides and the painful and tragic lessons of her thousand-year history should be sufficient proof that only when she has a powerful army capable of attacking can she hope to assert herself.' He further pointed out the dangers of the Social Democratic youth movements, with their emphasis on anti-military propaganda, before the young men were called up. With Bernhardi he stressed the evil influence of the towns, and commented earnestly 'thank God for the country folk!' To excite the wrath of patriotic Germans he reminded his readers how the Social Democrats had referred to the victorious army of 1870–1 as 'bloody villains', '*Landsknechte*' and 'cut-throats'.[1]

The determination to fight Social Democracy was common to officers of all political persuasions. Even von Stosch, who because of his opposition to Bismarck was often considered a liberal, believed that 'powder and lead' was the only possible answer to the increasing influence of Social Democracy.[2] In their struggle the officers were supported throughout by the conservatives. The Social Democrats' demands for promotions according to ability, severe restrictions on the luxurious life in the officers messes, reductions in the amount of time spent in a needless cleaning of equipment, proper controls to stop the appalling number of cases of ill-treatment, the abolition of the use of batmen for officers, and the elevation of medical officers to full officer rank, were all turned down by the combined efforts of the conservatives and the War Ministry. As one prominent conservative put it, 'the accumulation of perfectly natural demands obviously had the tendency to make it seem as if conditions in the army were impossible and unbearable'.[3] In other words, even the minimum demands of the Social

[1] Generalleutnant von Liebert, *Die Entwicklung der Sozialdemokratie und ihr Einfluss auf das deutsche Heer* (Berlin, 1906).

[2] Frederic B. M. Hollyday, *Bismarck's rival, a political biography of General and Admiral Albrecht von Stosch* (Durham, North Carolina, 1960), p. 261.

[3] Graf Westarp, *Konservative Politik*, p. 291.

Democrats for reform of the existing army were opposed as being the thin end of the wedge. The conservatives thought that if they gave way on any of these points a militia would be just round the corner, and the most important pillar of an essentially conservative state would then be removed. Conservatives and Social Democrats had, however, one thing in common, they both talked in terms of a People's Army, the important difference being that the conservatives thought that they already had one, whereas the Social Democrats knew that they did not.

Certain of the fact that the Officer Corps stood solidly behind them and that the conservatives agreed to most of their demands, the War Ministers continued to demand legislation to counter the successes of the Social Democrats within the army. In a memorandum of 1893 the War Minister pointed out that the army did not have adequate legal powers to deal with the activities of Social Democrats. As an example he cited the case of one Sgt. Neumann who on the Kaiser's birthday, a holiday which was reserved for patriotic demonstrations and magnificent parades to show the unquestionable fidelity of the army, had visited an inn where he had not only talked to some workmen but had also sung 'revolutionary' songs with them. In another case, after manoeuvres involving the Landwehr in Frankfurt an der Oder, Social Democratic literature was discovered in the beds of regular soldiers. In both of these cases the War Minister complained that it had proved impossible to take any disciplinary measures. At the present moment, the only way for the army to take steps to prevent soldiers coming into contact with Social Democratic ideas was to issue a specific order forbidding certain actions. Thus it had been possible to give some soldiers in Hanover 14 days' 'close arrest' for attending a Social Democratic meeting, because a regimental order had been issued forbidding soldiers to attend meetings of this sort, and thus disciplinary action could be taken. In a similar case, also in Hanover, a soldier was given the same sentence for saying, 'Long live Social Democracy!' The War Minister pointed out that although it was forbidden by military law for soldiers to attend political meetings, there was no punishment suggested for such activity. The War Minister concluded by saying that sterner measures had to be taken to combat 'the tendency of the Social Democrats to make unequivocal appeals to revolution'.

Both the Kaiser and the Chancellor agreed with the War Minister that more should be done to curb the influence of the Social Democrats. The majority of the ministers at a meeting called to discuss the War Minister's minute agreed that the Kaiser's power of command over the army should be used to punish soldiers who in any way supported, either actively or passively, the Social Democrats. It was agreed that soldiers should thus be ordered not to attend Social Democratic meetings, to sing Social Democratic songs, or distribute Social Democratic literature. Some ministers did not share the general enthusiasm for these measures. The Minister of the Interior had doubts whether, in fact, such measures would really be effective in curbing the activities of the Social Democrats. The Vice-President of the State Ministry thought that the projected measures were too severe. The War Minister had demanded that soldiers be forbidden to attend any meetings or clubs, regardless of whether they were Social Democratic or not; the Vice-President feared that this would be unfair to clubs that had nothing to do with the Social Democrats, and that the soldier would be converted into a mere machine if he had continually to ask permission. In practice, he argued, it would mean that a soldier would even have to ask permission before going to church. To this the War Minister replied that a soldier was more dependent on the views of his officers than a civilian might suppose, and that the Vice-President's fears were therefore not entirely justified. This seems to have settled the matter, and the meeting agreed that the army should use the power of command for a more intensive campaign against the Social Democrats.[1]

Although the War Minister did not achieve his primary aim, a law forbidding any activity of the Social Democrats within the army, he was encouraged by the support he had obtained for his policy of bringing in sterner measures against them. On 1 January 1894 he sent out a letter to all military commanders calling for unified action against the Social Democrats within the limits which had been given him. He proclaimed that, 'any

[1] BA Koblenz: P135-2325, and DZA, Potsdam: Reichsamt des Innern, 15185; Meeting 18-9-1893.

share in clubs, meetings, celebrations or collections for which special permission by superiors had not been given' should be strictly forbidden, for, 'it is obvious that these activities which, by attacking the authority of the state and its representatives, seriously endanger the idea of subordination in the army, must be countered decisively and with the utmost severity, and that all legal weapons must be employed to this end'. In order to avoid any possible criticism, such as that voiced by the Vice-President at the meeting of the State Ministry, he insisted that what might at first sight appear to be a perfectly harmless dance could very well turn out to be a secret socialist meeting.[1]

However, the War Minister was not content merely to take action against soldiers, he wanted powers to enable him to prosecute civilians who encouraged soldiers to have anything to do with the Social Democrats. 'Since . . . the practice of proven revolutionary or Social Democratic ideas is generally considered an offence in the army, in my opinion it is also possible to prosecute any civilians who encourage soldiers to take such illegal action.' The Minister of Justice tried to avoid giving any answer to this request, and clearly did not wish to have anything to do with the War Minister's activities, which were constitutionally somewhat dubious. In point of fact a number of state prosecutors (*Staatsanwälte*) were prepared to co-operate with the War Minister, and prosecuted Social Democrats, who had tried to influence soldiers, on charges of undermining the discipline of the army. An example of this was the case of a worker, Karl Zinne, who, in November 1895, received 6 months' imprisonment for telling recruits that they should 'do their duty for the Social Democrats when they are in the army and spread Social Democratic views among the soldiers'. He was also found guilty of distributing 'revolutionary' literature among the troops.[2] Clearly for the Minister of Justice this was going far enough, and he did not wish to confirm this practice by a law.

Since the army's measures against Social Democracy were not determined by civil laws it was left to individual commanders to publish orders at their discretion. This was not a

[1] BA Koblenz: P135-2325, and DZA, Potsdam: Reichsamt des Innern, 15185; Meeting 18-9-1893.
[2] Ibid.

particularly satisfactory situation, as many soldiers, who were brought before military courts for such breaches of discipline, could successfully plead ignorance of the orders. The War Minister therefore decided to publish the orders in the *Staats-anzeiger* which would give them something approaching the authority of an actual law. After lengthy discussions, during which the War Minister had to accept the criticisms of his colleagues, having tried to make the order as harsh as possible, a final draft was adopted, and published in 1896. Henceforth, no soldier was allowed to attend any sort of meeting without the express permission of an officer; no soldier was allowed to utter any sentiments which might in any way be construed as being Social Democratic in tone, nor was he allowed to sing Social Democratic or revolutionary songs; and no soldier was allowed to possess, or to pass on to another, any form of Social Democratic literature. Perhaps the most obnoxious of all was the provision which stipulated that soldiers were in duty bound to denounce any of their fellow-soldiers if they suspected them of having anything to do with the Social Democrats. In order to make certain that in future soldiers would not be able to plead ignorance of these orders the War Minister insisted that they be printed annually in the *Reichsanzeiger*. The Minister of Justice objected to this, but the War Minister took no notice of his strictures and the orders were in fact printed every year. It was not until 1908 that the then War Minister, von Einem, began to have doubts as to the wisdom of continuing to print the orders, as he felt that they might well be used by the Social Democrats as propaganda against the army.[1]

In June 1913 legal measures against the Social Democrats and the army were again discussed. It was proposed to punish with up to three years' imprisonment 'whoever wilfully tries to undermine military morale and discipline, or influence people against doing their military duties by openly, or in front of a crowd, or any large assembly, insulting or mocking military organizations or military orders, or spreads false rumours about them which are likely to make them contemptible'. It was even considered that a 'private insult' to the army should be prose-cuted, and this was to include remarks made at work, or even at home. The Minister of the Interior, impressed perhaps by the

[1] BA Koblenz: P135-2325.

War Minister's drastic description of the dangers of Social Democracy, agreed that he would co-operate, and mentioned that it might be possible to push a law quickly through parliament if needed. But he made his support dependent on the War Minister bringing concrete proofs forward that the army really was endangered by the activities of the Social Democrats, and that the military security of the Reich could not be guaranteed without such measures. This proof was, predictably, not forthcoming, and once again the War Minister failed to obtain specific laws enabling him to hit back at the Social Democrats.[1]

Deprived of the legal backing it had hoped for, the army laid great stress on the closest possible co-operation with the police, so that it would be well informed on any Social Democratic activity. On 20-3-1890 the War Ministry issued an order to all Commanding Generals instructing them to keep a close watch on the Social Democrats in their respective areas, and urging the closest possible co-operation with the local police so that speedy action could be taken in the event of a revolt, or should war break out, to stop any Social Democratic efforts to hinder mobilization. The order was repeated in the next month with particular reference to possible disturbances on the 1 May.[2] The army also required the police to inform them of any recruits who were members of the Social Democratic Party, but this proved to be an almost impossible task. On 19-7-1905 the Bavarian Ministry of the Interior wrote to the Bavarian War Ministry that they could only keep a check on people who played a leading part in the party.[3] Since the Social Democrats behaved in an exemplary fashion whilst in the army the civil police were not particularly interested in spending a great deal of time and energy hunting for suspected Social Democrats, and such reports to the army diminished in number as time went on. However, such reports did continue to be sent in; for example in Essen the Landwehr inspection reported to the area commander in Düsseldorf that the police had discovered that six men who were candidates for promotion to be N.C.O.s were party members. Although the men were refused promotion the writer of the report did not believe that, in the event of

[1] BA Koblenz: HO2-1/22.
[2] Bayr. HSA, Abt. IV, KA, Alt Reg. 18, Band I.
[3] Ibid.

war, there would be a mass desertion of Social Democratic sympathizers, as many officers feared.[1]

Faced with the growing reluctance of the police to co-operate in the witch-hunt against the Social Democrats the army called upon the local corps commanders to send in yearly reports on the progress of Social Democracy. These reports were mostly hair-raising diatribes on the imminent danger of revolution and civil war, which only served to raise the passions of the military authorities and were not capable of giving them an objective picture of the true aims and policies of the Social Democrats. A quotation from one such report gives an adequate picture of the general tone. In December 1912 the report of the VIth Corps said that: 'The Social Democrats have an unscrupulous and demagogic press and purposefully use terror', and demanded 'legal rights in peace time to take severe action against the treacherous activities of their inflammatory press'.[2] The tone of such reports goes some way to explain why the War Ministers constantly demanded increased powers against the Social Democrats. They implicitly believed all that was reported to them from the corps, and regarded any civilians who did not share these drastic views as simply misinformed as to the real nature of Social Democratic activity.

Control of soldiers attending Social Democratic meetings proved difficult, and again the police were reluctant to co-operate too closely with the army. At first the army demanded the right to appoint special military patrols to control Social Democratic meetings. This was clearly an encroachment on the rights of the police, and was flatly turned down by the civil authorities.[3] As a compromise solution the police agreed to try to check the number of soldiers at such meetings, and to report their names and numbers to their regiments.[4] The problem of stopping soldiers who were on leave from attending these meetings proved even more difficult. On 2-4-1913 the Governor of the Residence in Berlin wrote to the War Minister that there were far too many reports of soldiers attending Social Democratic meetings, and that regimental commanders should in future warn their soldiers not to go to such meetings when on

---

[1] BA Koblenz: HO2-1/22.   [2] Ibid.
[3] Staatsarchiv Ludwigsburg: E150-1186.
[4] Ibid.

leave.[1] The War Ministry took prompt action, and circulated a note throughout the army that steps should be taken to warn the soldiers properly not to attend such meetings.[2] In the same year the War Ministry found it necessary to repeat the prohibition of attendance at Social Democratic functions.[3]

The army was highly alarmed at the idea that Social Democrats might become N.C.O.s in the army, and thus gain a position of authority which they might very well use to win supporters for the movement. On 5-3-1896 the War Minister issued an order that 'people who are known for their Social Democratic views before being called up may in no circumstances be promoted during their regular service'. The Minister insisted that this must remain an iron rule, as no matter how well a man behaved during his time of service, and regardless of the fact that he might be an exemplary soldier and born leader, it should never be forgotten that the Social Democrats were anxious to avoid trouble in the army and therefore expressly told members to do their utmost during their military service. The army could not tolerate potential traitors in positions of authority.[4]

The same principle also applied to volunteers. These volunteers enjoyed the privilege of a short term of service and also, because they were selected according to their intelligence, stood far better chances of promotion when they joined the reserve after their term of service. On 19-9-1894 the War Minister issued an order that no Social Democrat was to be allowed to serve as a volunteer, and that checks should be made where possible to ensure that no Social Democrat had slipped into the volunteer army.[5] As far as the military authorities could find out no known Social Democrat was ever allowed the privilege of serving as a volunteer. Proof of allegiance to Social Democracy was often somewhat slender. In one case a young man was turned down because he had been seen reading the Social Democratic paper *Schwäbische Volkszeitung*. This case caused a public uproar, but the army stood solidly behind the sergeant who had turned down the young man's application.[6] The army

[1] BA Koblenz: HO2-1/22.
[2] Bayr. HSA, Abt. IV, KA, M.Kr.2466.
[3] BA Koblenz: HO2-1/22.
[4] Bayr. HSA, Abt. IV, KA, M.Kr.2283.
[5] Ibid., Abt. IV, KA, M.Kr.2466. [6] Ibid., Alt Reg. 18, Band I.

was unable to refuse a man the right to serve as a volunteer on the specific grounds that he was sympathetic to the aims and views of the Social Democrats, for this was constitutionally inadmissible and would have certainly led to a scandal. The established formula was therefore to turn down a man on the grounds that he lacked 'moral qualities', a favoured phrase which was also used in the case of Jews who applied for commissions, and which did not even disguise the real motive.[1]

Equally the army tried to prevent any Social Democratic sympathizer from being promoted in the reserve. In 1904 the War Minister cited the example of a man who had served a 9-months' prison sentence for '*lèse-majesté*', and had subsequently been promoted to the rank of sergeant in the reserve where he had used his position to try to win fresh voters for the Social Democrats. The man had, in fact, been on the staff of a socialist newspaper. The Minister used the case as a warning that every possible precaution must be taken to stop the promotion of Social Democrats, even in the reserve.[2]

The army also kept a tight control on Social Democratic literature, and any soldier found in possession of such material was severely punished. This rule also applied to recruits or men coming back from leave whose mothers, without stopping to think, had wrapped up sandwiches in a local Social Democratic paper; if this was discovered on his return to the barracks it could lead to harsh measures being taken against him.[3] Once again the legal position of the army was not clearly defined, and frequently roundabout methods had to be used. Thus on 12 December 1912 the Minister of the Interior wrote to the War Minister that anarchists and socialists were about to launch an onslaught of propaganda leaflets; 'in view of the confidential nature of this information I would ask you, so far as official measures, such as legal confiscation etc., are not concerned, to be discreet about it'.[4] The Minister of the Interior's readiness to back up the War Minister in his efforts against the Social Democrats, was heartily endorsed by the Prussian Police President, Jagow, who constantly agitated for greater powers to enable the police to take more drastic measures against anti-

---

[1] Staatsarchiv Ludwigsburg: E150-1186.
[2] Bayr. HSA, Abt. IV, KA, M.Kr.2283.
[3] BA Koblenz: HO2-1/22.   [4] Ibid.

military literature.[1] The army was never granted any further legal weapons with which to beat the Social Democrats, and had to use more subtle and indirect ways of curbing the flow of anti-military literature into the army. Thus, in one typical case, a trainee teacher, one Falkner, nearly lost his job at the instigation of the War Ministry, which accused him of having given an 'unpatriotic' book to an N.C.O. Falkner concocted an ingenious tale to show that the book only landed in the N.C.O.'s hands by pure chance, and the educational authorities were prepared to accept his version of the story.[2]

In order to increase the effectiveness of the army's policy of weaning recruits away from Social Democracy the War Minister decided, in an order of 21-4-1890, that henceforth recruits who were known to sympathize with the Social Democrats were to be posted away from areas where the Social Democrats were particularly strong. This meant in practice that recruits from industrial areas tended to be posted to garrisons in small country towns. Similarly in 1894 the War Minister ordered that no known Social Democrat should be allowed to serve with the guards. The *élite* of the German army had to be preserved from the infiltration of treasonable ideas.[3]

The 1896 order had successfully enabled the army to take stern measures against soldiers who attended meetings without permission from an officer, although the effectiveness of the measure was diminished owing to the difficulties of exercising adequate controls. The military were, however, not content to rest there. They were particularly alarmed by the possibility that soldiers might come into contact with Social Democrats in inns during their time off duty. The army therefore put out of bounds to soldiers any inn which was under the slightest suspicion of having Social Democrats among the guests. Such measures were often arbitrary and could cause considerable hardship to landlords who depended on the custom of soldiers. Particularly at election times, when excitement was high and the bar-room politicians at their most vociferous, a chance remark by a guest could bring severe financial losses down on the head of an unsuspecting landlord. Protests were frequent,

[1] BA Koblenz: HO2-1/22, folio 221.
[2] Bayr. HSA, Abt. IV, KA, Alt Reg. 18.
[3] Ibid., Pr. KM, 13-4-1894.

but the army, hand in hand with the civilian authorities, remained adamant. In 1900 the *Schwäbische Tagwacht* printed an article claiming that such measures were a violation of the constitutionally guaranteed 'right of assembly'. The paper was promptly sued by two civil servants, and obliged to pay a fine of 150 marks on the grounds that it was purely a matter of military discipline.[1] The army's attempts to bring direct political pressure to bear on the landlords was naturally enough resented, but mainly for economic rather than political motives. In Saxony, it was agreed in 1904 that inns, which were suspected of being the meeting places of Social Democrats, should only be placed out of bounds to military personnel on days when an actual political meeting was held. In Prussia, however, the old methods remained in force. It was not until 1905 when the *Deutsche Gastwirtverband*, the professional organization of the landlords, protested to the War Minister that many of their members were losing a considerable amount of business owing to the arbitrary intervention of the military authorities, that the War Minister agreed to make some concessions. Shortly afterwards, the Minister wrote to the general commands that care should be taken to check closely whether, in each individual case, it was really necessary to place an inn out-of-bounds.[2] This was but a small concession, and the practice of placing inns out-of-bounds at the slightest excuse remained in force. Thus, when the band-masters of the IVth army corps arranged to have a meeting at the *Blauer Elefant* in Magdeburg, in March 1913, this had to be cancelled as the War Minister personally intervened on the grounds that the inn was frequented by Social Democrats.[3] Whether the Minister feared that the band-masters would return to teach their bands to play the Internationale is not recorded.

If the army was determined to place its anathema on inns which showed the slightest signs of harbouring Social Democrats among their clienteles, even stronger was its determination to sever links between the army and organizations which were in any way connected with the Social Democratic movement. One such example is that of the co-operative shops (*Konsum-*

[1] *Schwäbische Tagwacht*, 14-11-1900 and Staatsarchiv Ludwigsburg: E150-1219.
[2] Bayr. HSA, Abt. IV, KA, Alt Reg. 18.
[3] Ibid., KA, M.Kr.2285, Pr. KM, 14-3-1913

vereine). Owing to their low prices and system of dividends these shops were particularly favoured by soldiers, whose pay was not generous enough to allow them to ignore a good offer. In 1914 soldiers were forbidden to use these shops:

According to official information these co-operatives are in many ways closely connected with the Social Democratic Party, therefore, according to existing law and military orders, it is not permissible for members of the regular army, so far as they belong to the peace-footing, to be members of this organization.[1]

Sometimes the army's zealous hunt for Social Democrats caused direct violations of the law. In 1895 the Bavarian War Minister had to warn the Bavarian army that it was not permissible to open soldiers' letters in order to see whether or not they sympathized with the Social Democrats.[2]

The army was not content with defensive measures against the Social Democrats and, wherever possible went over to the offensive by playing a vital role as a strike-breaker and taking steps against even the slightest suspicion of an armed revolt. From the point of view of the army these measures worked well and, as far as strike-breaking was concerned, there was the closest possible co-operation between civilian and military authorities. In all recorded cases of the army being called in to break a strike the formula was similar. The civil administration in the area in which a strike was threatened, or had actually broken out, wrote to the army authorities, usually to the local corps commander, asking for military support. This was almost automatically granted. The army was only too anxious to prove the loyalty of the troops in what seemed to many a hot-headed officer to be a dress rehearsal for the inevitable armed clash with Social Democracy. The usual ground given for calling in the troops was not to force the workers back to work at the point of the bayonet but to give adequate protection to plant and equipment against possible sabotage by the strikers. But the psychological effect was well calculated to persuade all but the hardiest to return to work.

The ultimate decision as to whether the troops should be called in to intervene in a civil strife rested with the Kaiser, but the army could be certain of his support. In August 1890

[1] Bayr. HSA, Abt. IV, KA, M.Kr.2284, Pr. KM, 1-5-1914.
[2] Ibid., KA, Alt Reg. 18, Band I, KBKM, 8-11-1895.

William II ordered an infantry brigade of the IIIrd Army Corps to Berlin to threaten the Social Democrats who were meeting in the capital, without informing the Chancellor, or the War Minister, or the Chief of the Civil Cabinet.[1] Moreover, in his more expansive moments, the Kaiser was all too prone to underline in dramatic terms his wish to use force against the Social Democrats. Thus his remark to Bülow in 1905: 'First shoot, behead and get rid of the Social Democrats, by a bloodbath if need be, and then fight a war outside. But not beforehand and not a tempo.'[2]

Much of what the Kaiser said was mere bluff, but the tone which he set had a profound effect on the army. The cases of army commanders urging restraint on the use of troops against strikers were rare indeed. General Albedyll, who commanded the VIIth Army Corps in Münster, wrote to the Kaiser in 1891 that he did not think the troops should be called in against the Westphalian miners who were on strike unless all other methods failed. Although he managed on this occasion to convince the Kaiser, some eighteen months later he alerted the troops under his command on the direct orders of the Kaiser.[3]

Once the army was called in by the civilian authorities, usually by the local district officer (*Kreisdirektor*), they had to ask for the permission of the Kaiser and of the War Ministry before they could actually take any action.[4] This permission was in practice given almost automatically, and the only recorded case where the demands of the civil authorities were not met was that of Albedyll; he had to persuade the Kaiser not to intervene, and his objections were not so much caused by any objections to using the army against strikers, but rather because this interfered with the army's training programme.

The strikes in the slump years of 1889 and 1890 provide examples of the army's role as a strike-breaker in the pre-war years. At the first sign, or even rumour, of a strike the army was at once alerted. Once the strike broke out the troops were called in, but the strikers were usually so well disciplined that incidents were very rare, and in the majority of cases the troops

[1] Schmidt-Bückeburg, *Das Militärkabinett*, p. 189.
[2] Bülow, *Denkwürdigkeiten*, ii. 198.
[3] BA Koblenz: HO2-1/20, 154.
[4] Von Einem, *Erinnerungen*, p. 166.

returned to barracks having merely stood idly by. But the phantom of a Social Democratic revolt, or of workers running amuck, remained with the army; although, as the years went by, it became increasingly obvious that this was highly unlikely to happen, the army continued to alert troops at the slightest provocation.[1]

The army did not confine its activities merely to standing by, waiting for the moment when it could put its bayonets to good use. During the strike at the Berlin electricity works of A.E.G. in 1905, the Commanding General wrote to the Kaiser demanding that troops be sent to the factory, although there had been no trouble at all. Among the troops sent were armed soldiers of the Railway Brigade and the Guard Pioneers who were to work in the factory; but by the time the troops arrived the workers had already returned to work.[2]

Every year there were similar incidents, but it was only occasionally that force was used, such as during the Mansfeld miners' strike of 1909 and the Ruhr miners' strike of 1912. Although highly placed officers called for armed action against any strike, the army was on the whole reluctant to shoot first. They knew perfectly well that whenever the army resorted to force this merely weakened the reputation of the army among many civilians otherwise sympathetic to it, and strengthened the class-consciousness of the workers.[3]

Since the army was quite often called in to assist in putting down a strike a number of different plans were produced in an attempt to find a more effective way of dealing with them. In 1889 Albedyll, the general in command of the VIIth Corps, suggested that, since the use of ordinary units for strike-breaking seriously hindered training programmes, special units should be created within the army to deal specifically with strikes. Albedyll suggested a programme of training with practice alarms and special tactics to deal with riots. Although both the Kaiser and the Military Cabinet agreed with these proposals nothing in fact came of them.[4] It may have been that once the wave of strikes had subsided after the slump of 1889 to 1890 it

---

[1] BA Koblenz: HO2-1/20–25.   [2] Ibid.
[3] Dieter Fricke, *ZfGW* Heft 6 (1958) 1298–1310, and *Hamburger Nachrichten*, 4-1-1906.
[4] BA Koblenz: HO2-1/20, 92.

13—G.O.C.

was no longer thought necessary to keep special units throughout the Reich on constant alert, or possibly political considerations may have played a part in that the army feared that such
units would merely provide valuable propaganda material to
the Social Democrats. In June 1894 the question was again
raised, but again nothing came of it.[1]

Once these proposals had been dropped the army had no
unified programme for putting down strikes or revolts, so that
individual commanders were left very much to their own
resources. Many commanders were somewhat impetuous in
their attitude to any possible unrest and issued orders that the
army should resort to force at the first signs of unrest. Although
these orders were well known to the highest ranking officers in
the Reich there is no recorded evidence to suggest that they
called for somewhat less drastic action, preferring to leave the
local commanders the power of final decision. Mercifully none
of the more drastic orders were ever brought into effect, but it is
significant that no one saw fit to urge restraint over the wilder
plans.

An example of such an order is that of the Supreme Commander in Brandenburg, dated 19-1-1906. The Social Democrats had announced their intention to organize demonstrations in favour of the reform of Prussian electoral law, which
was carefully designed to keep the Social Democrats out of the
Diet, on what became to be known as 'Red Sunday'. The army
immediately feared that the demonstrations would end with
the erection of barricades in the streets. The order read: 'If
barricades are built they are to be bombarded with grenades
before they are stormed by the infantry.'[2] Once again the
demonstrations passed without an incident, and such draconic
measures were never needed.

The most notorious of these orders was that of the Commanding General of the VIIth Army Corps, Freiherr von
Bissing, issued on 30-4-1907. Three years later the order landed
in the hands of the Social Democrats, who were able to use it to
support their arguments against the projected increases in the
army which were debated in the Reichstag in the following year,
thus causing the army considerable embarrassment. Bissing's

---

[1] BA Koblenz: HO2-1/20–159.
[2] Dieter Fricke, *ZfGW* Heft 6 (1958) 1298–1310.

order dealt with the action his corps should take in the event of 'troubles in the interior', and urged that the severest possible measures should be taken. He did not think that the army should wait until shots had been fired from the other side, but rather that at the first signs of civil unrest the army should at once use force:

> There must be absolutely no doubt about the fact that even in the event of passive resistance the necessary result will be the use of weapons . . . if it is necessary to use rifles even against an unarmed crowd, it is quite unnecessary first of all to send warning shots over their heads. It is far better to show the rebels straight away one's determination to strangle all revolutionary attempts from the outset.

The army's distrust of the civilian authorities and its conviction that they were too feeble-minded are eloquently shown in the order: 'It has always proved disastrous to declare a state of siege too late, and to make the military commander responsible to a higher, or equally ranking civilian authority.' Developing this theme Bissing showed that the army had scant respect for constitutionally guaranteed liberties.

> The first measures which must be taken, at the same time as the state of siege is proclaimed, are the suppression of all papers which follow the revolutionary line, and the arrest of their editors, along with all persons known to be leaders and agitators, without taking any notice of the immunity of the Reichstag members. In any case those arrested must be handed over to the military authorities who must immediately take them to a safe place . . . under no circumstances may higher or lower commanders begin negotiations with the revolutionaries. There can be only one condition—unconditional surrender. All ringleaders or whoever is caught with a weapon in his possession are to be executed. The full severity of the law is to be applied mercilessly.[1]

Bissing's order was by no means the work of an isolated individual of particularly radical views, but was based on an official publication of the General Staff of 1907, *Fighting in Insurgent Towns*. The General Staff had taken the Russian revolution of 1905 as a timely warning that a similar revolt might occur in Germany, and the Historical Section of the General Staff was instructed to examine revolts, such as the

---

[1] DZA, Potsdam: Reichskanzlei 1271 (47–50) full text in Dieter Fricke, *ZfGW*, Heft 6 (1958) 1298–1310.

Paris Commune and the revolts of 1848, in the hope that suitable lessons could be drawn from these examples as to how a revolution could best be put down by the army. The conclusions of the study were pessimistic. The General Staff feared that over the years the working class had become increasingly dangerous. The working class, it was argued, was much better organized than it had been, it was better financed and could rely on the support of sympathizers abroad. It was particularly dangerous that workers had been trained and disciplined during their period of military service and were thus well prepared to fight in a revolution. In the light of these prognostications the General Staff decided that the only hope of dealing with a revolt was to go straight over to the attack. Artillery was to be used against barricades, as all other methods had proved worthless in the past. The army was determined to have a free hand against any revolt, and to be free from any interference by civilians. In order to avoid the possibility of such interference the army decided that the government should be evacuated as soon as possible: 'A government which is acting with the memory of such terrible scenes fresh in its mind is liable to influence the military commanders to make concessions or to negotiate.' The fear that officers might be tempted to reach a compromise agreement with the revolutionaries led the General Staff to insist that 'the senior commander must make it his fundamental principle to impress upon his subordinate officers that they may not start negotiations with the revolutionaries'. As in the Bissing order, the General Staff also declared that 'the immunity of the Reichstag members is no longer to be respected'. In the copy of the work in the Württemberg War Ministry this sentence is carefully crossed out in red ink, suggesting that at least in some quarters there were doubts as to the legality of such an order.[1]

The extreme nervousness of the army, fearing that at any moment a revolution might break out, was often shared by civil ministries. Thus in September 1906 the Ministry of the Interior sent a leaflet entitled *Tactics and Fortifications for Revolutions* to the War Ministry as virtual proof that a revolt was about to break out. The leaflet was the work of an extreme

[1] Heeresarchiv Stuttgart: Württ. KM Persönliche Angelegenheiten der Württ. Kriegsminister, Band 19.

anarchist group and gave somewhat muddle-headed advice as to how barricades should be built. The fact that such a leaflet was treated with deadly seriousness by the highest authorities is eloquent proof of the deep-rooted fear that revolution was always near at hand.[1]

The army's campaigns against the Social Democrats met with some criticism within the army itself. The too frequent reiteration, of the theme that the country stood on the brink of revolution, coupled with the fact that the revolution showed no evident sign of actually breaking out, led many to adopt a somewhat sceptical attitude towards the diatribes of the higher authorities of the Reich. Since the Social Democrats laid great stress on the fact that their members should behave in an exemplary fashion during their period of service many officers admired the military qualities of their Social Democratic soldiers, and were prepared to turn a blind eye to their political beliefs. Furthermore, the whole system of controlling the political opinions of soldiers and their activities outside the barracks proved singularly inefficient. Nor was it possible for the police to give sufficient information as to the number of Social Democrats among the new recruits. An example of the growing impatience with these methods can be seen in a report of the General Command of the Ist Bavarian Army Corps to the Bavarian War Minister of 1905. The report insisted that the practice of making yearly reports on the progress of Social Democracy within the army was a pure waste of time. Although it was evident that the Social Democratic party was gaining new members at a remarkably high rate, the number of Social Democrats within the army was dropping according to military reports. This discrepancy was proof of the inefficiency of the methods used by the army, and the writer doubted whether a better method was possible. The reports were based on highly dubious material, in that soldiers were often falsely accused of being Social Democrats, and conversely many Social Democrats had successfully managed to cover up their traces. The report closed with the observation that, since the Social Democrats on the whole behaved well in the army, there was no real justification for such practices.[2]

[1] BA Koblenz: HO2-1/21.
[2] Bayr. HSA, Abt. IV, KA, Alt Reg. 18.

With the mounting criticism and the lack of any significant success, the army tended to pay less attention to the policy of active restrictions on the political activities of soldiers, and tried to win them away from Social Democracy by a programme of political education. It was hoped that carefully prepared lectures would make soldiers see the errors and dangers of socialism and democracy and would leave the army as faithful subjects of the Kaiser and stalwart supporters of the established order.

One of the principal weapons in the army's fight against Social Democracy was the Christian religion. Religion was traditionally believed to be an essential part of army discipline, and officers were expected to be seen in the front pews of the garrison church. An officer, it was felt, had a duty to be religious, for religion was considered the basis of all honour and morality. Furthermore a belief in the after-life was a comforting stimulant to heroic deeds on the battle field.[1] Conversely many Social Democrats, including Bebel, were atheists, and on the left of the party religion was dismissed as a cunning instrument of class oppression. This fact helped to convince the army that one of the most effective antidotes to socialism was the Church.

This liaison between throne and altar against the dark forces of the revolution was a favourite theme of William II, and the topic of characteristic pronouncements. The Kaiser demanded, 'Christian soldiers who say the Lord's Prayer . . . no blasphemers'.[2] Convinced that he himself was part of God's order he thought the same of the army. Just as the throne, 'is nothing without altar and crucifix, so is the army nothing at all without the Christian religion'.[3] A soldier who was not a Christian was, in the Kaiser's eyes, worthless: 'Whoever is not a Christian is not an upright man and is not a Prussian soldier and under no circumstances can he do what is asked of a soldier.'[4] On another occasion he returned to this theme. 'Whoever among my soldiers thinks nothing of religion and of God is no good. He is without honour, and is not worthy of wearing my uniform! . . . only he who trusts implicitly in his God can be a real soldier.'[5] Young recruits were called upon to join in the crusade

---

[1] See von Schaible, *Standes und Berufspflichten des deutschen Offiziers* (Berlin, 1891).

[2] Kaiser Wilhelm II, *Rekrutenvereidigung*, 16-11-1893 in, R. Höhn, *Die Armee als Erziehungsschule der Nation* (Bad Herzburg, 1963), p. 189.

[3] Ibid., 12-11-1896.   [4] Ibid., p. 189, 18-11-1896.

[5] Ibid., p. 189, 10-11-1909.

against materialism and atheism: 'Never forget that you are obliged to defend order and religion in the country.'[1] The Kaiser was quite clear as to who was the real enemy of his devout army which he called 'into battle for religion, morals and order, against the revolutionary parties'.[2] To recruits he spoke in the same vein: 'Just as I as Kaiser and Monarch do everything for the Fatherland, you are duty bound to devote your entire lives to me, for you have given your oath as Christians and the two servants of God have spoken to you in the Christian manner.'[3]

Similarly the evangelical Chaplain General (*Feldprobst*) of the Prussian army called upon all army chaplains to co-operate in the fight against socialism, pointing out, in a memorandum of 18-9-1890, the opportunity which the army had to reform the wayward.[4] He had no doubts as to the dangers of Social Democracy. In the future socialist state, he claimed, 'there is no room for the King by the Grace of God, for the authorities as representatives of God or for sovereign power which acts in the name of God'. He agreed with the army that it was the army alone which stood between order and morality and the revolutionary hordes. 'This revolutionary power would like, above all, to overthrow the army, since the army is based on the very foundations of human order: the fear of God, loyalty to the King and obedience.' It was the duty of the chaplains to do everything in their power to warn soldiers of the errors of Social Democracy and to lead back any lost sheep into the fold of the established order. The army was not without its own powerful ideology which was as capable of inspiring men as any idea that the Social Democrats might concoct: 'The army places the individual in the service of an idea which inwardly inspires his whole being, patriotism: "With God for Kaiser and Fatherland".' The Chaplain General, carried away perhaps by these lofty sentiments, went on to claim that the army was essentially a socialist society, that was therefore easy to defend against the onslaughts of the Social Democrats: 'The social gap between

[1] Kaiser Wilhelm II, *Rekrutenvereidigung*, 16-11-1893 in, R. Höhn, *Die Armee als Erziehungsschule der Nation* (Bad Herzburg, 1963), p. 189, 15-11-1894.

[2] Wilhelm II, *Rede beim Festmahl für die Vertreter der Provinz Ostpreussen*, 6-9-1984, ibid., p. 189.

[3] Ibid., p. 189, 5-3-1895.

[4] Dieter Fricke in *ZfGW* Heft 6 (1960) 1378–95.

rich and poor which, in its gaping width, is one of the main sources of the present socialist agitation, does not exist in our army, in which everyone who serves is judged and accepted purely according to his worth and achievements.' He closed with the popular notion that God was on the side of the Prussian army, and would not fail to support it in the fight against the Social Democrats. 'The army is the finest institution of the earthly kingdom and God Almighty will help it to become the nursery of the Kingdom of God.'

This exalted view of the army as a band of self-effacing Christian soldiers living in a state of uncorrupted socialism and fighting the good fight for God and morality proved somewhat tricky to uphold. Great was the alarm when Field Marshal Moltke's *Trostgedanken* were published posthumously in 1892. Saint Moltke, as Engels called him, was always regarded as the paradigm of the Prussian soldier, a man whose military qualities rested on the firm foundation of a devout Christian soul. The *Trostgedanken* showed that he was in fact, in matters of religion at least, a sensitive rational deist in the fashion of the 18th century, who looked upon the Evangelical Church with critical scepticism.[1] Such was Moltke's prestige that the Church did not dare to lead a frontal attack against these heresies, but pastors spoke of their sadness and pain that such a great man had not found the way to bliss in the bosom of the Evangelical Church.

The fact that the army's greatest man had turned out to be a deist did not augur well for the project of converting soldiers away from socialism by means of the Christian religion. In 1899 a book appeared which examined in some detail the religious beliefs of the Officer Corps.[2] The author did not believe that the army could be treated as the pillar of a Christian society. He felt that the older officers were deists in the Moltke fashion, and that the younger officers were little concerned with religion and were on the whole what he described as 'materialists'. For these reasons he did not believe that religion could be used effectively as a method of combating Social Democracy in the army, for only a small minority of the officers were

[1] Höhn, *Die Armee als Erziehungsschule der Nation*, p. 209.
[2] Oberstleutnant Ulrich von Hassel, *Christentum und Heer* (1899); see also Höhn, pp. 214 ff.

sincere Christians; in any case officers and men hardly ever came together outside duty hours, so that the men were unlikely to be influenced by their officers' religious beliefs.

The attitude of the majority of officers in matters of religion did not qualify them to play a particularly active part in converting the Social Democratic soldiers to the search for Eternal Truth. The chaplains, although they ranked as officers and could therefore use the officers' mess, had little influence over the religious beliefs of the officers. In the mess there was a strict rule that religious matters were not to be discussed, and only the most devout Christians among the officers were prepared to discuss religious matters with the chaplains in their free time. Thus the chaplains were left very much on their own, and had to rely almost exclusively on the weekly sermon as a means of political and religious education.

In their sermons the chaplains were severely restricted. If they hinted at the sins of officers and N.C.O.s this was at once regarded as an attempt to undermine military discipline. A chaplain wrote in a magazine for the evangelical chaplains in the army, in 1908, that it was not possible 'to prick the consciences of the officers and N.C.O.s who attend the services so far as their treatment of subordinates is concerned; whoever did that would soon have preached his last sermon in the army'.[1] Great tact was needed to avoid saying anything that might be considered to weaken the position of officers and N.C.O.s in the eyes of the soldiers. Thus the chaplains concentrated on rousing patriotic sermons, which revealed that God was on the side of Germany and the German army and that even the humble private soldier played his part in the army of God, fighting for freedom, justice, peace, and the German cause. An example of such heart-rending pathos is taken from a sermon given in 1904.

The German army is God's tool which has made the German people great once more, and brought honour to it. The generation still lives which saw with its own eyes how the Almighty took the scales and said of our hereditary enemy: thou art weighed in the balance, and art found wanting. The German sword is still an important weight in the scales of world history.[2]

---

[1] Höhn, *Die Armee als Erziehungsschule der Nation*, p. 222.
[2] Ibid., p. 232.

Examples of army sermons show the way in which the chaplains used every opportunity to support the government against
any criticism from the Social Democrats. God was, for the
chaplains, a loyal German and His voice spoke forth in favour
of a larger army and navy, thundered against the pacifists and
the hopeless utopists who dreamed of eternal peace. He was
also on the side of His representative on earth, the Kaiser,
particularly in times of trial, and His support for German
foreign policy was unconditional. In this activity the chaplains
were following the express instructions of the Kaiser himself. In
Strasburg in 1899, the Kaiser called upon the chaplains to
co-operate with him and his government in the struggle against
his political enemies.

Above all I should like to impress upon the worthy gentlemen of the
church, who have such a great influence on our people, that they
must work with all the strength at their disposal to ensure that
respect for the Throne, and trust in the Government becomes
stronger and stronger, for in the tempestuous time in which we live,
when the spirit of atheism rides abroad, the only protection the
church has is the hand of the Kaiser and the Coat of Arms of the
German Empire.[1]

Apart from the sermons, which cannot have had any significant effect in changing the political views of the soldiers, the
greatest opportunity the chaplains had of influencing soldiers
was in the preparation for the Oath to the Flag (*Fahneneid*). The
Fahneneid was regarded as one of the most important steps in a
soldier's training. It not only marked the end of a recruit's
period of basic training, but even more important it was an
outward and visible sign of the inward and spiritual trinity of
throne, altar, and sword. Hardly a year went by in which the
Kaiser did not visit the ceremony of the swearing-in of the
troops, usually in Potsdam or Berlin, but sometimes further
afield. It is at these ceremonies that some of his most famous
and characteristic remarks were made, many of which caused
political scandals. The oath was considered to bind a soldier for
the rest of his life to be the faithful subject of His Majesty. Since
the Social Democrats were not faithful subjects it was felt that
the *Fahneneid* was an effective method of ensuring that soldiers

---

[1] Kaiser Wilhelm II, Strasburg 5-9-1899, in Höhn, *Die Armee als Erziehungsschule
der Nation*, p. 239.

did not fall into their hands. As one chaplain put it: 'You will be asked about your oath to the flag on God's day of Judgment, see to it that a broken oath does not rob you of eternal bliss'.[1] Another opportunity for the chaplains to influence the politics of the soldiers was the *Kasernen-Abendstunden*. The War Ministry had ordered in 1856 that from time to time an hour or two should be reserved in the evenings when the chaplains could give religious instruction to the soldiers. Attendance at these meetings should be voluntary. But religion soon gave way to politics, and once again soldiers were treated to their chaplain's patriotic rhetoric. In a projected programme for such a meeting a military chaplain suggested the following headings for a lecture on the role of the Hohenzollern in German history.

The influence of the Hohenzollern on building the character and spirit of our people. Training for freedom and self-sufficiency, saving their subjects from the excessive power of the robber barons, towns, clergy, and aristocracy. Abolition of thraldom, serfdom, labour services and bondage. Granting a constitution, the imperial constitution. This was largely the work, labour and the gift of the Hohenzollern. Examples of real passion for duty, their feeling for truth and justice, German approach (*wesen*), their domestic bliss which was cultivated and fostered by the Hohenzollern and their wives and through them has become the common inheritance of our people, who are duty bound to be grateful.[2]

The chaplains soon found out that use of the evening meetings could work both ways. Soldiers who sympathized with the Social Democrats had the unfortunate habit of asking them awkward questions, and most chaplains whose political ideas did not go much beyond a few well-worn slogans soon found themselves defeated in political arguments. Some chaplains argued that they should make a close study of social and political conditions, and read at least one Social Democratic paper, so that they could reply to such questions. Others, influenced by the fact that the Church did not favour the active participation of pastors in politics, thought that the chaplains should refrain from such activities altogether.

In Bavaria, where the majority of soldiers were Catholics,

---

[1] Höhn, *Die Armee als Erziehungsschule der Nation*, p. 242.
[2] Höhn, ibid., p. 262.

there was no organized Chaplain's Corps. There were in fact only nine military chaplains in the entire Bavarian army, for the rest the duties of chaplain were performed by the local priests. The military chaplains merely acted as advisers and co-ordinators to the priests in the various garrisons.[1] Indeed the army resented the interference of the clergy with military affairs and turned down the suggestion of the Archbishop of Munich that a proper chaplains corps be founded in the Bavarian army, as local priests were overworked.

Similarly, in Württemberg the army gave financial support to priests in garrison towns, and allowed soldiers free time to go to church.[2] The fact that in Bavaria and Württemberg the work of army chaplains was done by local priests led the military writer, Colonel Gädke, to suggest that the chaplains corps be abolished in the Prussian army, as in peace-time the institution was a mere waste of public money.[3]

Although the army continued to make an ostentatious display of the links between the army and the Church with church parades, *Fahneneid*, and patriotic sermons, the policy failed in its essential purpose of enforcing moral and political orthodoxy among the soldiers. Little or nothing was done to convert the heathen or strengthen the faith of the wavering; indeed, the chaplains' policies were well calculated to turn people away from the Church and to strengthen the arguments of the Social Democrats that the Church was misusing its power and acting as a heavy-handed advertising agency for the established reactionary order.

Similar to the use of religion for political purposes within the army was the use of 'heroic' history to inspire loyalty to the house of Hohenzollern and to the destiny of the German Reich. Indeed history and religion were closely intermingled. William II would speak of God as 'the old ally of Rossbach and Dennewitz', and liked to insist that the course of German history was the steady revelation of divine favour. The Kaiser's cult of his grandfather, William I, is a case in point. William II thought of his grandfather as a more suitable hero for his people than Frederick the Great, since he had been an orthodox Christian,

---

[1] Höhn, *Die Armee als Erziehungsschule der Nation*, p. 254.
[2] *Berliner Tageblatt*, 29-12-1909.
[3] Ibid.

and he began to refer to him as the 'Heroic Kaiser' or the 'hero of victory surrounded with a halo'.

The cabinet order of 13-2-1890 stressed the importance of officers knowing their history and of teaching it to their soldiers as a means of patriotic education. The order was discussed in the *Militär-Wochenblatt* the following week in an article which stressed the importance of the teaching of history in the army, both militarily and politically. 'This unparalleled history must be made available to the people and made their common inheritance. The army, which is the nation in arms, is the ideal medium for this purpose.'[1]

The Kaiser had begun his campaign for 'patriotic' history the year before when he called upon the schools to pay more attention to history as an effective weapon to combat the Social Democrats. This had been welcomed in the army, but very soon it began to criticize the schools for failing in their duty in this respect, thus leaving to the army the brunt of the work as a school of the nation. This criticism was voiced in a regimental history of the Ist Guards Regiment: 'The schools' specific duty to act as a preparation for the army by teaching patriotism through knowledge of history, &c., and to inspire the soldierly virtues of obedience, courage, and a sense of duty, was either not fulfilled or only insufficiently.'[2]

Although the army was not tired of blaming the schools for failing to teach history effectively it did little better itself. The 'patriotic history teaching' was usually left to the younger lieutenants, who were singularly ill-equipped to undertake it. Things were not made easier by the fact that there were very few text-books available, and those in circulation were of a very poor quality. The most important text-book on the subject did not see fit even to mention the names of Scharnhorst or Stein, and Gneisenau was merely described as an assistant of Blücher's. The whole problem of pre-March liberalism was omitted, and in general the book was highly selective.[3] The army was thus ill-equipped to deal with the Social Democrats in the field of history, the more so since the Social Democrats were particu-

---

[1] *Militär Wochenblatt*, Nr. 16, 22-2-1890.

[2] *Geschichte des Königlich-Preussischen Ersten Garde-Regiments zu Fuss 1871–1914* (Berlin, 1933), p. 66.

[3] Lehmann und Von Estorff, *Dienstunterricht des Offiziers* (1909); see also Höhn, *Die Armee als Erziehungsschule der Nation*, pp. 321 ff.

176   THE ARMY AND SOCIAL DEMOCRACY

larly interested in Scharnhorst and Gneisenau, whom they regarded as examples of a progressive element within the army, and whose work could be used as a starting point for future reforms.

In an attempt to strengthen the patriotic campaign against the Social Democrats the army produced a number of newspapers for the men's reading rooms with articles designed to rouse their patriotic feelings. In the words of one such paper, 'understanding for the past, contentment with the present, and unshakeable confidence in the future of our German Fatherland, under the victorious leadership of its Monarch, is to be spread, and the troops are to be made more resilient, even after they have left the army, against erroneous teaching'.[1]

Two of these papers, *Nach dem Dienst* and the *Soldaten Hort*, were published by the War Ministry. A third paper was added later, *Der Soldaten Freund*, which was bought from a private publishing house. As a rule about 150 copies of each of these papers were sent to the general commands, and these copies were then distributed among the various units. No political papers whatsoever were allowed in the men's reading rooms; the only papers allowed were the *Allgemeine Zeitung*, a paper which specialized in rousing tales of the heroic deeds of the Hohenzollern, the Catholic *Sonntagszeitung*, and the military paper the *Militär-Wochenblatt*. The Prussian War Ministry also advised the various armies of the Reich as to which books were suitable for use in the soldiers' reading rooms, and recommended 'safe' booksellers. The only thing which was not provided was sufficient funds to buy more than a few books. The publishers, however, saw a chance here to increase the sales of their books, and various units were flooded with samples of patriotic literature and prayer books, in the hope that they might be ordered for the reading rooms.[2]

Soldiers found little incentive to read these papers and books, for they were hardly the sort of reading material most suited to arouse the interest of a soldier in his leisure hours. Moreover, even if the soldiers actually bothered to read any of these publications it is doubtful whether the constant reiteration of the

[1] Programme of *Nach dem Dienst*, in Höhn, *Die Armee als Erziehungsschule der Nation*, p. 331.
[2] Heeresarchiv Stuttgart: WKM, AApA (A), Band 601 and 670.

theme that everything was for the best in the best of possible worlds was likely to win over a potential Social Democrat.[1] Once again the army failed to find an effective ideological alternative to Social Democracy.

The army was greatly alarmed by the steady migration from the country into the towns, which naturally followed on Germany's increasing industrialization. The army resolved to do all it could to stop this tendency. The method chosen was to give soldiers training in agricultural skills, in the hope that they might become so interested that they would wish to work on the land on leaving the army.

Agricultural instruction usually took place on Saturday afternoons and lasted for some $1\frac{1}{2}$ hours. In some regiments, in order to keep up flagging enthusiasm, competitions were organized in ploughing, mowing, or milking. The Prussian War Minister required annual reports on progress throughout the Reich in accordance with the 'guiding principles for the experimental introduction of agricultural instruction in the army (1908)'.

The practice of giving soldiers lectures in agriculture soon became the topic of debate. Major Brandenburg, who was the chief theoretical spokesman of the movement, wrote in the *Deutsche Tageszeitung* that: 'only by preserving and strengthening the rural population can the German Reich maintain its position, therefore everything must be done to make agricultural instruction, which is concerned with this problem, a permanent and obligatory feature in the army'.[2] The Bavarian Ministry of the Interior agreed, and thought that it was possible 'by lectures on general agricultural topics to preserve interest and love for the home soil among those soldiers among us who come from the country, and to prevent them giving up jobs in agriculture on leaving the army'.[3] This enthusiasm was shared by other ministries, but the farmers' organizations were not impressed. The Farmers' League (*Bauernbund*) thought it would be better if the soldiers played football on Saturday afternoons rather than wasting their time playing farmers. The Agricultural Council of the Wiesbaden area announced that it did not think

[1] *Berliner Tageblatt*, 3-10-1907.
[2] Quoted in *Bayerische Staatszeitung*, 20-11-1913.
[3] Memo Bayr. Staatsministerium des Innern, 7-11-1913 Bayr. HSA, Abt. IV, KA, M.Kr.2327.

that the lessons would do much good.[1] The *Bayerische Landeszeitung*, the mouthpiece of the Bavarian farmers, considered the lessons useless: the army had more than enough to do without trying to turn out first-class farm labourers as well as highly trained soldiers.[2]

The army was on the whole pleased with the results of this agricultural instruction, but even within the army criticism was voiced. In Bavaria the corps commanders, in their reports for 1908 on the progress of agricultural lessons, were unanimously critical. Among the reports the IInd Corps feared that some of the instructors might very well be 'enemies of the state or of the army', and the IIIrd Corps thought that party political questions might well arise.[3] Once the novelty of the experiment wore off soldiers tended to regard the whole thing as an additional burden. Soldiers from the land regarded the whole idea as a joke, and referred to their instructors as spreaders of artificial manure (*Kunstdünger*). The farmers were not won over to the idea that the 'People's university of the nation' should include agriculture in its curriculum, the more so as the cost of the lectures, and even the heating and light used in the lecture rooms, was borne by the local agricultural councils.

The most important attempt by the army to cure soldiers of Social Democracy was also its most spectacular failure. It was expected of officers to bring up social and political questions during instruction periods (*Dienstunterricht*) and to convince soldiers of the advantages of the existing order. This did not mean that soldiers were allowed to ask questions on political matters, for this was thought to be bad for discipline and would place the men on the same level as their officers.

This system had its passionate defenders. The *Jahrbücher für die deutsche Armee und Marine* in 1905 said that all officers should be politically engaged, for, 'this sort of preparation for war is just as important as weapon training'. General von Eichhorn, Commanding General of the XVIIIth Army Corps, was even more emphatic. 'I must stress that the officer today has a political duty to train his subordinates to be loyal citizens and to stand up against the pernicious influence of Social Demo-

[1] *Bayerische Staatszeitung*, 20-11-1913.
[2] *Bayerische Landeszeitung*, 12-2-1913.
[3] Bayr. HSA, Abt. IV, KA, M.Kr.2327.

cracy. The disease is still superficial, and the period of service must act as a healing spring which will wash away the disease.'[1] Eichhorn suggested that the advantages of the existing system should be carefully explained, with emphasis on social legislation, particularly for invalids and the sick. This suggestion, which was widely published in the military press, was regarded by many officers as the thin end of the wedge, for it was bound to lead to discussions in which the well-trained Social Democrats would be at an advantage. Once again the cry was raised that the army should remain unpolitical.

The reason behind the distrust of Eichhorn's suggestions was that the officers were singularly ill-equipped to provide adequate lectures on social and political affairs. Since most officers did not even know the outline of the constitution, and the Supreme Warlord boasted that he had never read it, it is hardly surprising that lessons in civic studies (*Staatsbürgerkunde*) were usually rather poor. Officers, who came almost exclusively from the landed gentry and the upper *bourgeoisie*, had no idea of industrial conditions, and were therefore incapable of discussing the social problems of many of their soldiers. Efforts to improve relations between officers and men were thought of as concealed attempts to undermine military discipline. Any suggestions by more imaginative officers that they should keep in close touch with the realities of the industrial world by visiting factories, examining the living conditions of the working class, or by discussions with the workers themselves, were inevitably turned down. Any attempt at an intelligent appraisal of the real issues involved behind the rise of Social Democracy was too radical, for it meant an opening up and in some sense a liberalization of the attitude and even of the structure of the officer caste.[2] A discussion with the proletariat would, in the army's eyes, lead automatically to a loss of status and prestige.

The ideology of a sophisticated political party could not be fought with the crude weapons used by the army, and difficulties with the discussions of political issues in the army steadily increased. The army, aware of the demands of modern technical warfare, wanted soldiers to be able to think for them-

[1] Eichhorn memo, 19-9-1905, printed in Demeter, *Das deutsche Offizierkorps*, p. 291.
[2] See the works of Hauptmann Preuss; Höhn, *Die Armee als Erziehungsschule der Nation*, p. 392.

14—G.O.C.

selves, but in the political sense this could only lead to disaster, for the army was unable to counter the carefully posed questions that inevitably arose in lectures of this nature.

The army was therefore obliged to admit defeat. In the Cabinet Order of 3-1-1907 the Kaiser ordered that henceforth social and political questions were not allowed in the instruction periods. Although officers were still allowed to attack the 'Social Democratic Movement which is against Monarchy, state and religion', general problems of wages, living conditions, social legislation, and the like were no longer to be discussed. The cabinet order was regarded as so important that the War Minister, von Einem, sent an order to all units giving the text of the order; this was repeated three months later.[1]

Since political lectures were no longer allowed in the old form, the army relied more and more on appeals to the heart. Emphasis was laid on the brotherhood in arms, and the popular notion that since all soldiers, officers and men alike, wore the same uniform, they were all equals. In line with this new sentimental approach was an increasing emphasis on patriotic songs. Soldiers were called upon to bawl in unison songs such as *Als die Preussen marschierten vor Prag, O Strasburg, O Strasburg,* and *Das Volk steht auf, ein Sturm bricht los.* Unfortunately, most of the texts for these songs had been rewritten by the Social Democrats, so many mouthed the patriotic versions but thought of 'revolution'.[2]

The army began to lose heart. The whole idea of 'the school of the nation' had failed to bring any results, and increasingly lost supporters. The belief was gaining ground that the only hope was to put down Social Democracy by force of arms, and to many this seemed to be the most important task of the army. 'Let revolution shake its fist at throne and altar, the German knights assembled round their holy standard, armed with the holy power of God, will be ready with sharpened sword and shining buckler to fight victoriously with God for Kaiser and Reich.'[3] Others, outraged by the fact that Social Democrats were sitting in the Reichstag and even held positions on

---

[1] Bayr. HSA, Abt. IV, KA, M.Kr.2327.

[2] Höhn, *Die Armee als Erziehungsschule der Nation,* p. 437.

[3] *Jahrbücher für die deutsche Armee und Marine 1899;* Höhn, *Die Armee als Erziehungsschule der Nation,* p. 389.

parliamentary committees, despaired of the future of the Reich. The army having failed, they were not slow to find potential scapegoats. It was all the fault of the Reichstag, for tolerating Social Democrats in positions of authority, or of the schools for not giving children an adequate patriotic education, or of the employers for their greed and cupidity—in any case the army had done its best and could not be blamed.

The root cause of the army's failure to combat Social Democracy effectively was the political structure of the Officer Corps. The officer stood in a direct relationship with the Kaiser, and owed no allegiance to the people as such, nor to its representatives in the Reichstag. His power was based on his position within a hierarchical system; discipline and unconditional obedience were his greatest virtues. Isolated from the majority of his countrymen by the traditions of the officer caste, he was unable to appreciate the real issues that were at stake. Least of all could he understand the motive force behind Social Democracy, which stood for all that was most foreign to him: Equality, reason, the abolition of privilege and class. The officer's opposition to socialism was understandable, but it was also blind and uninformed. The attempt to destroy Social Democracy within the army was therefore doomed to failure; and the fact that many officers realized this goes much of the way to explain the violence, the rancour, and frustration of the Officer Corps in the face of a movement which they could not halt. In one particular field the army found it extremely difficult to counter the attacks of the Social Democrats who emerged as the champions of the ill-treated soldiers. Constantly attacked in the Reichstag, or at political meetings, the army was in a weak position to hit back, for even the officially printed statistics of ill-treatment and suicides gave an alarming picture of abused authority. Moreover, the more soldiers were ill-treated the more they turned to the Social Democrats for help, for the army's system for handling complaints was quite inadequate. Some officers realized that the ill-treatment of soldiers did nothing but harm the army in the eyes of the country at large, and helped to drive soldiers into the arms of the Social Democrats, but by no means all officers shared their view that drastic measures should be taken to cut back the number of cases of ill-treatment. For many these cases were all part of the natural order of things, and a change could only be for the worse. In the official history of the 1st Regiment of Foot Guards this theme is treated in some detail.

People who were hostile to the army often used the question of ill-treatment of soldiers as an excuse for agitation. It is well known that ill-treatment occurred. Temperament, attitude of mind and authority over subordinates lead all too easily to it . . . but it must also be stressed that the stubbornness or cussedness of a subordinate can drive an N.C.O. to the limits of his patience, and N.C.O.s were not little weaklings who were prepared to accept this sort of thing.[1]

In a similar way the appallingly high suicide rate in the army could be dismissed as the result of 'a wounded sense of honour or fear of dishonour'.[2]

Fortunately this attitude was not the sole one, and some responsible officers were deeply concerned with the problem. In an edict of 8-6-1891 Prince George of Saxony tackled the problem of ill-treatment, and spoke of 'an extremely reprehensible situation . . . refined tortures . . . the result of brutality and demoralization'.[3] General von Loë wrote that: 'Ill-treatment of the soldiers by N.C.O.s is a cancerous growth within the army'.[4]

The problem of suicides was directly linked with that of ill-treatment. Statistics published in the *Militär Wochenblatt* gave an alarming picture of the high suicide rate.

Between 1876 and 1890 the yearly average of suicides in the Prussian army alone was 216. By way of comparison the paper published figures for the British army where the average number of suicides during the same period was 12. Even taking into account the fact that the British army was considerably smaller the difference was remarkable. From 1890 to 1895 the average for Prussia was 200, and the paper suggested that since this meant a decline there was no immediate cause for alarm.[5] In Württemberg, according to the official statistics of the War Ministry, there was an average of 18 suicides per year between 1897 and 1911.[6]

---

[1] *Geschichte des Königlich Ersten Garde-Regiments zu Fuss 1871–1914*, p. 73.
[2] Höhn, *Sozialismus und Heer*, ii. 249.
[3] Karl Liebknecht, *Gesammelte Reden*, (Berlin, 1958) i. 314.
[4] Leopold von Schlözer. *Generalfeldmarschall Freiherr von Loë* (Berlin, 1914), p. 184.
[5] *Militär-Wochenblatt*, No. 9, 29-1-1896.
[6] Heeresarchiv Stuttgart: Denkschriften Sammlung, Band 452.

On an average there were approximately 14 times more suicides in the army than among civilians.[1]

It was not possible for the army to deny these facts, and week
by week a watchful opposition collected fresh material with
which to attack the army. The complacency of the War Minister
von Kaltenborn, who announced in the Reichstag on 13 March
1891 that as far as ill-treatment was concerned there was really
nothing to get worked up about, became a thing of the past, at
least in official circles.[2] On 17-9-1892 William II issued an order
to the Commanding Generals pointing out that, although the
number of cases of ill-treatment had been reduced, there were
still too many. He called upon all officers to exercise a stricter
supervision of the N.C.O.s, to set a better example and to take
swift action when a case of ill-treatment came to light. He
added that any offenders would be severely punished.[3] In
general this order had little effect, and the punishments of
N.C.O.s who had ill-treated soldiers remained comparatively
mild. On 30-7-1910 the Bavarian War Minister sent out a
sharply worded note accusing officers of not taking adequate
steps to stop ill-treatment and of failing to set a good example
to the N.C.O.s. 'The damage caused by blunders, hot-headed-
ness and lack of understanding in the training and treatment
of soldiers is so fundamental that an officer must take this into
account.'[4] This general warning was followed on 20-7-1912 by
a warning to ensigns. 'The repeated instances of irregular
treatment and ill-treatment of subordinates by ensigns have
caused me to beg commanders to pay close attention to the
training of these young men.'[5] Almost certainly as a result of
the wide publicity afforded to the Rosa Luxemburg trial, which
was due to begin, the Prussian War Minister, von Falkenhayn,
sent out an order on ill-treatment of soldiers on 28-5-1914. He
pointed out that the large number of cases of ill-treatment in
the army had caused a considerable sensation among civilians,
that this was quite understandable, and had severely damaged
the reputation of the army. He called upon military courts to
impose stricter sentences, for they had often been far too

[1] Dieter Fricke, *Militarismus und Klerus. ZfGW*, Heft 6 (1960) 1378–95.
[2] *Steno. Bericht*, 13-3-91.
[3] Demeter, *Das Deutsche Offizierkorps*, p. 297.
[4] Bayr. HA, Abt. IV, KA, M.Kr.1711.   [5] Ibid., M.Kr.2031.

lenient in cases where no permanent bodily harm had been inflicted. This leniency was unjustified, and served to damage the reputation of military justice.[1]

Certainly sentences were mild. One N.C.O. convicted for 100 cases of ill-treatment was given nine months' imprisonment; another who had tortured a recruit, who later died as a result, got one year. An N.C.O. guilty of 145 cases of ill-treatment got 18 months, another guilty of 280 cases 9 months; another received 15 months for 600 cases, and finally an N.C.O. guilty of 229 cases of ill-treatment was punished with a mere 2 months' imprisonment. The number of cases of ill-treatment was equally alarming. In Prussia an average of 800 cases per year was brought before the courts.[2] In Württemberg there were 3,247 cases between 1902 and 1913.[3] Since it was extremely difficult for a soldier to bring a complaint against his N.C.O. for ill-treatment it can safely be assumed that the actual number of cases was considerably higher than the number which reached the courts.

The problem of the ill-treatment of soldiers was illuminated in the trials of Rosa Luxemburg. Although she was found guilty the trials led to the severe humiliation of the War Minister, and this directly through the question of ill-treatment. On 26-9-1913 in Bockenheim near Frankfurt-am-Main, Rosa Luxemburg addressed a meeting and in the course of her speech said: 'If we are called upon to use these murderous weapons against the French or any other of our brothers then we will cry: "We will not do it!"'[4] For this remark Rosa Luxemburg was tried on 20-2-1914, was found guilty of inciting soldiers to disobey orders, and was sentenced to one year's imprisonment.

Since the verdict had to be confirmed by the Reichsgericht she was set free until that court had done so. Rosa Luxemburg wasted no time in continuing her attacks on the army, and this time tackled the specific problem of ill-treatment. In a speech on 7-3-1914 in Freiburg she mentioned a recent incident in

---

[1] Demeter, *Das deutsche Offizierkorps*, p. 296.

[2] Dieter Fricke, *Militarismus und Klerus*. *ZfGW*, Heft 6 (1960), 1378-95; *Frankfurter Zeitung*, 5-9-1908.

[3] Heeresarchiv Stuttgart: Denkschriften Sammlung, Band 384, memo. WKM 1913.

[4] *Leipziger Volkszeitung*, 21-2-14.

Metz where a soldier was found dead having been beaten up by an N.C.O.; the authorities were unable to decide whether he had committed suicide as a result of this ill-treatment, or whether he had died as a result of the ill-treatment and his head had then been placed in a noose by his torturer so as to simulate a suicide. She added: 'It is certainly one of the countless dramas which occur day by day in German barracks, and the groans of the tortured only seldom reach our ears.'[1] As a result of this remark the Prussian War Minister von Falkenhayn demanded that a charge be brought against her.

Before the trial started the Social Democratic press called for witnesses to prove the high incidence of ill-treatment in the army. Within a few days 922 men came forward declaring themselves ready to stand in the witness box, and daily further candidates wrote in.

The trial began on 29-6-1914. On the second day witnesses began to give painful accounts of ill-treatment in the army. Faced with the possibility of nearly one thousand witnesses coming forward with examples of ill-treatment the War Minister wanted to stop the case as quickly as possible. On the third day the State Prosecutor (*Staatsanwalt*) demanded that the case be adjourned since the War Minister had not yet been able to examine the cases which the defence intended to use. In a telegram to the State Prosecutor he said, 'although I cannot see any reason for hearing the evidence unless it is confined to recent events and to the so-called "barrack dramas", I should like to have the one-sided statements of the defence witnesses checked; on the other hand proceedings should be taken under military law, so long as they are not subject to the statute of limitations.'[2] The defence protested violently against adjournment:

It is precisely the handling of cases of ill-treatment by the courts martial which should be illuminated by the defendant here in a civil court, yet the War Minister wants the exact reverse, namely that the witnesses who are to give evidence in a civil court on ill-treatment should be called to account before courts martial.[3]

The efforts of the defence to stop an adjournment were without success, and the case was adjourned, never to be taken up

[1] *Volkswacht Freiburg (Breisgau)*, 9-3-14.
[2] *Vorwärts*, 4-7-14.   [3] Ibid.

again. On 22 October the verdict of the first trial was confirmed by the Reichsgericht.

Although the War Minister had managed to avoid too many witnesses appearing in a civil court and giving wide publicity to cases of ill-treatment in the army, and although Rosa Luxemburg was well out of the way as far as he was concerned, the case was a severe set-back for him. A large section of the press, in no way sympathetic to the ideas of Rosa Luxemburg, criticized the War Minister for his inept handling of the case. To those who could remember the speech of Falkenhayn in the Reichstag in May, admitting the high number of cases of ill-treatment in the army, and pledging that he would do everything to try to stop them, the whole affair made the minister appear a hypocrite. Many of those who were heartily glad to see Rosa Luxemburg locked away had to admit that she had bravely stood out against a well-known abuse, openly admitted by the military authorities, but about which very little had been done.

VIII

THE ZABERN AFFAIR

IN spite of the many cultural and linguistic links between Alsace-Lorraine and Germany the annexation of the area after the Franco-Prussian war met with the resolute opposition of a large majority of the population. The decisive date in the history of the relations between Alsace-Lorraine and Germany was 1789. Until the time of the French Revolution the links between Alsace-Lorraine and France had been neither strong nor heart-felt, but the revolution was met with tremendous enthusiasm in the area. The abolition of the old trade barriers bound the economy closely to that of France, and a protective barrier was erected against Germany. The abolition of seigneurial rights weakened the position of German aristocrats who still held lands in Alsace-Lorraine. The rise and fall of the Napoleonic empire forged a close link between the soldiers of Alsace-Lorraine and those of France. Symbolically it was in Strasburg that the 'Marseillaise' was composed and first sung.

The freedoms won in the revolution, in spite of many setbacks in subsequent years, convinced the inhabitants that their future lay with France, rather than with a politically backward Germany. The fact that, in spite of the centralizing forces of France, Alsace-Lorraine had preserved a German dialect and many essentially German customs convinced the Germans that they would greet the annexation of 1871 with cries of joy. When it became painfully obvious that exactly the reverse was true bitter disappointment turned to rancour. It was argued that the inhabitants of Alsace-Lorraine had been drugged by the dangerous opiate of the French Revolution into denying their real selves. They must be forced to be free, to be German. Thus Heinrich von Treitschke,

these lands are ours by right of the sword, and we wish to govern them in accordance with a higher right, the right of the German nation, which cannot allow its lost sons to remain for ever separated from the German Reich. We Germans, who know Germany and France, know better what is good for the Alsatians, than those unfortunates themselves who, due to their degeneration under the French, remain alien to the new Germany. We want to force them against their will to find themselves again.[1]

The policy of *Germanisierung* had begun.

The united front against the annexation soon began to weaken. At first the abrupt severing of the economic links with France had cut back profits, but soon profitable new links were forged with Germany and industrialists and merchants enjoyed a period of industrial expansion. The ore mining and smelting industries profited considerably with the expansion of German heavy industry. As the bulk of trade moved from West to East, so did the sympathies of many among the ruling classes. Instead of hatred and antipathy a new creed of 'realism' was preached, which reflected the view that as annexation had to be accepted, the most that could be hoped for was moderate reform. On the other hand, the increasing industrialization of the area caused a large number of workers from other parts of the Reich to settle there, and they tended to sympathize with indigent workers in their more radical demands and with their struggle against Prussianism.

The attitude of the Reich government towards Alsace-Lorraine changed, though at a snail's pace, with this weakening of antagonism in the upper echelons of society in the *Reichsland*. At first the area was controlled by a *General-gouvernement*, then by an *Oberpräsident* directly responsible to the Kaiser. In 1874 the affairs of the *Reichsland* were placed under the control of the Reichstag and the Bundesrat with a *Statthalter* at the head of the administration. In May 1911 the *Reichsland* was granted its own constitution and a two-chamber parliament. These concessions were in fact minimal, and direct control from the Reich remained, even if in a changed form. Thus although the second chamber with sixty members was elected by universal male suffrage and by secret ballot, every projected law had to be ratified by the upper chamber: of its 41 members 18 members were directly nominated by the Kaiser, 5 sat automatically by virtue of their official positions, and the rest were appointed by

[1] Treitschke, *Aufsätze, Reden und Briefe* (Meersburg, 1929), Vol. 3, p. 454.

a complex system from various bodies and institutions. As an extra guarantee all laws had to be ratified by the Kaiser. As far as basic freedoms were concerned, such as free speech, freedom of the press, and of assembly, there were severe restrictions, and it was not until 1908 that these prescriptions were ameliorated to the extent that they were now in accordance with the laws applying in the rest of the Reich. However, even this concession was constantly attacked by many in the Reich, from the Kaiser downwards, as a severe danger to national security.

The higher ranks of the administration, with very few exceptions, were in the hands of Prussians, many of them with a military background. But an even more significant cause of bad feeling was the large number of military personnel in the area. As hostile feelings between France and Germany intensified, the army tended increasingly to regard Alsace-Lorraine as being virtually enemy territory, as a spring-board for an eventual war and, owing to the hostile attitude of the population, as a danger point in the defences of the Reich. Thus in 1905, for every 100 inhabitants of the Reich there were 1·1 soldiers, in Alsace-Lorraine however the figure was 4·47. In the Reich for every 45 male inhabitants there was 1 soldier, but in Alsace-Lorraine there was 1 soldier for every 11 males.[1]

The large number of soldiers in the *Reichsland* was not in itself the sole reason for mounting antagonism. The arrogant attitude of the military was offensive, and since they were the flag-bearers of the policy of Germanization they were not trusted. Their frequent parades and festivals, particularly the *Sedan Tag*, wounded local pride and patriotism. Manoeuvres caused a considerable amount of damage and financial hardship, particularly in the country districts and compensation for damage caused during manoeuvres was often paid as a form of subsidy to pro-German elements. The constant attempts of the military to gain direct effective control over the area led to continuous strife with the members of the emergent local administration.

As Sedan retreated into the past and the population enjoyed a moderate degree of economic prosperity the German authorities had an increasingly good chance of winning over the people. In spite of official half-heartedness and often even ill-will, this

[1] Stenkewitz, *Gegen Bajonett und Dividende*, p. 130, footnote 284.

might have been possible, at least to a limited extent, had it not been for the direct interference of the army, which constantly attacked reforms promoted by the civil administration as endangering the security of the Reich. The culmination of the army's influence in the development of relationships between Germany and the newly annexed territories was the tragicomedy of Zabern.

Part of the army's scheme to gain absolute control over the *Reichsland* was to demand an all-out attack on the clubs and societies which flourished there. Thus on 3-2-91 the War Minister wrote to the *Statthalter* demanding that any meetings which had the slightest suspicion of being sympathetic to France should be closed down.[1] In September he wrote again complaining that he had had no reply. He added that the Catholic Church was a particular danger in that it remained largely faithful to France, and demanded further restrictions on the travel of Frenchmen into the area. This time Hohenlohe, the *Statthalter*, replied promptly. Although he may have been impressed by the War Minister's threat to report the whole matter directly to the Kaiser, where he almost certainly would have found an appreciative audience, he was none the less not particularly impressed by the call for a *Kulturkampf* or for draconic measures against the clubs. He pointed out that the military authorities tended to exaggerate the dangers of the situation in Alsace-Lorraine, and added that to forbid French officers to visit their families in the area would cause quite unjustified hardship. The Chancellor, Caprivi, agreed with Hohenlohe, and added that as about one third of the applications for passes were turned down anyway, further restrictions would be too harsh. Faced with the combined opposition of the Chancellor and the *Statthalter* the War Minister was forced to climb down.[2]

The problem of passes for Frenchmen to visit Alsace and Lorraine caused endless difficulties between France and Germany. In general it was the army, supported by the Kaiser, which demanded a high degree of restriction; whereas the civil administration, and particularly the diplomats, favoured a more liberal attitude. On 1-3-98 the Kaiser, acting on the specific

[1] DZA, Potsdam: Reichskanzlei, 172.
[2] Ibid.

recommendations of the War Ministry, forbade Frenchmen who did not themselves own land in the area to visit Alsace-Lorraine for hunting.[1] The following year the problem of passes turned up again. The German ambassador in Paris, Münster, had complained to Bülow that the whole problem was endangering Franco-German relations. Bülow replied on 9-2-1899 that the Commanding Generals and the War Minister would not hear of any relaxation of the passport regulations for Alsace-Lorraine, insisting that many of the French acted as spies and that Germany's military position in the area was extremely weak. Münster was not convinced by these arguments and pointed out that 'if we want to be good neighbours with the French, then we should not treat them worse than our other neighbours'. Here again the military had forced through its ideas, and had managed to convince the Chancellor with arguments as to the strategic necessity of stringent controls. Portales had reported on 6-12-1898 that Schlieffen was against the idea of giving passes as those to whom they were granted were quite likely to indulge in espionage, nevertheless Schlieffen thought that they could be used to get concessions from the French.[2] Against the demands of the diplomats that loosening of restrictions was essential for the development of normal relations between France and Germany, the army kept up a strong opposition, hinting that they knew best what was right for the security of the Reich. Thus the Commanding General of the XIVth Army Corps wrote directly to the Kaiser in 1912, repeating the old charge that most French officers who came to Alsace-Lorraine on the pretext of visiting their families were, in fact, spies. The *Statthalter*, Wedel, was furious at this report, and insisted that the military had hopelessly exaggerated the situation.[3]

After the annexation all young men in Alsace-Lorraine, who were due for military service, had to serve in other parts of the Reich. This was for two reasons; firstly it was felt that, should they serve in the area, they would be highly unreliable in time of war, and in peace-time might well pass military secrets to French agents; and secondly, it was argued that service in other parts of the Reich would convince them that their future

[1] DZA, Potsdam: Reichskanzlei, 172.

[2] *GPEK*, xiii. 254.

[3] DZA, Potsdam: Reichskanzlei, 169.

lay with Germany and not with France. The army would thus serve as a school for patriotic German attitudes. This policy turned out to be a complete failure. A large number of recruits deserted rather than be posted so far away from home, and desertions in Alsace-Lorraine soon became the highest in the Reich. The War Ministry was slow to realize that by allowing recruits to serve near their homes they could only profit, both by having fewer deserters and by creating a happier atmosphere among the civil population. It was not until 18-9-1902 that the War Minister wrote to the Chancellor suggesting that recruits be allowed to serve in Alsace-Lorraine. The topic was discussed in the government, and although Hohenlohe, whose advice was asked, felt that the Alsatians were proud that their sons served with the Guards regiments, and would feel insulted if this was no longer possible, most agreed that the measure was a wise one. The War Minister assured Hohenlohe that he did not intend to cut down the numbers serving with the Guards, but said that in future fewer troops would be sent to other regiments in the Reich and could serve in Alsace-Lorraine instead.[1] The results of this change in policy were not spectacular. Only a few recruits served in Alsace-Lorraine, and these formed small minorities within the various regiments, a fact that led to frequent trouble. In 1910 Wedel suggested that as an act of good will the deserters in Alsace-Lorraine should be pardoned. He pointed out that of the 2,423 registered deserters many were between the ages of 39 and 59 and therefore too old for military service. He also mentioned that such an amnesty would be an important step in normalizing the relationships between the military and the civilians. Von Einem, who as War Minister had urged that recruits from Alsace-Lorraine be allowed to serve near their homes, was in favour of such a step, but Heeringen regarded it as a dangerous weakening of military discipline and the Kaiser agreed with him. Perhaps as a demonstration that he was on the right side, and that his call for an amnesty was not caused by any great sympathy for the aspirations of the *Reichsland*, Wedel wrote of the Press in Alsace-Lorraine: 'Recently I have often regretted that I did not have the effective weapon of the "Dictator Paragraph" any more.'

---

[1] DZA, Potsdam: Reichskanzlei, 168/3.

The Kaiser wrote in the margin 'me too!', but the idea of an amnesty was dropped.[1] Although Wedel himself was an old soldier, and certainly no liberal, he constantly complained that the military, by interfering in the internal affairs of Alsace-Lorraine, made his task increasingly difficult, and that they did all they could to undermine the authority of the *Statthalter*. Thus on 19-4-1911 he wrote to Bethmann,

lastly I should like to point out that I am perfectly willing to give the War Minister information on the internal affairs of the country if he considers it necessary for his job, but I think I should emphasize that I consider myself alone responsible for the actions of the state police which is responsible to me, especially as far as watching foreigners and the control of the press are concerned, and that I can fulfil these duties without interference from outside with the legal powers granted to me.[2]

In this struggle with the military Wedel was at a considerable disadvantage. The military authorities made a habit of making long reports on even the most trivial incidents, using them as evidence of the imminent danger to the security of the Reich that a liberal policy in Alsace-Lorraine would only serve to enhance. Their reports were often sent direct to the Kaiser, so that by the time the Chancellor discussed such problems with him he had already made up his mind in favour of the military. Backing up the military against the lame policy of *Wedelei* stood an influential section of the pan-German Press, which was also eagerly read by the Kaiser. In this situation Bethmann, who, on the whole, favoured a liberalization of conditions in Alsace-Lorraine, and who agreed largely with Wedel, was placed in a difficult position. The Kaiser regarded any criticism of the military as a direct attack on his power of command, and Bethmann was thus obliged to attempt reform by round-about methods, which naturally made progress extremely slow and difficult.[3] Wedel was unfortunate to have among the Commanding

[1] DZA, Merseburg: Civil Kabinett, 89H:I Elsass-Lothringen 6, Band 1. The Dictator Paragraph of 30-12-1871 allowed the *Oberpräsident* in Strasburg to use armed force, censor the Press, deport people, &c. The Paragraph was repealed 2-6-1902.
[2] DZA, Potsdam: Reichskanzlei, 168/4.
[3] Hans-Günter Zmarzlik, *Bethmann Hollweg als Reichskanzler 1909–1914* (Düsseldorf, 1957), p. 92.

Generals in Alsace-Lorraine General Huene. As military attaché in Paris Huene had been a constant headache to the Embassy and had eventually been removed under the combined pressure of the Foreign Office and Caprivi. However he remained an intimate of the Kaiser who regarded his wild reports as revealed truth. Posted to Alsace-Lorraine Huene continued his habit of sending hair-raising reports on the imminent danger of France and the evil deeds of the French in Alsace-Lorraine. The Kaiser, predictably, was highly impressed by these reports. Huene's activities soon brought him up against Wedel, who found a valuable ally in Lyncker, the head of the Military Cabinet. After a ferocious attack on the clubs, which Huene claimed were in close liaison with pro-French elements in the active army and the reserve, and therefore should be treated as a purely military problem, Lyncker wrote to Huene that, although the Kaiser was pleased with Huene's 'energetic' attitude in Alsace-Lorraine, it would have been better if 'the General's report, which was on the whole estimable, had been expressed in somewhat less drastic terms, so that the misunderstandings which have occurred could have been avoided'. Huene was in no way put out by this criticism, and the Kaiser continued to support him, and to use the Commanding Generals as a direct source of information for developments in the *Reichsland*.[1]

Huene again stepped into the limelight in November 1909 in the 'Mulhouse Affair'. In the Central Hotel in Mulhouse, the most luxurious hotel in the town and much favoured by German officers, the band played the 'Marseillaise' amid the applause of the listeners, whereas *Heil Dir im Sieger-Kranz* was booed. Huene at once placed the hotel out-of-bounds to army personnel, and wrote a tirade to the Kaiser who was furious at the incident. Wedel, as usual, tried to calm everyone down, and pointed out a number of mitigating circumstances. After a few weeks the ban was lifted, for the officers missed the comforts of the Central Hotel, even if the band, which had been bribed, had shown alarmingly republican sentiments. However, in 1911 Huene again closed the hotel, although there had been no further incidents of this type, when it was suggested that a group of German airmen should be received there by a group of officers.

---

[1] DZA, Merseburg: Civil Kabinett 89H:I Elsass-Lothringen 6, Band 1.

The situation was further complicated by the fact that Prince Heinrich of Prussia, who was to be at the reception, refused to come if he could not stay at the Central Hotel. Wedel wrote to the Kaiser that 'the measure had not only an inconsequential character but also a flavour of malicious resentment'.[1]

In the Mulhouse affair Huene got his way, but in the next incident, which resulted from the first, the combined forces of Wedel and the Civil Cabinet managed to convince the Kaiser that Huene and his friends had gone a little too far, though the result of the affair was far from satisfactory for Wedel. General-major Schmundt, a friend of Huene's, who had gained quite a reputation for himself in Alsace-Lorraine through a number of exceptionally offensive remarks about the local population, and also some extreme jingoistic utterances, joined with Huene in an out-and-out attack on the Police President whom, as a civilian, they regarded as utterly incompetent and weak-kneed. Dieckmann, the Police President, had supported Wedel against Schmundt and Huene in the Mulhouse affair, in the hope that Prince Heinrich's visit would better the atmosphere between Alsace-Lorraine and Prussia. Wedel, Lyncker, and Valentini managed to persuade the Kaiser to tell the Military Cabinet to call Huene and Schmundt to order. However the pan-German press, particularly the Kaiser's favourite *Correspondenz Wedekind*, joined in the attack on the Police President, described Alsace-Lorraine as 'a wasps' nest of anti-German agitation', and called for a firm hand from the authorities there.[2]

A compromise solution was decided upon, in that both Schmundt and the Police President should be posted elsewhere. Unfortunately the story leaked to the press, whereupon the army insisted that Schmundt should stay at his post; otherwise it would lose face, by seeming to give way in the face of public opinion. Wedel refused to accept this rather lame argument, and threatened to resign if Schmundt was not posted. After some prevarication the Kaiser gave way and Schmundt was posted, having first been awarded the Order of the Red Eagle 2nd Class with laurels and the royal crown. Wedel was angry that Schmundt had been decorated, and wrote to Valentini, the

[1] DZA, Merseburg: Civil Kabinett 89H:I Elsass-Lothringen 6, Band 1, Wedel to Kaiser, 7-6-11.
[2] *Correspondenz Wedekind*, 24-8-11.

15—G.O.C.

Chief of the Civil Cabinet, that it was extremely unwise to give him such a high honour, as it could only serve to encourage the military to be even more extreme. Valentini heartily agreed and wrote 'Huene and Deimling are the real wire-pullers'.[1] Indeed although Wedel and the Civil Cabinet had managed to remove Schmundt from the scene, Huene, who was a much more dangerous rival, remained, and continued to enjoy the particular favour of the Kaiser.

In Alsace-Lorraine Huene's career was watched with careful interest and indeed anxiety. Huene's wife was a Freiin von Tionauth and related to a number of industrial magnates in Alsace-Lorraine, Belgium, and Luxembourg. This placed Huene in a particularly strong position, not only financially, but also politically. Many feared that Wedel, who enjoyed a certain amount of popularity, would be replaced by Huene and that he would then bring in his policy of 'Germanization at the double'.[2]

The army was not content with attacking Wedel and the civilian administration, but also tried to remove real or imagined enemies from the political scene. Thus in 1913 the *Generalkommando* of the XVth Army Corps tried to remove the Mayor of Colmar, Blumenthal, whom they accused of being a lackey of the French. As significant proof of his treachery they pointed out that he often went to visit his wife who was in hospital in Paris, although there were enough good hospitals in Germany. Similarly Moltke in the same year asked the War Ministry to try to remove the Alsatian member of the Reichstag, Wetterle, for, he said, the French only laughed at the Germans for putting up with his 'insults, defamations, and malicious insinuations'.[3]

Seen against this background the Zabern affair was not merely an isolated case, dependent on a few personalities, as some historians have suggested, but rather the culmination of a number of smaller operations which resulted in a head-on clash between the civilian and the military authorities. The fact that the Kaiser listened all too readily to the exaggerated reports of the military, and refused to take seriously the more

---

[1] DZA, Merseburg: Civil Kabinett 89H:I Elsass-Lothringen 6, Band 1.
[2] *Neue Mülhauser Zeitung*, 4-1-12.
[3] BA Koblenz: HO2-1/22.

balanced accounts of the civilians, only served to encourage the
army to step well outside its legal powers, and to treat the rights
and duties of the civilians with contempt. Although the population of Alsace-Lorraine had tolerated many injustices and
provocations with good humour and forbearance the steady
accumulation of grievances drew the anti-German elements
closer together again. At the same time the civilians and the
Kaiser were becoming equally impatient. Even Wedel, usually
a moderate as we have seen, wrote to the Kaiser 25-11-12:

from the German point of view obviously a new victorious war
against France would mean a final solution of the so-called 'Alsace-
Lorraine' question, even though it does not exist from the point of
view of international law. For the blood of Alsace-Lorraine let
under the German flag would build an unbreakable link between the
Reichsland and Germany.

The Kaiser for his part was in favour of anti-press laws and
dictatorial powers, and wrote in a marginal note: 'This is a
pretty mess! It could almost be Bohemia or Bosnia!' And elsewhere, 'if this continues I'll smash their constitution to bits!
Then I'll make a Prussian province out of Alsace-Lorraine!'
On all sides tension was high. The scene was set for the Zabern
affair.

The affair began on 28 October 1913 when Lieutenant
Freiherr von Forstner and Sergeant Höflich of the 5th company
of the 99th infantry regiment, which was stationed in Zabern,
were giving a lecture to recruits on the relations between the
military and the civilians in Alsace-Lorraine. Turning to a
soldier, who had already been charged with knifing, the Lieutenant said, 'if you knife an Alsatian 'wackes' you won't get 2
months for each dirty 'wackes' you bring me—you'll get 10
marks'. Whereupon the sergeant added, 'and from me one
taler in addition!'[1] Unfortunately for the army this incident
leaked to the press, and was published in the *Zaberner Anzeiger*
on 6-11-1913 with further details two days later. The paper
demanded that the commanding officer of the regiment should
apologize for this incident, and that he should take steps against
Forstner and Höflich. The commanding officer, Colonel von
Reuter, refused any sort of apology, and excused the remarks of

---

[1] *Zaberner Anzeiger*, 6-11-13.

Forstner and Höflich by claiming that they had no intention of insulting the entire population of Alsace-Lorraine and had merely meant the rowdies.[1] On the 12 November the *Generalkommando* at Strasburg issued a statement which largely repeated the attitude of the colonel.[2]

Although this incident seems trivial, and many much more serious cases of this type had happened previously, relations between the army and the civilian population had become so bad that a wave of indignation spread throughout the country.

After the *Zaberner Anzeiger* had published details of the affair the *Generalkommando* in Strasburg asked Reuter for his version of the incident, whereupon Reuter replied that the account given in the press was accurate, although perhaps a little exaggerated. Yet he could see no reason why it should have caused such a stir. He assured the *Generalkommando* that Lieutenant von Forstner had only wished to refer to rowdies and other undesirables, and that he entirely agreed with his point of view. Reuter added that he felt Forstner had been a little impetuous in offering ten marks reward, and that the sergeant's offer of a taler was 'absolutely improper!' After this nice example of excusing an officer and condemning an N.C.O. for exactly the same offence, Reuter continued that the case had been passed on to the Press by irresponsible elements among the recruits, who if they had really felt insulted, should have complained in the proper fashion to their company commander. He concluded that he felt that there was no valid reason for condemning Forstner's attitude, but rather that the *Zaberner Anzeiger* should be brought to heel 'for insulting Lt Freiherr von Forstner'. On 13 November General von Deimling was obliged to reconsider the position in the face of demonstrations in Zabern; he considered that Forstner had been altogether too imprudent and that in future he should weigh his words somewhat more carefully; Höflich's remarks he called 'thoroughly improper and unmilitary'. In view of the fact that there was considerable ill-feeling in the population Forstner should be confined to his rooms and Höflich put under close arrest, leaving it to Reuter to decide for how long. Whereupon Reuter gave Forstner 6 days for using the word '*Wackes*' when a regimental

[1] *Zaberner Wochenblatt*, 8-11-13.
[2] *Strassburger Post*, 12-11-13.

order had forbidden the use of this word, and Höflich got 10 days for ordering Alsatian recruits to report to him saying 'I am a "*Wackes*"!'[1]

The word '*Wackes*' was much discussed during the Zabern affair, and many ingenious interpretations were concocted. This was merely an attempt to try to defend Forstner, for everyone knew perfectly well that it was the established derogatory term used by Germans for the Alsatians, a term which Alsatians found naturally enough to be highly insulting.

On 9 November, that is to say the day after the names of Forstner and Höflich had been published in the Press, there were elections for the local *Krankenkasse* in Zabern. As it was a Sunday there were many people in the streets. Also on this day Forstner was duty officer, which meant that he had to march round the town with his escort. Fearing the hostility of the Zaberners, he had arranged for a police escort. Forstner behaved during his rounds in his usual arrogant manner, and was very shortly followed by a crowd, mostly women and children, who jeered at him. Reuter, who was informed of what was happening, at once thought in terms of revolution, and hoped that at last he would have a chance to have a crack at the Alsatians. Sentries were doubled, machine guns got at the ready, and all soldiers were ordered back to barracks. Reuter also sent a note to the District Officer (*Kreisdirektor*) saying that if the troubles did not quieten down at once he would declare a state of siege and rule by military law. The District Officer was appalled at Reuter's exaggerated view of the dangers, and wrote immediately that it was impossible to declare a state of siege without first informing the Kaiser. Reuter replied: 'I am perfectly aware of my rights and duties'. He added that the *Gendarmerie* was quite unable to deal with the situation. The District Officer, Mahl, declared that as yet the *Gendarmerie* was quite sufficient and that he would let Reuter know if he needed military support. Reuter wrote back, 'I am always at your disposal and ask you, sir, to let me know when you intend to come to see me'. Mahl replied in the same coin 'I am also ready to see the Garrison Commander, at any time, even this evening, at the District Office'. Next day Reuter announced in public in a loud voice that it was a scandal that Mahl had not come to consult

[1] Kurt Stenkewitz, *Immer feste druff!* (Berlin, 1962), p. 21.

him as 'he was inferior in rank to him'. Although Mahl had managed to restrain Reuter and the army to a certain extent, by insisting on the legal superiority of the civilian administration over the army in cases of civilian unrest, he nevertheless took measures against the demonstrators. He called upon the mayor to take a firm line, strengthened the police force, and called out the fire-brigade, a cause of some merriment once it was discovered that an umbrella gave adequate protection against this weapon. Some twenty persons were arrested, to be released next day after paying a small fine.[1]

On the following day there were some further demonstrations, particularly in front of the barracks of the 99th regiment, but the demonstrators were dispersed by the police and no serious incident occurred. The newspapers backed up the civilian authorities' plea for order, and by the 11th things were back to normal. The fact that Forstner remained in the barracks and only a few other officers appeared on the streets also directly influenced the attitude of the civilians. The affair took a curious turn in that Reuter asked for leave from the 11th, claiming that his health was poor. It seems likely that this was on the express wish of Reuter's immediate superior, Major General von Harbon.[2] The sight of a removal van outside Reuter's quarters suggested that the colonel was unlikely to return.[3]

Although tempers had cooled the Alsatians were anxious that action should be taken against Forstner. The report of the *Generalkommando* of the 12th did not make it seem probable that anything would be done. Although Forstner had not appeared on the 11th, it was well known that he was still with his regiment. Indeed Forstner was in excellent form and on the 14th started off a fresh incident. During a lecture to his troops on the foreign legion he said 'As far as I'm concerned you can **** on the French flag!' A remark which was reported in the Press on the following day.[4] The '*Wackes* incident' had not been particularly embarrassing to the army, as they felt that they could deal with the Alsatian subjects of the Kaiser in their own way, but such a direct and widely publicized insult to France was alto-

[1] DZA, Potsdam: Reichskanzlei, 171.
[2] Arnold Heydt, *Der Fall Zabern* (Strasburg, 1934), p. 10.
[3] Erwin Schenk, *Der Fall Zabern* (Stuttgart, 1927), p. 16.
[4] *Der Elsässer*, 15-11-13.

gether a different matter. The Commanding General in Strasburg acted quickly, and on the 18th published a statement
saying that Forstner had not mentioned the French flag, but
had been merely referring to the Foreign Legion. It was
threatened that anyone spreading such untruths about the
army would in future be prosecuted.[1] The Press at once replied
that 79 recruits had heard Forstner's remarks and were prepared
to swear that the original version was the correct one, and not
that given by the *Generalkommando*, and that they were also
prepared to give further specimens from the Forstner reper-
toire.

On 16 November Wedel sent a report to Bethmann on the
'*Wackes* incident', in which he sharply criticized the army. 'The
behaviour of certain officers, particularly that of Lt von Forstner,
has a strong smack of provocation, and unfortunately shows
that in military circles a proper sense of responsibility is not
always present.' On the same day he wrote to the Kaiser, in
less drastic terms, excusing Forstner by saying that by '*Wackes*'
he had only meant 'argumentative characters and rowdies',
and not the Alsatians in general. However in view of the scanda-
lized attitude of the population he recommended that Forstner
be posted elsewhere. He vigorously defended Mahl in his
struggle with Reuter, and included in his report a strong word
against the press, which he claimed was responsible for the
whole unfortunate affair.[2]

In the meantime the military advisers of the Kaiser had
recommended that Reuter should remain as commanding
officer of his regiment, so as not to give way too easily to civilian
pressure. On 17 November Reuter returned to his regiment.[3]
He, quite naturally, regarded the express order of his Kaiser
to return to his regiment as proof that the Kaiser and his military entourage stood behind him and supported his tough line
against that of the civilian authorities. At once he set about
trying to find those responsible for informing the press of what
had happened in the barracks, claiming that they had broken
their oath to the flag and covered the regiment with disgrace.
Shortly afterwards nine men and a sergeant, all of them

[1] *Strassburger Post*, 18-11-13.
[2] DZA, Potsdam: Reichskanzlei, 170.
[3] Stenkewitz, *Immer feste druff!*, p. 37.

Alsatians, were arrested, but all were set free shortly afterwards owing to a complete lack of incriminating evidence. Reuter then posted all Alsatian recruits in the 5th company to other units.

On 23 November Wedel sent in further reports. To Bethmann he wrote that he had asked General von Deimling to post Forstner elsewhere in order to reduce the tension which had been increased by the second incident, and added that Deimling had refused on the grounds that the army would only lose face. To the Kaiser he wrote: 'In my view the prestige of the army will not suffer but will gain if an injustice which really happened is not covered up but is punished.'[1] Wedel's comments were underlined in a letter two days later by Baron Hugo von Türkheim to the Civil Cabinet in which he sharply criticized the policy of the army in Alsace-Lorraine, particularly General von Deimling, and the ruthless attitude of the Generals, particularly over the question of passes, which had done much to make the work of the civil administration virtually impossible. He wrote, 'it is really no exaggeration when people here claim that the *Statthalter*, the Secretary of State, the District President and the *Kreisdirektor* no longer rule, but rather the General Commands of the XIVth, XVth and XVIth Corps!' He added that he wondered whether the army was deliberately trying to stir up a revolt in order to be given the chance to push through its radical policy.[2]

As Wedel indicated in his reports of the 23rd, tension had risen once again. The return of Reuter and his action in arresting the 10 soldiers, and posting Alsatian recruits, was further proof to the population that nothing would be done to ensure satisfaction for their grievances. At the same time Wedel told the District Officer to take harsh measures against any further demonstrations and to call in the army if needed. The mayor of Zabern called upon the citizens to keep the peace. These stern measures might have been successful had the 99th Regiment been able to restrain its enthusiasm for the '*Wackes Jagd*'. Quite the reverse happened, and Reuter continued the offensive.

On Reuter's orders an officer and four policemen searched

[1] DZA, Potsdam: Reichskanzlei, 170.
[2] DZA, Merseburg: 89H:I Elsass-Lothringen 6, Band 2.

the offices of the *Zaberner Anzeiger* in the hope that they would find some evidence as to who had betrayed Forstner to the paper. This action was strictly illegal, as Reuter acted entirely of his own accord and did not have the permission of the responsible authorities. In fact the search revealed nothing of any value to them, and they reported back to Reuter with empty hands. At the same time officers, among then the inevitable Forstner, began to appear more frequently in the town, this time with an armed guard of four men. The sight of officers doing their shopping with an armed guard was met with the chortles and derision of the inhabitants of Zabern.

Reuter was acting in an illegal and provocative way, but this was not enough for General von Deimling. Looking back perhaps to the good old days when he had helped to massacre the Hereros he urged Reuter to even more desperate action, and accused him of not being as 'dashing' (*schneidig*) as an officer of His Majesty was expected to be. Reuter promptly ordered that in future civilians who in any way insulted the army should be promptly arrested, whereupon a number of arrests took place.

In the first wave of arrests, on 26 November, an apprentice baker, Daehn, was arrested for laughing at a military patrol, and passers-by who had witnessed his arrest and been unable to restrain their mirth were also arrested. In another incident a bank clerk was arrested because he was suspected of having laughed. The army handed all the arrested men over to the police, who, unable to find any charge on which to detain them, promptly set them free.

Reuter clearly expected that at any moment a revolt would break out; it seems likely that the arrests were designed to encourage the population to take some more desperate steps, thus giving the army the long-awaited chance to hit back. Unfortunately for Reuter there were no demonstrations, and the people continued to be amused rather than to plan a revolt. Reuter strengthened the guard and issued the machine-gun sections with live rounds.

On 28 November a fresh round of arrests took place. Although even the official accounts of these arrests read like extracts from a highly imaginative farce, not everyone had cause to laugh. A number of those arrested, almost all on charges of laughing, or the favourite military charge of dumb insolence, were insulted by the officers and some seriously maltreated. As a climax to the day Reuter appeared with some officers and about 60 men on the Schlossplatz, and although there was no demonstration whatsoever, ordered the people to disperse. Not all obeyed the order, but with a drum roll and a charge with fixed bayonets, even the most hardy took to their heels.

That day some 30 people were arrested, among them an official of the state court and the state prosecutor (*Staatsanwalt*) whom the colonel set free when they were brought to him. The others were thrown into a cold, damp, inadequately ventilated cellar, where they were kept throughout the night and most of the next morning. No form of sanitary arrangements was made, which increased their discomfort, the prisoners' repeated request to be allowed to leave the room at least for this purpose was refused, so that they had to make do with a corner of the small room.

On that evening District Officer Mahl was dining in Strasburg, and among the guests was General Deimling. Mahl was informed of the events in Zabern that day by the mayor, the deputy District Officer, and a member of the Alsace-Lorraine Landtag, who all called upon him to take steps to restrain the military. Mahl asked Deimling to order Reuter to curb his martial ardour, but Deimling merely replied that he had every confidence in Reuter, and that he was sure that he would do the correct thing. Mahl, who had shown some courage in dealing with Reuter, was clearly not in the mood to argue with Deimling, and accepted his assurances.

Back in Zabern the deputy District Officer, Grossmann, went to the barracks of the 99th Regiment and asked Reuter to reduce the number of patrols, so that any further incidents might be avoided. Reuter was furious, and said that since the civilian authorities had been utterly incompetent and had failed to give adequate protection to the troops, he had been forced to take action on his own account. In spite of the fact that the army had dispersed the people from the Schlossplatz they seemed unperturbed. Pointing this out to Grossmann, Reuter said, 'look here, the people are standing there again. If the Schlossplatz and the Hauptstrasse are not kept free, if people hang around and laugh, then I shall take action. There will be shooting; I have given the orders.' Grossmann could only con-

clude from the colonel's words that he was all out to provoke
an incident which would give the army the chance to shoot. In
order to avoid giving Reuter the slightest chance to take such
drastic steps Grossmann strengthened the police force and
ordered them to stop any loitering and to keep the streets as
clear as possible. Although the police proved perfectly adequate to keep people on the move, Reuter still made a number
of military patrols march through the streets.

The next day, a Saturday, the unfortunate prisoners were
removed from their cellar and brought before the military
judge—an illegal proceeding, since they could only be tried by a
civil court as a state of martial law had not been declared. They
were then marched, under heavy escort, to the civil courts where
they were shortly afterwards set free, as once again there was no
charge which could be brought against them.

On that day there were three further arrests, and the prisoners
were turned over to the police, but only after the repeated
protests of the civil authorities. On Sunday the town was quiet,
with constant patrols by the army and police. On Monday
Zabern was like a ghost town. The military patrols were then
stopped.

On the 29th, a Saturday, the local council (*Gemeinderat*) of
Zabern sent a telegram to the Chancellor, complaining about
the activities of Reuter and the army, and asking for adequate
legal support against the 'continual openly provocative actions
of Colonel von Reuter, which are a mockery of the whole con-
cept of law'. Bethmann replied at once by telegram saying that
he had asked Wedel for a report as soon as possible. Wedel's
report was sent off the next day to Bethmann; in it he gave a
factual account of the events in Zabern, stressing the way in
which the prisoners had been ill-treated, and questioning the
legality of Reuter's conduct. On the same day Pauli, from the
Ministry of the Interior, sent in his report in which he quoted
Deimling as having said: 'I have, furthermore, personally told
the Regimental Commander, Colonel von Reuter, to act energetically, to make arrests, and to use weapons mercilessly
against any resistance . . . this order is the natural consequence
of the sloppy and passive attitude which the local authorities in
Zabern have shown recently.' Wedel refused to accept Deimling's point of view, and further telegraphed to the Kaiser, saying,

I have to report to Your Majesty that the investigation set in motion by me has shown such serious excesses and such illegality by Colonel von Reuter in Zabern, that I consider that a remedy is absolutely essential. I beg Your Majesty most urgently for an audience, and ask that Secretary of State Freiherr Zorn von Bulach as well as Pauli, who led the investigations, should be allowed to accompany me.[1]

Unfortunately General Deimling had already sent in his report on the Zabern affair the day before Wedel, and obviously gave a very different account of the events there. The Kaiser then telegraphed Deimling telling him that he held him responsible for keeping 'peace and order'. The Kaiser, relying on the advice of the army, and clearly regarding Wedel's report as altogether too drastic, telegraphed to the *Statthalter*, 'The Chief of the Military Cabinet will discuss the steps taken by Colonel von Reuter as soon as the report of the General Commands is at hand, until then I would ask Your Excellency for written reports.'[2] In spite of Wedel's sharply worded note the Kaiser did not consider it worthy of discussion, and made no mention of Deimling's report, a severe breach of faith in that Deimling stood under Wedel as far as police measures in Alsace-Lorraine were concerned.

On the 29th Huene visited the Kaiser, who was staying at the time at Donaueschingen with Count Fürstenberg. Certainly he influenced the Kaiser, if influence was needed, to back up the military. An intimate of Bethmann's, who was with the Kaiser, described Huene's presence as ominous (*'verhängnisvoll'*). Bethmann for his part supported Wedel, and in a telegram to the Kaiser declared that in his opinion the army had acted illegally. On 2-12-1913 Wedel sent in a further report to Bethmann, which merely served to underline his criticisms of the military: 'As far as I know there was no friction between civil and military in Zabern before Colonel von Reuter arrived. Its citizens have a right not to be treated like Hereros and not to be made responsible for the cheeky insults of immature boys who knew how to escape the hands of the police and the army.' Meanwhile the Kaiser received further reports, from Reuter and Deimling, laying the blame for the whole affair on the

---

[1] DZA, Merseburg: 89H:I Elsass-Lothringen 6, Band 2.
[2] Ibid.

civil authorities and the local police for failing to take adequate measures. The Kaiser accepted this view wholeheartedly and covered Wedel's and Bethmann's reports with marginal notes to the effect that the police had been inadequate and the army had acted correctly. In further notes he claimed that 'this swinish press is ¾ responsible', and that the Alsatians had been bribed by English money. It was hardly surprising therefore that the army continued in its own sweet way. Reuter congratulated his men in a regimental order for their 'dashing behaviour'. On 2 December the Chief of the General Staff of the XVth Army Corps issued an order that, if the *Gendarmerie* still refused to give adequate protection to officers, then officers should continue to be given an armed escort, and any offenders should be handed over to the police. It was at this stage that the Crown Prince sent his famous telegrams, the first to Deimling ('Bravo!') and the second to Reuter ('Beat 'em up!'). On the 3rd the War Minister, von Falkenhayn, refused to issue an order forbidding the use of the word '*Wackes*' in the army, on the grounds that if he did this he would have to forbid the use of all sorts of nicknames.

Forstner was to be involved in one further incident. On 2nd December he was marching a column of soldiers through the village of Dettweiler, near Zabern. The inhabitants of the village recognized him at once and a number of none too flattering comments were passed. Forstner at once ordered his soldiers to arrest whoever was shouting at him. The only person they were able to catch was a lame shoe-maker by the name of Blank. Blank denied that he had said anything, whereupon an ensign hit him in the face with the butt of his rifle whilst some soldiers held on to him. This was altogether too much for Blank, and he tried to escape. In the struggle although he was still held by several soldiers Forstner drew his sword and hit the unfortunate man across the head, so that he fell to the ground with a severe head injury. Blank was taken to the mayor's office, given first aid and his statement was taken down.[1]

At this stage it may have seemed that the military party had won a convincing victory over the civilians, and that the 'hard line' in Alsace-Lorraine had triumphed. However events in Zabern had not escaped the eye of certain members of the

[1] See DZA, Potsdam: Reichskanzlei, 170/171 for all the above.

Reichstag. On 28 November the first questions were asked, though they had been tabled three days before when the House reassembled after the recess.[1] Falkenhayn was asked what he intended to do to protect the people of Alsace-Lorraine from the insults of officers and N.C.O.s. Falkenhayn repeated the official army line that Forstner had not been referring to Alsatians as a whole, and that the army had to take adequate steps to protect itself against impertinence and insolence. Falkenhayn's answers were not thought to be very satisfactory, but the Zabern case at this stage was not considered very important and the house moved on to other matters.

These first questions were asked on the very day that Reuter had taken the law into his own hands, and on Monday most members were well informed as to the events in Zabern either directly by telegram from Zabern or through the press. Fresh questions were tabled and on the 3rd and 4th the Reichstag discussed the Zabern affair in one of its most lively debates. The debate began with speeches from three members from Alsace-Lorraine, from the Progressive People's Party, the Social Democrats and the Centre. They accused the army of having erected a military dictatorship in Zabern, of having insulted the entire population and of trampling the law of the land underfoot. They emphasized that the whole affair would never have occurred if the army had taken adequate and proper steps in the first place. The Chancellor spoke next. He was in a tricky position, for although he knew perfectly well from Wedel's reports that the military had acted well beyond the bounds of legality and had by their actions directly caused the crisis, and although he had passed on these thoughts to the Kaiser, yet he did not want to denounce the army in the Reichstag. At first he tried to say nothing at all by making a number of nebulous remarks, but after frequent interruptions he was forced to make some definite statement. He claimed that at this stage, when he had not had a full report on the events in Zabern, it was not possible for him to say which of the two parties, the civilians or the military, had acted correctly; but he added that the army had the right and the duty to defend itself against the attacks of the population. He was however to make a slight concession in that he said that the 'limits of the law were not observed'.

---

[1] Steno. Bericht, 25-11-1913 and 28-11-1913.

The next speaker was the War Minister, von Falkenhayn. Falkenhayn's biographer describes the scene in melodramatic terms. 'On one side the slim military figure with a tight-fitting uniform and the eyes which were lit with fearlessness and rising determination: I will fight this battle to the end! On the other side—there are no other words for it—a mob no longer in control of its senses, no longer aware of the dignity of Parliament.'[1] No doubt Falkenhayn thought of his performance in the Reichstag in these terms, but in fact his speech did more than anything to bring a number of waverers over to the side of the opposition. He gave unconditional support to the army, attacked the people of Alsace-Lorraine, and defended the provocative actions of the army as being in the interest of the population in that they had obviated any more serious incidents. His speech ended in an uproar which he had done even more than Bethmann to provoke. Members from the Centre and Right spoke next, their sense of justice outraged by Bethmann's and Falkenhayn's speeches. The Centre member Fehrenbach said, 'I never expected to speak like this. It is in no way in accordance with my disposition as I know it.' Similarly the National Liberal van Calker said, 'My whole disposition is turned upside-down by the Chancellor's speech.' Thus much against their will and their deepest convictions many speakers from Centre and Right Wing parties were obliged to join forces with the Social Democrats in condemning the excesses of the military in Zabern. At the end of the first day of the Zabern debate a member of the Progressive People's Party proposed a vote of no confidence (*Missbilligung*) against the Chancellor. A similar proposal was brought forward the next day by the Social Democrats. On the second day of the debate Bethmann (whose commitment to a policy of reform in Alsace-Lorraine and support for Wedel's position took second place to his loyalty to the Kaiser and to his concern with the prestige of the army) declared his unconditional support for the War Minister, a move which only served to harden the fronts. The Social Democrats spoke of military dictatorship, and the Progressives of the injured rights of the people of Alsace-Lorraine. The debate closed with a speech from the president of the second chamber of the Alsace-Lorraine Landtag, who assured the

[1] Zwehl, *Falkenhayn*, p. 47.

house that the people of Alsace-Lorraine would continue the struggle for their rights against the excesses of the army, certain of the support of their many sympathizers in Germany. In the vote which followed 4 abstained, 54 voted for the Government, 293 against.

In the face of such a severe defeat in the Reichstag Bethmann decided to travel to Donaueschingen next day to report personally to the Kaiser. Also present would be Wedel and Deimling. The Kaiser, who was due to travel that afternoon to Stuttgart for a celebration, only gave three quarters of an hour's time to the discussion of the Zabern affair. In the course of this interview it was decided that the 99th Regiment should be removed from Zabern temporarily to a manoeuvre ground, and that responsible officers of the regiment should answer for their activities before a court martial. Further the Kaiser guaranteed Wedel that the Constitution of Alsace-Lorraine would be closely observed in future.[1]

The Reichstag debate had at least achieved something. Although there was no constitutional reason why Bethmann or Falkenhayn should resign after the vote of no confidence, thus causing a major political crisis, the Kaiser and the government had been forced to realize that something had to be done. The matter had been kept on the boil and the longer the Zabern affair was discussed the more the position of the military party was eroded. For the civilian administration in Alsace-Lorraine Bethmann's defeat and the Kaiser's reluctant acceptance of at least some of their demands was a welcome change in the course of developments. The Secretary of State Zorn von Bulach told a Berlin newspaper that he no longer intended to resign.[2]

Back in the Reichstag the Social Democrats, encouraged by the result of the Zabern debate, tried to hold together the 'Zabern coalition' and to force the Chancellor to resign, by refusing to vote for the estimates. On 9 November, in a debate on foreign policy, Scheidemann said those who had supported the vote of no-confidence should refuse to vote for the estimates. The subsequent debate showed that in the face of such a radical demand parties other than the Social Democrats were unwilling to continue the attack on the government and thereby force

---

[1] Schenk, *Der Fall Zabern*, p. 48.
[2] Ibid.

through a major constitutional change. The Centre, National Liberals, and Progressive People's Party felt that the vote of no confidence had put sufficient pressure on the government to bring the Zabern affair to a satisfactory conclusion, and were held back by constitutional scruples from going any further.

Meanwhile on 8 December the courts martial began in Strasburg. Not, as many had hoped, of the officers, but of the soldiers who had reported the various incidents to the press. The first of these received 5 weeks' close arrest, although the War Ministry had to admit subsequently that he had been unjustly convicted.[1] On the 11th three further soldiers were tried, this time in connexion with the insult to the French flag. Although the prosecution demanded sentences of several months, the court decided, possibly with a view to the wide publicity afforded to the trials, on six weeks' close arrest for one and on 3 weeks for the other two. Although the trials were clearly further proof of the army's attempt to exercise complete control over soldiers, both inside and outside the barracks, and further to protect the army from any form of criticism, the sentences were favourably received in the press, although some right-wing papers considered that they were far too mild.[2]

On 19 December Forstner stood before the court martial on charges of illegal use of a weapon and causing wilful injury in the case of the shoemaker Blank. Forstner's attempts to excuse himself by claiming that he had acted in self-defence failed to convince the court, and he was sentenced to the minimum sentence of 43 days' imprisonment. He at once said that he would appeal against the sentence. Whereas the sentences against the soldiers were used as proof of the clemency of military justice, Forstner's sentence caused loud cries of horror in the right-wing press which argued that it undermined the authority and honour of the Officer Corps, and that the sentence was far too severe. For the left it was at least encouraging that Forstner had been found guilty, but compared to the sentences on the soldiers he seemed to have got off lightly.[3]

The article which caused the greatest sensation at this time was one by the police chief of Berlin in the *Kreuzzeitung*.[4] Jagow

---

[1] Arnold Heydt, *Der Fall Zabern*, p. 32.
[2] Schenk, *Der Fall Zabern*, p. 54, for examples from the press.
[3] Schenk, ibid., p. 56.   [4] *Kreuzzeitung*, 22-12-13.

claimed that Forstner had only been doing his duty, and that the fact that he had been brought before a court martial was scandalous in that 'military exercises are sovereign acts and thus cannot possibly be punished by law'. Furthermore Forstner was 'almost in enemy territory', and therefore his actions were even easier to excuse. Wedel was furious with Jagow, and wrote a strong note of protest to Bethmann on 30-12-13, whereupon the government made a semi-official statement against Jagow in the *Nord-deutschen Allgemeinen Zeitung.*[1]

On 5 January began the third and largest court martial against Reuter and Lieutenant Schad. Reuter was charged with illegally acting in a public function which was not allotted to him, for arresting people without authority to do so, and several similar charges. Schad was in addition charged with trespassing and ill-treatment. Whereas in the case of Forstner it had proved impossible not to convict him, as the act against Blank could not be denied, Schad and Reuter were both acquitted, for the charges rested on a slightly more abstruse point of law. The court accepted the original version of the military, that the civilian authorities had failed to do their duty and to preserve the peace and that therefore Reuter had felt obliged to step in. Reuter's defence rested on the Cabinet order of 18 October 1820 which read: 'If the military commander having appraised the situation feels, according to his sense of duty and his conscience, that the civilian authorities have waited too long before asking the army to aid them, in as much as they are no longer strong enough to ensure peace and quiet, then he is permitted and duty-bound, even without a request from the civil authorities, to take action and to take over command, which is to be accepted by the civilians.' The court also accepted Reuter's argument that he had been forced to lock his prisoners away in the cellar, because had he handed them over to the civil authorities that evening it would have led to a revolt, and very possibly to loss of blood. Similarly Lieutenant Schad was acquitted; the charges of causing bodily harm were this time dropped merely on the strength of Schad's statement denying the charge. The sentences were greeted in the court with cries of joy, and officers rushed forward to congratulate Reuter and Schad.[2] Predictably the press reacted differently to

---

[1] DZA, Potsdam: Reichskanzlei, 172.   [2] Schenk, *Der Fall Zabern*, p. 58.

this decision: on the right there were cries of glee, on the left the conviction that this was yet another example of *Moloch Militarismus* trampling down justice and law. Indeed the trials had been a travesty of justice, civilian witnesses were treated with a distasteful arrogance, and wherever their statements differed from those of the two accused the court preferred to turn a deaf ear. The argument that officers, as 'representatives of the majesty and authority of the state', had to be protected, used as an excuse for Reuter's and Schad's activities, was to say the least of it, a highly dubious interpretation of the law.[1]

On 10 January, that is on the day that Reuter and Schad were acquitted, Forstner's appeal came before the *Oberkriegsgericht* in Strasburg.[2] The defence insisted that it was immaterial whether Blank intended to attack Forstner or not, the important fact was whether Forstner thought he was going to be attacked. At the same time the fact that Blank had a penknife in his pocket was used as evidence that he was going to use it, and the defence asked rhetorically if Forstner was expected to stand there and be stabbed in the ribs. The court accepted Forstner's appeal on the grounds that he had acted in self-defence, in the words of the verdict: 'The accused in the view of the court restricted himself to that degree of self-defence which was objectively necessary for defence against a possible attack.'

The army was delighted with the outcome of these trials, and the Kaiser shared their joy. On the 18th he awarded Reuter the Order of the Red Eagle Third Class.[3]

A number of other trials remained to be dealt with, mainly of some of the men arrested on 8 and 9 November. One man received a month's imprisonment for singing the 'Marseillaise' whilst under arrest, and another the same sentence for threatening a policeman. Most of the other charges were dropped. Deimling's, Forstner's, and Höflich's action against the *Zaberner Anzeiger* was withdrawn, 'in the interests of a desirable reconciliation and mollification'. Similarly those who had spent the night in the cellar also withdrew their charge against the military authorities.[4]

The Minister of Justice was unhappy about the outcome of

[1] DZA, Potsdam: Reichskanzlei, 172.   [2] Ibid.
[3] Stenkewitz, *Immer feste druff!*, p. 109.   [4] Schenk, *Der Fall Zabern*, p. 62.

the courts martial. The Imperial Department of Justice (*Reichs-Justiz-Amt*) wrote a number of memoranda on the legal aspects of the Zabern affair all of which came to the conclusion that the army had acted illegally. The memoranda were sent to the Minister of Justice on 19 January 1914, and on the following day the Minister wrote to the War Minister that the army could not justify its actions by referring to the Cabinet order of 17 October 1820 for 'an unpublished instruction designed for the authorities does not have the force of law'. The Minister went on by saying that even if the Cabinet order could be enforced it would still be rendered null and void by article 36 of the constitution. The War Minister flatly refused to accept these arguments.[1]

Whilst the legal complexities of the affair were discussed in a lengthy correspondence between the Ministers for War and Justice, the Social Democrats organized a number of protest meetings throughout the Reich. At the same time the affair was widely discussed by many parliamentary bodies. On 10-1-1914 the Prussian upper house heard with delight a tirade by Graf Yorck von Wartenburg on the dangers of allowing the army to come under the control of parliament, and of allowing the Prussian army to slip out of the hands of Prussia into the hands of a democratic Reich.[2] The Prussian lower house debated the Zabern affair from 13 to 15 January. The Right pointed out the danger of allowing the army to be controlled by the Democrats, as it was the main pillar of the state and had to be ready to put down by force any attempts by the Social Democrats to seize power or to ruin the economy by strikes. The National Liberals, who had voted against Bethmann in the Reichstag, stood solidly behind the Conservatives, and the Centre claimed that they had only voted against Bethmann because he had failed to make his position clear. The house demanded even stronger 'Prussian' methods in Alsace-Lorraine either by strengthening the army, and having more Prussians as civil servants, or by abolishing the constitution and making the *Reichsland* a Prussian province.[3] Karl Liebknecht was unable to speak, being howled down by the Conservatives.

[1] BA Koblenz: P135-2245.
[2] *Verhandlungen des preussischen Heerenhauses 1914–15*, 10-1-1914.
[3] *Verhandlungen des preussischen Hauses der Abgeordneten* 22 Leg., Period 2, Session 1914–15, Band 1.

The Zabern affair was again mentioned in the Reichstag on 13 January with questions from the Social Democrats, and again on the 23rd and 24th, the questions tabled this time by the Progressive People's Party. The debate showed clearly that the Zabern coalition had no hope of survival. One by one those who had voted against Bethmann declared their faith in the army and their determination not to undermine the Kaiser's power of command by establishing parliamentary control over the army, and attacked their erstwhile allies, the Social Democrats, for their desire for a 'revolutionary democratization' of the army. The Reichstag decided to establish a commission to investigate certain legal aspects of the affair, but the so-called *Zabernkommission* never reached any positive conclusions.[1]

The Landtag of Alsace-Lorraine also discussed the Zabern affair, first in the Second house from 13 to 15 January. The debate was lively, and the actions of the military were sharply criticized, as was the government of Alsace-Lorraine for failing to take adequate measures against the excesses of the army. At the end of the debate a resolution was passed demanding proper control over the actions of the army, a reform of military legal practice, and further constitutional rights for Alsace-Lorraine.[2]

The Upper House of the Landtag, although its members were carefully chosen by the Prussian administration, came to a similar conclusion. In its debate of 19 January the house passed a resolution saying that the army had acted illegally, and demanded guarantees that a similar case would not recur.

The collapse of the united front in the Reichstag against the army gave the signal for reaction to set in. The 18th January saw the first meeting of the *'Preussenbund'*, an organization built up of members of a whole range of reactionary and para-military organizations. Among the speakers was Lieutenant General von Wrochem who said, 'Since 3 December a dreadful danger threatens our army. When the rabble from all classes emerges victorious a hole will be bored in the imperial army. At last the voice of Colonel von Reuter rings clearly above the insane ravings of the mob. He acted in a true Prussian manner.' General Schmidt described the Alsatians as 'flabby, sloppy,

---

[1] *Steno. Bericht*, 23-1-1914, 24-1-1914.
[2] *Verhandlungen der zweiten Kammer des Landtags für Elsass-Lothringen*, Band 94.

dastardly creatures'. The General came before the police for
this remark, only to be excused for his words on the strength of
his military temperament and glowing patriotism. The meeting
heard many speeches against Alsatians, Democrats and even
the Bavarians, who were accused of cowardice in the Franco-
Prussian war. A resolution was passed that Prussia must preserve
her individual identity, and her constitutional rights as an
independent state, and that she must ever be a fortress against
the evil powers of democracy.[1]

On the same day as the *Preussenbund* meeting the Prussian
State Ministry met to discuss the Zabern affair.[2] By this time
Bethmann, after private discussions with Reichstag members,
was certain that a vote of no confidence would no longer be
passed against him in the Zabern affair, and was anxious to
placate the War Minister. He said:

The position would be much better, especially for the War
Minister, if one concentrated on the serious doubts as to the legal
position. Otherwise the army will immediately be accused of using,
as a basis for the use of weapons, an instruction which for decades
has been in contradiction to the law, and it will appear that everything that has happened in Zabern is without any legal justification.

Bethmann thus watered down the Justice Ministry's notes that
the military had acted illegally, and that the cabinet order no
longer had the force of law. The War Minister saw Bethmann's
statement as the green light, and replied:

I admit that the old regulations are not quite clear, but in Zabern
these proved excellent (*sic*) and similar cases could easily happen
again . . . if, for example, the police chief somewhere in Alsace-
Lorraine was malevolent and hesitated to bring in the army, under
the new regulations the local commander could only act in self-
defence.

The wheel had in fact turned full circle, and the military
emerged triumphant. In order to avoid any legal difficulties the
Cabinet Order of 1820 was replaced by the 'regulations on the
use of weapons by the army', which was published on 19 March
1914. The new regulations stipulated that the army could only

---

[1] DZA, Potsdam: Reichskanzlei, 173; *Freisinnige Zeitung*, 21-2-14; *Kreuzzeitung*,
19-1-14.
[2] BA Koblenz: P135-2245; DZA, Potsdam: Reichsjustizamt, no. 3613.

use their weapons when directly attacked, but the whole complex of relations between civil and military authorities in the event of unrest was never properly clarified, and this remaining confusion could only be to the advantage of the army, as the Zabern affair had clearly shown.[1]

As the reaction set in, criticisms of Wedel were voiced, and a campaign was launched to remove him from the post of *Statthalter*. In the papers of the Chancery is a letter addressed to Wahnschaffe, an Under-Secretary in the Chancery, typical of many others, which reads, 'As far as the *Statthalter* is concerned it is well known in the army that as a general he was useless, thus he was pushed off into the Foreign Office as a General Attaché and we laughed a lot about this in the Foreign Office.' The letter went on to describe the feebleness of Wedel's policy, and to claim that it was for this reason that the military had been obliged to step in.[2] Likewise attacks were made against Wedel's wife. It was rumoured that she was friendly with the Reichstag member Wetterle, whom the army had tried to remove, and that she was on intimate terms with a number of Alsatian nationalists.[3] It was even suggested that the Gräfin preferred to speak French rather than German, an appalling crime in the eyes of the Pan-Germans.[4] At the same time it was clear that the outcome of the Zabern affair had done nothing to bring the military closer to Wedel. The army remained adamant in its original position. On 17 January Falkenhayn wrote to Bethmann that the army could never share Wedel's concern for the feelings of the population of Alsace-Lorraine. 'As far as the emotions of the populace are concerned it is ridiculous to regard them as decisive for the distribution of troops in the Reichsland.'[5] The army continued its offensive against the mayor of Colmar, Blumenthal, and Wedel wrote to Bethmann on 28 February complaining that this was nothing but a direct interference of the army in politics, adding that the reports of the Commanding Generals in Alsace-Lorraine could only lead to what he described as 'lynch justice'.[6]

The army won a considerable victory over Wedel in the question of recruits serving in Alsace-Lorraine. The Command-

---

[1] DZA, Potsdam: Reichskanzlei, 1271.   [2] Ibid., 155.
[3] Ibid. 169.   [4] Ibid., 159.
[5] Ibid., 172.   [6] Ibid., 169.

ing Generals of the XIVth, XVth, XVIth, and XXIth Corps wrote to the War Minister that they considered that, in view of the recent events in Zabern, recruits from Alsace-Lorraine should no longer be allowed to serve at home. Falkenhayn passed these memoranda on to Bethmann on 10 February, with a note that 'the situation which has come to light proves that recruits from the Reichsland are under the influence of the demagogic nationalist press of Alsace-Lorraine, and the frequent close family ties and business relationships with France render their absolute reliability questionable'. The frontier, he argued, had to be defended by reliable men. The Kaiser gave his blessing to this measure, and on 13 April 1914 the War Ministry issued an order to the effect that, in future, recruits from Alsace-Lorraine would have to serve in other parts of the Reich.[1]

This measure made nonsense of Wedel's policy of trying to placate the feelings of the population of Alsace-Lorraine, and to promote a policy of moderate reform. Faced with the united and successful opposition of the army, the Pan-Germans and the Conservatives, his days were numbered. On 1 May Wedel was retired.[2] But the Wedel administration went down fighting. The report of the Ministry for Alsace-Lorraine to Bethmann of 30 April, the day before the retirement, read, 'Your Excellency, and certainly also the War Minister, would agree with me that neither the *Statthalter* nor I would be able to take on responsibility for general policy in Alsace-Lorraine if the present arrangement is not equally strictly respected by the military authorities, as it has always been respected by us.'[3] The news of Wedel's retirement was greeted with dismay in Alsace-Lorraine and the citizens of Strasburg gave him a torch-light procession as a token of their sympathy.[4] Wedel's successor, Dallwitz, was an impeccable Prussian and conservative, who regarded Wedel's politics in Alsace-Lorraine as an expression of 'impotence and feebleness'. Ominously Wahnschaffe wrote, when the appointment of a successor to Wedel was being discussed, 'above all Dallwitz will have respect for and authority

[1] DZA, Potsdam: Reichskanzlei, 169.
[2] Ibid., 159/1.
[3] Ibid., 173.
[4] Schenk, *Der Fall Zabern*, p. 99.

with the army'.[1] The army had indeed won yet another significant victory.

On 18 April the 99th Regiment returned to Zabern and to an icy reception in the town. They returned, however, without the heavily compromised officers. Reuter took over the command of a regiment in Frankfurt an der Oder, Forstner went to Bromberg and Schad remained in Alsace, but was posted to the 3rd Battalion of his regiment in Pfalzburg.

The Zabern affair had an important effect on foreign affairs in that it quite naturally increased France's distrust of Germany. The Russian ambassador in Paris described the situation in a dispatch to his Foreign Ministry.

Recently, even before the incidents in Zabern, Pichon often spoke to me anxiously about the increase of anti-French sentiment in Germany. According to some very reliable information which he had, apparently from H. J. Cambon, Kaiser William, who so far has personally shown thoroughly peaceful sentiments towards France, and who always dreamed of an understanding with France, is beginning to come round to the view of those among his entourage, particularly those from military circles, who are convinced that a Franco-German war is inevitable, and therefore believe that such a war would be better for Germany the sooner it should start. According to the same source this change in the attitude of Kaiser William is partly explained by the impression made by the Crown Prince's attitude on him, and by fear that he might lose his prestige in the German army, and in all sections of the German people.

The French government was anxious to avoid a clash with Germany over Zabern, as the army was in the middle of a difficult reorganization to bring in the three-year service. For this reason the French government told the press to play down the Zabern affair, and Jagow admitted to the French Ambassador in Berlin that this had been effective. The French feared the possible consequences of an open split between the military and the civil authorities in Germany over Zabern, the more so as the radical anti-French faction in the army had won such significant victories.[2] The Kaiser's reactions to French criticism show that many of their fears were justified. 'Let them come! Then

[1] H-G. Zmarzlik, *Bethmann Hollweg als Reichskanzler 1909–1914* (Düsseldorf, 1957), p. 127.
[2] *Der Diplomatische Schriftwechsel Iswolskis 1911–1914*, Ed. Friedrich Stieve (Berlin, 1926), Vol. iii, No. 1154, p. 368.

with God's help we will have a final reckoning with them. For we have been abused and insulted in the last two years not only by the entire French press, technical and otherwise, but at home by the '*Wackes*' who have been enticed by French money! No wonder we lose our patience!'[1] The outcome of the Zabern affair only helped to widen this gap between France and Germany. The army stepped up its anti-French witch-hunting campaign in Alsace-Lorraine, and the French saw their worst fears confirmed.

In Germany itself reaction to the Zabern affair was very mixed. The army stood united in condemning the civil administration, and particularly the press. Groener, for example, blames the affair on the 'undisciplined' press.[2] Ludendorff was even more outspoken, predictably enough, and spoke of the 'revolting and hysterical way in which the affair was handled by the press, and the insanity of the Reichstag which showed how far the agitation against the Officer Corps and army had developed'. He also saw a dark plot of Catholics, Jews, and Freemasons behind the affair.[3] Similarly the conservatives stood solidly behind the army.[4] Among the more moderate conservatives many had serious doubts as to the wisdom of letting the army have a free rein. Baroness Spitzemberg, an intelligent and sensitive recorder of the epoch, and of impeccably conservative political views, roundly opposed the army in Zabern.[5] Another conservative, Hutten-Czapski, wrote to Bethmann on 4-12-13 'my close political friends, whose leaders I have just spoken to, naturally want to be able to stay loyal to the army (*militärfromm*) but must have certain guarantees'.[6] On the left the Social Democrats were united in condemning this ominous outburst of militarism. In the last resort those who wished to remain *militärfromm* did so, once the danger of a red coalition raised its ugly head, and the fear that the army might come under direct democratic control became widespread in conservative circles. In the face of a challenge from the Left all

[1] *GPEK* xxxix. 230.
[2] Groener, *Lebenserinnerungen*, p. 140.
[3] Ludendorff, *Mein militärischer Werdegang*, p. 168.
[4] Westarp, *Konservative Politik*, p. 318.
[5] See Spitzemberg, *Tagebuch*, 18-12-1913, p. 565.
[6] Hutten-Czapski, *Sechzig Jahre Politik*, ii. 128.

scruples were forgotten. Nonetheless the Zabern affair is important in that it showed that there were fundamental divisions in
German society, between the army and the civilians, and if
these divisions could, for the time being, be easily healed in the
face of a common danger, it became clear to many a contem-
porary that the army was lagging behind the times and was
supporting by brute force an ideology that no longer corres-
ponded to the fundamental realities of the age. Zabern showed
the split that was there, a grave warning for the future. Lenin
wrote that 'not "anarchy" has "broken out" in Zabern but the
true order in Germany, the rule of the sword by semi-feudal
Prussian landowners has become more severe.'[1] This is a somewhat drastic formulation of an essential truth, but even more
interesting is the fact that an ever-widening number of the
bourgeoisie no longer had an interest in supporting the political
ambitions of a junker-dominated army. That was the real
lesson of Zabern, and the fact that the common fear of the left
blinded many could not disguise the fact that power was
beginning to slip, however slowly, from the hands of the extreme right.

[1] W. I. Lenin, *Über Deutschland und die deutsche Arbeiter-bewegung* (Berlin, 1957),
p. 291.

CONCLUSION

WILLIAM II's accession in 1888 marked a turning point in the history of the German Officer Corps. Under William I the army had been content to bask in the glories of the Kaiser's past campaigns, and its contribution to the unification of the Reich insured its popularity. Bismarck resisted any attempts by the army to interfere with his policies, and relations between the army and the government were, at least on the surface, correct. Although Bismarckian Germany saw profound economic and social changes, the effects of those changes did not have acute political consequences until the Wilhelmine era. Once again the army was to attempt to play a political role by trying to preserve the conservative order against changes that were threatening a social structure that preserved the army's pre-eminent position in the state.

The swashbuckling and aggressive attitude of the Kaiser reflected the feeling of the younger generation of officers with whom he liked to mix in the messes of Potsdam and Berlin. Like William himself the Officer Corps was eager to emulate the deeds of their fathers and to lead the Reich to higher pinnacles of glory. This was not only the result of a desire to prove to their elders that they too were capable of equal or even greater feats of valour and military ability, but it also reflected the growing *malaise* in Germany. It was felt that, although the industrial and commercial strength of Germany had increased, her political power in the world was not compatible with this wealth. Many felt that Germany had been wilfully denied that place in the community of nations which by wealth, strength, and history was her due. It seemed to them that the Reich was hemmed-in by envious and suspicious powers, determined to do everything in their power to deny it its rightful place in the sun.

The army's belief in the inevitability of a European conflict was not primarily a corollary of the euphoria of *Weltpolitik*. More important was the belief, which was first voiced by the elder Moltke, that the Franco-Prussian war had failed finally to settle the question of German security in Europe. Bismarck had been short-sighted in his policy in not allowing the army to crush France once and for all, and he had failed utterly to recognize the danger of a revived France. From the initial premise that Germany would have to fight another European war to ensure her lasting security it was only a very short step to claim that another war would secure German hegemony over Europe. In Wilhelmine Germany with its over-confidence in the future, its constant posturing and its aggressive commercial policy it was this latter thought which came increasingly to dominate men's minds. Problems of long-term security gave way to irredentist and expansionist dreams. The elder Moltke had demanded that the Danube become a German river, Bernhardi preached the need for natural frontiers and a revival of the Holy Roman Empire (presumably with the inclusion of Prussia), the younger Moltke thought in terms of a radical struggle between Teuton and Slav, others, like von der Goltz, believed that war was desirable for its own sake, to create a dynamic sense of national unity and purpose that was stifled by the clash of political parties and by conflicting interest groups. The dictatorial powers granted to the Commanding Generals in time of war would ensure that the army would no longer have to submit to the wishes of vacillating civilians or be frustrated by the politicians.

In practical terms this attitude meant that there was pressure brought to bear on the government to take an even firmer line during the two crises over Morocco, even if that meant the serious risk of war. The army was directly instrumental in strengthening the war party in Austria, and played a critical role in the July crisis of 1914. The army's growing frustrations with German foreign policy led to an increasingly antagonistic attitude towards the diplomatists. Since the Foreign Office was to blame for the parlous position of Germany in the world, an attempt was made to by-pass the traditional diplomatic channels by the use of the military attachés. This attempt was thwarted by Caprivi, but it is unlikely that the military attachés could have caused any significant changes in foreign policy, partly because of the constitutional position of the Chancellor and of the State Secretary in the Foreign Office, and partly because the Kaiser lacked the determination and the application to rule by means of a 'personal regiment'. After the defeat of the attachés the army no longer actively interfered with the course of German foreign policy and concentrated on the purely technical details of strategic planning. Thus the Schlieffen plan was drawn up without proper consultation with the government, and its inflexibility was to have important and disastrous political effects. Strategy and politics are always intimately linked, and the blame rests on Bismarck's successors for insisting that they could not hope to understand the complexities of military thinking, just as much as it does on the army for exploiting this situation to the full.

The Officer Corps was as determined to fight the enemy within the Reich as it was to assert Germany's position in the world. The struggle against Social Democracy was one of the main points of the army's peace-time programme. Once the extremists had learned by bitter experience that William II's call for a conservative *coup d'état* could not be taken seriously, the army concentrated on a two-point programme against Social Democracy. First they developed elaborate plans for the suppression of a socialist revolt, which they were convinced was imminent. Secondly they instituted a programme of political re-education for soldiers, in the hope that the army could become the 'school of the nation', to teach those who might be tempted by democratic ideas to be true and loyal subjects of the Kaiser and Reich. This attempt was ill conceived and badly executed, and only helped to increase the army's sense of frustration, and gave an additional impetus to the ideas of those who thought that only war could give Germany a sense of united purpose. The constant iteration of the theme that revolution was only just around the corner blinded the army's eyes to the fact that the majority of the Social Democrats had no intention at all of overthrowing the existing state by force. It also increased the army's frustration with the government which seemed almost perverse in its resolute refusal to see the dangers that lay ahead. Conversely the army's actions as a strike-breaker, which were sometimes unnecessarily brutal, made the Social Democrats all the more determined to press for reforms in the army.

The ever-widening gulf between the ideology of the Officer

Corps and the political realities of Wilhelmine Germany helped
to strengthen its sense of caste, its determination to preserve its
privileged position, and its direct allegiance to the Kaiser as
Supreme Warlord. Separated from the rest of society by its
social exclusiveness, its elaborate code of honour which often
was in direct contradiction to existing laws, and by its resolute
refusal to make any concessions to a changing world, the Officer
Corps maintained a position of extreme conservatism. Although divided into four armies this ideological solidarity gave a
homogeneity to the Officer Corps which transcended local
patriotism. This further strengthened the hegemony of the
Prussian army, ensured by the responsibility of the Prussian
General Staff for strategic planning, and by the fact that the
Prussian War Minister answered for the army as a whole in the
Reichstag.

Although the Wilhelmine army seems at first sight to be
united in its allegiance to the Kaiser, dedicated to a common
ideology, and with the dominant position of the Prussian army
ensuring its unity, there was an important structural weakness
at the very top. The rivalries between the General Staff, the
Military Cabinet and the War Ministry, and the extreme
difficulty of defining the sphere of competence of each institution greatly weakened the unity of the army, and made any
sort of long-term planning exceedingly difficult. This made the
army an unsuitable instrument of any attempted 'personal
regiment'. The clash between the General Staff and the War
Ministry also meant that the effective strength of the army was
not large enough to meet the demands of its own war plan.

The failure of the attempt to settle the differences between
the parties which upheld the *status quo* in the face of a threat
from the left caused a growing sense of frustration, and even of
fatalism, in conservative circles. This feeling was echoed in the
attitude of the Officer Corps towards civilians. Although it was
hoped that the Officer Corps could be a self-perpetuating clique,
considerable concessions had to be made to the *bourgeoisie* to
meet the need for more officers in a larger army. Nevertheless
its system of recruitment was such that only those who fully
shared the fondest prejudices of the Officer Corps could hope
for a commission. The position of the army was greatly enhanced by the corps of reserve officers, uncritical in its admira-

tion for the regular army, and anxious to ape its ways. The number of para-military organizations, with their large membership, seemed further indication that the army's programme of stemming the tide of liberalism and democracy had some chance of success.

The common ideology of the extreme conservatives and the Officer Corps, and its increasing estrangement from the political realities of the day, parallel with the growth of economic liberalism and Social Democracy, forced the army to adopt an extreme position. Conscious that democratic ideas were on the march that might well shake the privileged status of the Officer Corps, it feared that it might be endangered from within. Thus it demanded wide powers to control the influx of known Social Democrats into the army, exercised strict censorship of all printed material coming into the barracks, and tried to ensure that no Social Democrat was given promotion. This programme also failed. The civilian authorities were unwilling to co-operate in what was clearly a fruitless task. It proved impossible to control a soldier's every movement, and the policy of the Social Democrats that its members should be careful to behave in an exemplary fashion whilst serving in the army meant that a large number of party members inevitably became N.C.O.s. The realization that this programme was failing only helped to spur on the army's demands for draconic measures against Social Democracy and liberalism.

The stronger the challenge became to the position of the Officer Corps, the louder became its criticisms of the civilians. Just as the diplomatists were accused of dewy-eyed optimism far removed from the harsh realities of the power struggle between states, so other ministries were accused of failing to see the dangers that lay ahead, of wilfully denying the army that degree of authority that was essential if the old order was to be preserved. Just as the Officer Corps was becoming increasingly estranged from the country at large, so the relations between civil and military authorities became more tense. This is clearly seen in the Zabern affair, a struggle not only between the army and the civilian population in a small town, but also between civilians and military at the highest levels of government.

The remarkable success of the para-military, youth, and veterans' organizations and the fact that the army had to make but few concessions to a changing world was encouraging to the Officer Corps. But all hopes of winning wide support for the conservative order proved illusory. In an industrial society of increasing strength and complexity an ideology based on the prejudices of East Elbian landowners could not hope to predominate. The Officer Corps became increasingly divorced from the majority of the people. Not even war helped to bridge this ever-widening gap. By 1916 the split between the army leaders and the government became so acute that Hindenburg and Ludendorff, drawing on a vast fund of popular support for the army, natural in time of war, were able to establish their 'silent dictatorship'. Even after the total defeat of the German army the Officer Corps was to emerge again with most of the fondest prejudices of the Wilhelmine period unchanged. After the bitter experiences of the war years and the humiliation of defeat, it proved once again a thorn in the side of the politicians and the diplomatists. By remaining an autonomous caste the Officer Corps proved an obstacle to the achievement of that degree of national unity which the liberals had achieved during the war against Napoleon and had failed to recreate in 1848, and which alone could have given a degree of political stability to Germany that might have averted the dreadful excesses which were to follow. The stubborn resistance of the Officer Corps of Wilhelmine Germany to any liberalization of the army, although this was vital, in the interests not only of political harmony but also of military efficiency, was a significant factor determining Germany's inability to achieve a political equilibrium that might have given the nation reserves of strength to withstand defeat and depression. The Officer Corps was to pay dearly for its stubborn refusal to move with the times.

BIBLIOGRAPHY

UNPUBLISHED SOURCES

BUNDESARCHIV KOBLENZ:
General-Akten des preussischen Justizministeriums:
P135-1057, 2039, 2165, 2223, 2245, 2264, 2265, 2266, 2282, 2285, 2286, 2306, 2325, 2342, 2869, 7801, 7870, 8037, 8040, 8041, 8042, 8582, 8583, 8588, 11578, 11651.

BUNDESARCHIV–MILITÄRACHIV:
Obere preussische Militärbehörden:
HO2-1/20, 1/21, 1/22.
Militärische Nachlässe:
HO8-32/11–14 Nachlass von Deines; 46/64, 46/78 Nachlass Groener; 52/1 Depot von Blomberg; 58/1 Nachlass Graf v.d. Schulenburg-Tressow.
KO8-7 Nachlass Gustav Freiherr von Senden Bibran.

BAYERISCHES HAUPTSTAATSARCHIV ABTEILUNG IV KRIEGS-ARCHIV.
M.Kr.1711, 1854, 1863, 1865, 1874, 1875, 1944, 1945, 1947, 1952, 1960, 2031, 2046, 2048, 2049, 2071, 2072, 2073, 2074, 2114, 2283, 2285, 2327, 2357, 2466.
Alt Register 18, Bund 1.

STAATSARCHIV LUDWIGSBURG:
E130 vV
E150 1156, 1186, 1219
F201 624

HEERESARCHIV STUTTGART:
Württembergischer Kriegsministerium—persönliche Angelegenheiten des Württembergischer Kriegsminister:
Band 2, 7, 8, 19, 25, 27, 34, 53.
Denkschriften Sammlung:
Band 3, 82, 173, 361, 365, 367, 384, 405, 452, 454, 527.
Württembergische Militärbevollmächtigte Berlin:
Band 41
Württembergische Kriegsministerium Abteilung für allgemeine Armee und für persönliche Angelegenheiten (A):
Band 601, 671, 932, 936, 937.
Kriegsministerium Verwaltungsabteilung:
Band 240

DEUTSCHES ZENTRALARCHIV, POTSDAM:
Reichskanzlei:
Band 159/1, 168/3, 168/4, 169, 170, 171, 172, 173, 192, 754, 1267/3, 1270, 1271, 1287, 1288, 1305, 2257, 2258, 2273.
Reichsministerium des Innern:
Band 12204, 15185.
Reichs-Justiz-Amt:
Band 3613
Auswärtige Amt:
Band 50265, 50645.

DEUTSCHES ZENTRALARCHIV, MERSEBURG:
Civil Kabinett:
89H: XXVI: Militaria 5, 6, 28.
89H: I Elsass Lothringen 6, Band 1, 2.
Rep 77, Tit. 924.
Rep 92 Waldersee:
A I-15
B I-1, 6, 7, 15, 16, 21, 22, 28, 53.
B II-7, 8, 13, 14, 18.

PUBLISHED SOURCES

Die deutschen Dokumente zum Kriegsausbruch 1914, ed. Graf Montgelas and Walter Schücking (Berlin, 1927).
Die grosse Politik der europäischen Kabinette, 40 vols., Ed. A. Mendelssohn-Bartholdy, I. Lepsius, and F. Thimme. (Berlin, 1922–26).
Österreich-Ungarns Aussenpolitik 1908–1914, 9 vols., Ed. Ludwig Bittner and Hans Uebersberger (Vienna, 1930).
Reichsarchiv: Der Weltkrieg 1914 bis 1918. Kriegsrüstung und Kriegswirtschaft. Die militärische, wirtschaftliche und finanzielle Rüstung Deutschlands von der Reichsgründung bis zum Ausbruch des Weltkrieges, 2 vols. (Berlin, 1930).
RITTER, Gerhard, 'Die deutschen Militär-Attachés und das Auswärtige Amt. Aus den verbrannten Akten des Grossen Generalstabs', Sitzungsberichte der Heidelberger Akademie der Wissenschaften, Jahrgang 1959, 1 Abhandlung (Heidelberg, 1959).
Stenographische Berichte über die Verhandlungen des Deutschen Reichstages.
Stenographische Berichte über die Verhandlungen des Preussischen Hauses der Abgeordneten.
Verhandlungen des Preussischen Herrenhauses.

MEMOIRS, DIARIES, LETTERS, &c.

BERNHARDI, Friedrich von, Denkwürdigkeiten aus meinem Leben (Berlin, 1927).
BÜLOW, Bernhard von, Memoirs, 4 vols. (London, 1931–32). Letters (London, 1930).
CONRAD, von Hötzendorff, Feldmarschall, Aus meiner Dienstzeit 1906–1918, 4 vols. (Vienna, 1921).

ECKARDSTEIN, Hermann von, *Lebenserinnerungen und politische Denkwürdigkeiten*, 2 vols. (Leipzig, 1919–20).

EINEM, Generaloberst von, *Erinnerungen eines Soldaten, 1853–1933* (Leipzig, 1933).

FONTANE, Theodor, *Briefe an Georg Friedlaender* (Heidelberg, 1954).

FREYTAG-LORINGHOVEN, Freiherr von, *Menschen und Dinge wie ich sie in meinem Leben sah* (Berlin, 1923).

GOLTZ, Generalfeldmarschall Colmar Freiherr von der, *Denkwürdigkeiten* (Berlin, 1929).

GROENER, Wilhelm, *Lebenserinnerungen: Jugend, Generalstab, Weltkrieg* (Göttingen, 1957).

GÜNDELL, General Erich von, *Aus seinen Tagebüchern*, ed. Walter Obkircher (Hamburg, 1939).

HINDENBURG, Generalfeldmarschall P. von, *Aus meinem Leben* (Leipzig, 1934).

HOHENLOHE-SCHILLINGSFÜRST, Fürst Chlodwig zu, *Memoirs*, trans. G. W. Chrystal, 2 vols. (London, 1906).

HUTTEN-CZAPSKI, Bogdan Graf von, *Sechzig Jahre Politik und Gesellschaft*, 2 vols. (Berlin, 1935–36).

KEIM, Generalleutnant A., *Erlebtes und Erstrebtes* (Hanover, 1925).

LANCKEN-WAKENITZ, Oscar Freiherr von der, *Meine dreissig Dienstjahre 1888–1918* (Berlin, 1931).

LUDENDORFF, E., *Mein Militärischer Werdegang* (Munich, 1933).

MACKENSEN, August von, *Briefe und Aufzeichnungen des Generalfeldmarschalls aus Krieg und Frieden*, ed. Wolfgang Foerster (Leipzig, 1938).

MEINECKE, Friedrich, *Erlebtes, 1862–1901* (Leipzig, 1941).

MEISNER, Heinrich Otto, 'Aus Berichten des Pariser Militär-Attachés Freiherr von Hoiningen gt. Huene an den Grafen Waldersee (1888–1891).' *Berliner Monatshefte* Jahrgang 15 (1937).

MOLTKE, Generaloberst Helmuth von, *Erinnerungen-Briefe-Dokumente 1877–1916*, ed. Eliza von Moltke (Stuttgart, 1922).

MOLTKE, Generalfeldmarschall Helmuth von, *Gesammelte Schriften und Denkwürdigkeiten* (Berlin, 1892).

MONTS, Anton Graf, *Erinnerungen und Gedanken*, ed. K. F. Nowak & F. Thimme (Berlin, 1933).

RENN, Ludwig, *Adel im Untergang* (Berlin, 1948).

SCHLIEFFEN, Generalfeldmarschall Graf Alfred von, *Gesammelte Schriften* (Berlin, 1913).

—— *Briefe*, ed. Eberhard Kessel (Göttingen, 1958).

SCHWEINITZ, General von, *Briefwechsel* (Berlin, 1928).

SEECKT, Hans von, *Aus meinem Leben 1866–1917* (Leipzig, 1938).

SPITZEMBERG, Baronin, *Tagebuch* (Göttingen, 1961).

STIEVE, Friedrich, *Der diplomatische Schriftwechsel Iswolskis 1911–1914*, 6 vols. (Berlin, 1926).

RATHENAU, Walter, *Briefe* (Dresden, 1926), Vol. I.

SWAINE, Major General Sir Leopold, *Camp and Chancery in a Soldier's Life* (London, 1926).

TIRPITZ, Alfred von, *Erinnerungen* (Berlin, 1927).
—— *Politische Dokumente* (Berlin, 1924).
TRESCKOW, Hans von, *Von Fürsten und anderen Sterblichen* (Berlin, 1922).
WALDERSEE, Generalfeldmarschall Alfred Graf von, *Denkwürdigkeiten*, ed. H. O. Meisner, 3 vols. (Stuttgart, 1923–25).
—— *Aus dem Briefwechsel*, ed. H. O. Meisner (Berlin, 1928).
WEDEL, Graf Carl von, *Zwischen Kaiser und Kanzler* (Leipzig, 1943).
WERTHEIMER, Eduard von, 'Ein k. und k. Militärattaché über das politische Leben in Berlin 1880–1895'. *Preussische Jahrbücher*, Band 201 (Berlin, 1925).
WIESE, Leopold von, *Kindheit. Erinnerungen aus meinen Kadettenjahren* (Hanover, 1924).
ZEDLITZ-TRÜTZSCHLER, Count Robert, *Twelve Years at the Imperial German Court*, trans. Alfred Kalisch (London, 1924).

REGIMENTAL HISTORIES

Geschichte des Königl. Leib-Kürassier-Regiments 'Grosser Kurfürst' (Schlesien) Nr. 1. (Berlin, 1906).
Aus der Geschichte des 1 Garde-Dragoner-Regiments Königin Viktoria von Grossbritannien und Irland 1815–1898 (Berlin, 1907).
2 Niederschlesisches Infanterie-Regiment Nr. 47 (Berlin, 1910).
Fusilier Regiment Prinz Heinrich von Preussen (Branden-burgisches) Nr. 35 (Berlin, 1910).
Geschichte des Infanterie-Regiments von der Marwitz (8 Pommerschen) Nr. 61 (Berlin, 1910).
Geschichte des Königlich Preussischen Ersten Garde-Regiments zu Fuss 1871–1914 (Berlin, 1933).
Geschichte des Infanterie-Regiments Prinz Louis Ferdinand von Preussen (2 Magdeburgischen) Nr. 27 1815–1895 (Berlin, 1896).

NEWSPAPERS AND PERIODICALS

Bayerische Landeszeitung.
Bayerische Staatszeitung.
Berliner Tageblatt.
Berliner Zeitung.
Correspondenz Wedekind.
Der Beobachter (Stuttgart).
Der Elsässer.
Frankfurter Zeitung.
Freisinnige Zeitung.
Hamburger Nachrichten.
Kreuzzeitung.
Leipziger Volkszeitung.
Militärwochenblatt.
Neue Mülhauser Zeitung.
Schwäbische Tagwacht.

Strassburger Post.
Volksstimme (Frankfurt am Main).
Volkswacht (Freiburg (Breisgau)).
Volkszeitung (Berlin).
Vorwärts.
Vossische Zeitung.
Zaberner Anzeiger.
Zaberner Wochenblatt.

PAMPHLETS

BEBEL, August, *Nicht stehendes Heer* (Stuttgart, 1898).
CARLEBACH, Dr S., *Das Heereswesen und die jüdische Erziehung* (Lübeck, 1915).
Lamms jüdische Feldbücherei *Der Krieg und wir Juden* (Berlin, 1915).
Comité zur Abwehr antisemitischer Angriffe in Berlin, *Die Juden als Soldaten* (Berlin, 1896).
KOPSCH, Julius, *Die Juden im deutschen Heer* (Berlin, 1910).
LOEWENTHAL, Max J., *Das jüdische Bekenntnis als Hinderungsgrund bei der Beförderung zum preussischen Reserveoffizier* (Berlin, 1911).
—— *Jüdische Reserveoffiziere* (Berlin, 1914).
NORDMANN, H., *Israel im Heere* (Berlin, 1879).
'R. VON RIJIN', *Individualismus und Schablone im deutschen Heer* (Berlin, 1892).
LIEBERT, Generalleutnant von, *Die Entwicklung der Sozialdemokratie und ihr Einfluss auf das deutsche Heer* (Berlin, 1906).
'K. VON R.', *Der nächste Krieg* (Berlin, 1886).
SELBACH, E. A., *Der Einjährige muss bleiben!* (Düsseldorf, 1895).
Soldaten Brevier (Berlin, 1907).
WESTPHAL, H., *Das deutsche Kriegervereinswesen* (Berlin, 1903).

SECONDARY SOURCES

ALTEN, Georg von, *Handbuch für Heer und Flotte* (Berlin, 1909).
ANDERSON, Eugene N., *The Social and Political Conflict in Prussia 1858-1864* (Lincoln, Nebraska, 1954).
ANDERSON, Pauline Reliyea, *The Background of Anti-English Feeling in Germany 1890-1902* (Washington, 1939).
ANDLER, Charles, *Le socialisme impérialiste dans l'Allemagne contemporaine* (Paris, 1918).
ARNOLD, Ernst, *Aus allerlei Garnisonen* (Leipzig, undated).
AYS, H., *Die Wahrheit über Zabern* (Kehl, 1914).
BALFOUR, Michael, *The Kaiser and his times* (London, 1964).
BENARY, Albert, *Das deutsche Heer* (Berlin, 1932).
BERGH, Max van den, *Das deutsche Heer vor dem Weltkriege* (Berlin, 1934).
BERNHARDI, Friedrich von, *Germany and the Next War* (London, 1914).
BEYERLEIN, Franz Adam, *Jena or Sedan* (London, 1904).
BIGELOW, Poulteney, *Prussian Memories 1864-1914* (New York, 1916).
BILSE, Lieutenant, *Life in a Garrison Town* (London, 1904).

BOETTICHER, Friedrich von, *Schlieffen* (Göttingen, 1957).

BOURDON, Georges, *The German Enigma* (London, 1914).

BOGUSLAWSKI, A. von, *Deutschland das Heer* (Berlin, 1904).

—— *Die Parteien und die Heeresreform* (Berlin, 1892).

—— *Die Ehre und das Duell* (Berlin, 1896).

BÜLOW, Kurt von, *Preussischer Militarismus zur Zeit Wilhelms II* (Schweidnitz, 1930).

CHAPMAN, Guy, *The Dreyfus Case* (London, 1963).

CHÉRADAME, André, *L'Allemagne, la France et la question d'Autriche* (Paris, 1902).

COCHENHAUSEN, Generalleutnant von, *Von Scharnhorst zu Schlieffen 1806–1906* (Berlin, 1933).

CONRING, Franz, *Das deutsche Militär in der Karikatur* (Stuttgart, 1907).

CONZE, Werner, *Polnische Nation und deutsche Politik im ersten Weltkrieg* (Köln, 1958).

CRAIG, Gordon A., *The Politics of the Prussian Army 1640–1945* (Oxford, 1955).

—— *From Bismarck to Adenauer: Aspects of German Statecraft* (Baltimore, 1958).

—— 'Military Diplomats in the Prussian and German Service: The Attachés 1816–1914'. *Political Science Quarterly*, 64 (1949), 65–94.

—— 'NATO and the New German Army', *Military Policy and National Security*, ed. William W. Kaufmann (Princeton, 1956).

CRAMB, J. A., *Germany and England* (London, 1914).

DANSETTE, Adrien, *Le Boulangisme* (Paris, 1946).

DEMETER, Karl, *Das deutsche Offizierkorps in Gesellschaft und Staat 1650–1945* (Frankfurt am Main, 1962).

EARLE, Edward Meade, *Makers of Modern Strategy* (Princeton, 1944).

ECKARDSTEIN, Hermann von, *Die Isolierung Deutschlands* (Leipzig, 1921).

EISENHART-ROTHE, General Ernst von, *So war die alte Armee* (Berlin, 1935).

ENDRES, Franz Carl, 'Soziologische Struktur und ihr entsprechende Ideologien des deutschen Offizierkorps vor dem Weltkriege', *Archiv für Sozialwissenschaft und Sozialpolitik*, 58 (1927), 293.

EPSTEIN, Klaus, *Matthias Erzberger and the Dilemma of German Democracy* (Princeton, 1959).

FICK, H., *Der deutsche Militarismus der Vorkriegszeit* (Potsdam, 1932).

FISCHER, Fritz, *Griff nach der Weltmacht* (Düsseldorff, 1961).

—— 'Weltpolitik, Weltmachtstreben und deutsche Kriegsziele', *Historische Zeitschrift*, 199 (1964), 265–346.

FOERSTER, Freiherr W., *Mein Kampf gegen das militärische und nationalistische Deutschland* (Stuttgart, 1920).

FOERSTER, Wolfgang, *Aus der Gedankenwerkstatt des deutschen Generalstabes* (Berlin, 1931).

FORNASCHON, Wolfgang, *Die politische Anschauungen des Grafen Alfred von Waldersee und seine Stellungnahme zur deutschen Politik* (Berlin, 1935).

FRIEDJUNG, Heinrich, *Das Zeitalter des Imperialismus, 1884–1914*, 3 vols. (Berlin, 1919).

FREYTAG-LORINGHOVEN, Freiherr von, *Krieg und Politik in der Neuzeit* (Berlin, 1911).

FRICKE, Dieter, 'Die Affäre Leckert-Lützow-Tausch', *Zeitschrift für Geschichtswissenschaft* Heft 7 (1960), 1579–1603.

—— 'Zur Rolle des Militarismus nach innen in Deutschland vor dem ersten Weltkrieg', *Zeitschrift für Geschichtswissenschaft*, Heft 6 (1958), 1298–1310.

—— 'Zum Bündnis des preussisch-deutschen Militarismus mit dem Klerus'. *Zeitschrift für Geschichtswissenschaft*, Heft 6 (1960).

—— 'Zur Militarisierung des deutschen Geisteslebens in Wilhelminischen Kaiserreich. Der Fall Lec Arons', *Zeitschrift für Geschichtswissenschaft*, Heft 5 (1960).

GASTON, Henry, *L'Allemagne aux Abois* (Paris, 1912).

GEISS, Imanuel, *Julikrise und Kriegsausbruch 1914*, 2 vols. (Hanover, 1963).

GERTH, Senator W., *Die unmöglichen Hohenzollern* (Berlin, 1925).

GLEICH, G. von, *Die alte Armee und ihre Verirrungen* (Leipzig, 1919).

GOLTZ, Generalfeldmarschall Colmar von der, *The Nation in Arms. A treatise on Modern Military Systems and the Conduct of War* (London, 1906).

GROENER, Wilhelm, *Das Testament des Grafen Schlieffen* (Berlin, 1927).

—— *Politik und Kriegführung* (Stuttgart, 1920).

HAAS, Ludwig, *Der deutsche Jude in der Armee. Im deutschen Reich*. (Berlin, 1913).

HALLER, Johannes, *Philip Eulenburg: The Kaiser's Friend* (London, 1930).

HALLGARTEN, Georg W. F., *Imperialismus vor 1914* (Munich, 1963).

HAMMANN, Otto, *The World Policy of Germany 1890–1912* (London, 1927).

HARDEN, Maximilian, *Köpfe*, 3 vols. (Berlin, 1921).

HART, B. H. Liddell, *The Ghost of Napoleon* (London, 1933).

HAUBACH, Theodor, 'Der Sozialismus und die Wehrfrage'. *Die Gesellschaft* (Berlin, 1926).

HEFFTER, Heinrich, *Die Kreuzzeitungspartei und die Kartell-politik Bismarcks* (Leipzig, 1927).

HERZFELD, Hans, *Deutsche Rüstungspolitik vor dem Weltkrieg* (Bonn, 1923).

—— 'Zur neueren Literatur über das Heeresproblem in der deutschen Geschichte', *Vierteljahrshefte für Zeitgeschichte*, Jahrgang 4 (1956).

HEYDT, Arnold, *Der Fall Zabern* (Strasburg, 1934).

HÖFLICH, Sergeant, *Affaire Zabern* (Berlin, 1931).

HÖHN, Reinhard, *Sozialismus und Heer. Die Auseinandersetzung der Sozialdemokratie mit dem Moltkeschen Heer 1871–1878* (Bad Homburg vor der Höhe, 1959).

—— *Die Armee als Erziehungsschule der Nation. Das Ende einer Idee* (Bad Herzburg, 1963).

HOLLYDAY, Frederic B. M., *Bismarck's Rival. A political Biography of General and Admiral Albrecht von Stosch* (Durham, North Carolina, 1960).

HOSSBACH, Friedrich, *Die Entwicklung des Oberbefehls über das Heer in Brandenburg, Preussen und im deutschen Reich von 1655–1945* (Würzburg, 1964).

HOWARD, M. E., *The Armed Forces*, New Cambridge Modern History, Vol. XI. (Cambridge, 1962).

HUBER, Ernst Rudolph, *Heer und Staat in der deutschen Geschichte* (Hamburg, 1938).

JANY, Kurt, *Geschichte der königlich preussischen Armee*, Band IV (Berlin, 1933).

JERUSSALIMSKI, A. S., *Die Aussenpolitik und die Diplomatie des deutschen Imperialismus Ende des 19. Jahrhunderts* (Stuttgart, 1954).

KANTOROWICZ, Hermann, *Der Offizierhass im deutschen Heer* (Freiburg, 1919).

KEHR, Eckart, 'Zur Genesis des kgl. preussischen Reserve-offiziers', *Die Gesellschaft* (1928), ii. 492 ff.

KESSEL, Eberhard, 'Die Tätigkeit des Grafen Waldersee als General-quartiermeister und Chef des Generalstabs der Armee', *Die Welt als Geschichte* (1954) Jahrgang 14.

KLOSTER, Walter, *Der deutsche Generalstab und der Präventivkriegs-Gedanke* (Stuttgart, 1932).

KOHN-BRAMSTEDT, Ernst, *Aristocracy and the Middle Classes in Germany* (London, 1937).

KUHL, H. von, *Der deutsche Generalstab in Vorbereitung und Durchführung des Weltkrieges* (Berlin, 1920).

LAMBSDORFF, Gustav Graf von, *Die Militärbevollmächtigten Kaiser Wilhelms II am Zarenhofe 1904-1914* (Berlin, 1937).

LIEBKNECHT, Karl, *Gesammelte Reden und Schriften*, Vol. I (Berlin, 1958).

LUDENDORFF, Margarethe, *My Married Life with Ludendorff* (London, 1930).

LUDENDORFF, E., *Französische Fälschung meiner Denkschrift von 1912 über den drehenden Krieg* (Berlin, 1919).

LUXEMBURG, Rosa, *Ausgewählte Reden und Schriften*, Vol. II (Berlin, 1955).

MACDIARMID, D. S., *The Life of Lt. Gen. Sir James Moncrieff Grierson* (London, 1923).

MCALEAVY, Henry, 'Sai-Chin-Hua 1874-1936', *History Today*, Vol. VII, No. 3 (1957).

MANN, Heinrich, *Der Untertan* (Munich, 1964).

MAURICE, Major-General Sir Frederick, *Haldane*, 2 vols. (London, 1937-9).

MEIER-WELCKER, Hans, *Deutsches Heerwesen im Wandel der Zeit* (Arolsen, 1954).

MEISNER, Heinrich Otto, 'Graf Waldersees Pariser Informationen 1887', *Preussische Jahrbücher*, Band 223/224 (1931).

MOHS, Hans, *Generalfeldmarschall Alfred Graf von Waldersee in seinem militärischen Wirken*, 2 vols. (Berlin, 1929).

LENIN, W. L., *Über Deutschland und die deutsche Arbeiterbewegung* (Berlin, 1957).

MOSER, Otto, *Ernsthafte Plaudereien über den Weltkrieg* (Stuttgart, 1925).

NICHOLS, J. Alden, *Germany after Bismarck. The Caprivi Era 1890-1894* (Cambridge, Mass., 1958).

NOWAK, Karl Friedrich, *Kaiser and Chancellor* (London, 1930).

—— *Germany's Road to Ruin* (London, 1932).

NIEMANN, Alfred, *Kaiser und Heer* (Berlin, 1929).

OBERMANN, Emil, *Soldaten, Bürger, Militaristen* (Stuttgart, 1958).

ONCKEN, Hermann, *Das deutsche Reich und die Vorgeschichte das Weltkrieges* (Leipzig, 1933).

PRIEBATSCH, F., *Geschichte des preussischen Offizierkorps* (Breslau, 1919).

PROSS, Harry, *Die Zerstörung der deutschen Politik* (Frankfurt am Main, 1959).

PURCELL, Victor, *The Boxer Uprising* (Cambridge, 1963).

PILANT, Paul, *Le Péril allemand* (Paris, 1913).

RASSOW, Peter, 'Schlieffen und Holstein', *Historische Zeitschrift*, 173 (1952) 297–313.

RITTER, Gerhard, *The Schlieffen Plan* (London, 1958).

—— *Staatskunst und Kriegshandwerk; das Problem des 'Militarismus' in Deutschland*. 3 vols. (Munich, 1954–64).

—— 'Das Verhältnis von Politik und Kriegführung im Bismarckischen Reich', *Deutschland und Europa*, ed. Werner Conze (Düsseldorf, 1951).

—— 'The Political Attitude of the German Army 1900–1944', *Studies in Diplomatic History and Historiography in Honour of G. P. Gooch* (London, 1961).

RÜDT VON COLLENBERG, Freiherr Ludwig, 'Die staatsrechtliche Stellung des preussischen Kriegsministers von 1867 bis 1914', *Wissen und Wehr*, Heft 5, Jahrgang 1927.

—— *Generalfeldmarschall von Mackensen* (Berlin, 1942).

—— *Die deutsche Armee von 1871 bis 1914* (Berlin, 1922).

SCHAEFFER, Dietrich, *Aufsätze, Vorträge, und Reden*, 2 vols. (Jena, 1913).

SCHAIBLE, von, *Standes und Berufspflichten des deutschen Offiziers* (Berlin, 1891).

SCHARFENORT, von, *Die königlich preussische Kriegsakademie 1870–1910* (Berlin, 1910).

SCHENK, Erwin, *Der Fall Zabern* (Stuttgart, 1927).

SCHIEMANN, Theodor, *Videant Consules—la Guerre est-elle inevitable* (Paris, 1890).

SCHLÖZER, Leopold von, *Generalfeldmarschall Freiherr von Loë* (Berlin, 1914).

SCHMIDT, Paul von, *Der Werdegang des preussischen Heeres* (Berlin, 1903).

SCHMIDT-BÜCKEBURG, Rudolph, *Das Militärkabinett der preussischen Könige und deutschen Kaiser* (Berlin, 1933).

SCHMIDT-RICHBERG, Wiegand, *Die Generalstäbe in Deutschland 1871–1945* (Stuttgart, 1962).

SCHÜSSLER, Wilhelm, *Weltmachtstreben und Flottenbau* (Witten, Ruhr, 1956).

SOSSIDI, Eleftherios, *Die staatsrechtliche Stellung des Offiziers im absoluten Staat und ihre Abwandlung im 19 Jahrhundert* (Berlin, 1939).

STADELMANN, Rudolph, *Moltke und der Staat* (Krefeld, 1950).

STENKEWITZ, Kurt, *Gegen Bajonett und Dividende* (Leipzig, 1960).

—— *Immer feste druff!* (Berlin, 1962).

TESKE, Hermann, *von der Goltz, ein Kämpfer für den militärischen Fortschritt* (Göttingen, 1957).

THIESSEN, Johannes, *Der preussische Militarismus* (Berlin, 1919).

THIMME, Anneliese, *Hans Delbrück als Kritiker der Wilhelminischen Epoche* (Düsseldorf, 1955).

THIMME, Friedrich, *Front wider Bülow* (Munich, 1931).

TOPHAM, Anne, *Memories of the Fatherland* (London, 1916).

TREVELYAN, G. M., *Grey of Fallodon* (London, 1937).

VAGTS, Alfred, *A History of Militarism, Civilian and Military* (London, 1959).

VOLKMANN, and HOBOHM, (eds.) *Die Ursachen des deutschen Zusammenbruchs im Jahre 1918*, 4 Reihe, Vol. 11 (Berlin, 1929).

WEBER, Marianne, *Max Weber, ein Lebensbild* (Tübingen, 1926).

WENDEL, Hermann, *Zabern—Militäranarchie und Militärjustiz* (Frankfurt am Main, 1914).

WEHLER, Hand-Ulrich, 'Der Fall Zabern', *Die Welt als Geschichte*, i (1963).

WERNER, Lothar, *Der Alldeutsche Verband 1890–1914* (Berlin, 1935).

WESTARP, Graf von, *Konservative Politik im letzten Jahrzehnt des Kaiserreiches*, Vol. 1 (Berlin, 1935).

WHEELER-BENNETT, John W., *Hindenburg, the Wooden Titan* (London, 1936).

WILE, Frederic William, *Men around the Kaiser* (London, 1914).

WITZLEBEN, E. von, *Adolf von Deines, Lebensbild 1845–1911* (Berlin, 1913).

WOLBE, Dr. Eugen, *Major Burg—Lebensbild eines jüdischen Offiziers* (Frankfurt am Main, 1909).

ZECHLIN, Egmont, *Staatsstreichpläne Bismarcks und Wilhelms II 1890–1894* (Stuttgart, 1929).

ZMARZLIK, Hans-Gunther, *Bethmann Hollweg als Reichskanzler 1909–1914* (Düsseldorf, 1957).

ZWEHL, H. von, *Erich von Falkenhayn* (Berlin, 1926).

—— *Generalstabsdienst im Frieden und im Kriege* (Berlin, 1923).

INDEX